CONFLICT AT COLOSSAE

A Problem in the Interpretation of Early Christianity
Illustrated by Selected Modern Studies

Revised Edition

CONFLICT AT COLOSSAE

A Problem in the Interpretation of Early Christianity
Illustrated by Selected Modern Studies

Revised Edition

Edited and Translated
with an Introduction and Epilogue by

Fred O. Francis
and
Wayne A. Meeks

Published by

Society of Biblical Literature

and

SCHOLARS PRESS

Sources for Biblical Study 4

1975

Distributed by

SCHOLARS PRESS
University of Montana
Missoula, Montana 59801

CONFLICT AT COLOSSAE
Revised Edition

Library of Congress Cataloging in Publication Data

Francis, Fred O   comp.
    Conflict at Colossae.

    (Sources for Biblical study ; 4)
    CONTENTS: Lightfoot, J. B. The Colossian heresy.--
Dibelius, M. The Isis initiation in Apuleius and related
initiatory rites.--Bornkamm, G. The heresy of
Colossians.--[etc.] Selected bibliography (p.   )
    1. Bible. N.T. Colossians--Criticism, interpre-
tation, etc. I. Meeks, Wayne A., joint comp. II. Ti-
tle. III. Series.
BS2715.2.F72 1975   227'.7'066   75-15737
ISBN 0-89130-009-0

Printed in the United States of America

Printing Department
University of Montana
Missoula, Montana 59801

To Paul W. Meyer

teacher and friend

CONTENTS

Acknowledgments   vi

Abbreviations   vii

Introduction   1

The Colossian Heresy   13
          J. B. Lightfoot

The Isis Initiation in Apuleius and Related Initiatory Rites . .   61
          Martin Dibelius

The Heresy of Colossians   123
          Günther Bornkamm

Paul's Adversaries in Colossae   147
          Stanislas Lyonnet, S. J.

Humility and Angelic Worship in Col 2:18   163
          Fred O. Francis

The Background of EMBATEUEIN (Col 2:18) in Legal Papyri and
Oracle Inscriptions   197
          Fred O. Francis

Epilogue   209

Selected Bibliography   219

ACKNOWLEDGMENTS

"The Isis Initiation in Apuleius and Related Initiatory Rites," by Martin Dibelius is taken from his collected essays, *Botschaft und Geschichte*, ed. Günther Bornkamm with Heinz Kraft, vol. 2, Copyright © 1956 by J. C. B. Mohr (Paul Siebeck). It is translated by permission of the publisher.

"The Heresy of Colossians," by Günther Bornkamm is taken from *Das Ende des Gesetzes. Paulusstudien.* (Gesammelte Aufsätze, vol. 1), Copyright © 1952 by Chr. Kaiser Verlag. It is translated by permission of the publisher.

"Paul's Adversaries in Colossae," by Stanislas Lyonnet, S. J., is from "L'Etude du milieu littéraire et l'exégèse du Nouveau Testament," *Biblica* 37 (1956) 27-38. It is translated by permission of the editors of *Biblica*.

"Humility and Angelic Worship in Col 2:18," by Fred O. Francis, appeared first in *Studia Theologica* 16 (1963) 109-34. It is reprinted by permission of *Studia Theologica*.

ABBREVIATIONS

ABSA	*Annual of the British School at Athens*
Ant.	Josephus, *The Antiquities of the Jews*
art. cit.	article cited previously
ARW	*Archiv für Religionswissenschaft*
b	Babylonian Talmud
BCH	*Bulletin de Correspondance Hellénique*
CD	Damascus Document (from Cairo Geniza)
CIL	*Corpus inscriptionum latinarum*
col.	column(s)
diss.	dissertation
DJD	Discoveries in the Judaean Desert
ed(d).	edition(s), edited (by)
ET	English translation
FRLANT	Forschungen zur Religion und Literatur des Alten und Neuen Testaments
HE	Eusebius, *Ecclesiastical History*
HTR	*Harvard Theological Review*
JBL	*Journal of Biblical Literature*
JÖAI	*Jahreshefte des österreichischen archäologischen Instituts*
JTS	*Journal of Theological Studies*
JW	Josephus, *The Jewish War*
LXX	Septuagint
Met.	Apuleius, *Metamorphoses*
MS(S)	manuscript(s)
MT	Masoretic text
n(n).	note(s)
NRT	*La nouvelle revue théologique*
n.s.	new series
NT	New Testament
NTS	*New Testament Studies*
OGIS	Dittenberger, *Orientis graeci inscriptiones selectae*
OT	Old Testament

PG	Migne, *Patrologia graeca*
RB	*Revue biblique*
RHR	*Revue d'histoire et de philosophie religieuses*
RevPh	*Revue de philologie*
RSV	Revised Standard Version
SAH	Sitzungsbericht der Akademie der Wissenschaften zu Heidelberg
SBT	Studies in Biblical Theology
SNT	Studien zum Neuen Testament
ST	*Studia Theologica*
STDJ	Studies on the Texts of the Desert of Judah
TDNT	Theological Dictionary of the New Testament
TLZ	*Theologische Literaturzeitung*
tr., trans.	translated by, translator
TS	Texts and Studies
TWNT	*Theologisches Wörterbuch zum Neuen Testament*
vs(s).	verse(s)
VD	*Verbum Domini*
VT	*Vetus Testamentum*
WMANT	Wissenschaftliche Monographien zum Alten und Neuen Testament
ZNW	*Zeitschrift für die neutestamentliche Wissenschaft*
ZTK	*Zeitschrift für Theologie und Kirche*
ZWT	*Zeitschrift für Wissenschaftliche Theologie*
1QpHab	Pesher on Habakkuk from Qumran Cave 1
1QS	Rule of the Community (Manual of Discipline)
1QSa	Rule of the Congregation (Appendix A to 1QS)
1QSb	Blessings (Appendix B to 1QS)

INTRODUCTION

One of the hallmarks of New Testament scholarship of the nineteenth and twentieth centuries has been the attention it has paid to conflict as a formative factor in Christianity's early development. "Even
in the New Testament," insists Ernst Käsemann, "we are compelled to admit
the existence not merely of significant tensions, but, not infrequently,
of irreconcilable theological contradictions."[1] While not all interpreters
would state the case so baldly or celebrate it with such relish, more and
more have come to see that tensions and contradictions abound in the
earliest stages of Christianity's life. Particularly since World War II,
first in German Protestant scholarship and in the American scholarship
directly influenced by the German, but then also in some circles of Roman
Catholic exegesis, this recognition of diversity has led to some quite
definite assumptions and procedures in the method by which the attempt is
made to explain difficult texts in the New Testament and other early
Christian literature.

It is not hard to see why investigators whose eyes are adjusted
to spy out conflict should focus first and foremost on the letters attributed to Paul. Paul was clearly a controversialist. Much of his writing
is polemical not only in style (the "diatribe" of the Stoic and Cynic
orators), but in actual situation. Therefore to read his letters is something like listening to a friend engaged in heated argument by telephone:
one can hardly make sense of what he is saying unless one can guess what
the party at the other end of the line is saying. Moreover, Paul occupied
such a pivotal position in the history of the first Christians--because
of the volume of his preserved writings, the early date of his conversion
and of his missionary and literary efforts, and the ambiguities of his
relationship to the traditions of Judaism and the syncretic culture of
Hellenism--that *his* conflicts have seemed prototypical for the whole
Christian movement. No wonder that "The Opponents of Paul in _____"
has become a standard topic for monographs and articles.

The Letter to the Colossians has some extraordinarily puzzling
passages which hint darkly of a "philosophy," embodying "human traditions,"
"dogmas," and special practices, by which the author fears the congregation

will be "led astray." Several of these statements are so cryptic that some commentators have despaired of being able even to translate them into English. The opaque phrases must allude to notions which were familiar to the addressees, so our only hope of understanding them seems to lie in attempts to reconstruct the complex of doctrine and practice which the author wishes to oppose. Colossians is therefore an apt subject for the detective procedures which we wish to illustrate. The classic and the more recent studies included below were selected to provide a paradigm of ways in which a growing segment of New Testament scholarship has learned to exploit new discoveries, to construct by more-or-less controlled imagination prolific "models" to make sense of new and old data, and to test its models by exegetical application and by the mutual questioning that occurs within the guild of scholars. Along the way, the reader may also discover more of the real complexity and dynamics of early Christianity, as well as both the excitement and the uncertainty of the historian's task. He may, indeed, come to recognize not only the problematic character of even the most finely honed of our historical methods, but also the incompleteness of our very notions of what "history" is.

The ancient church, by and large, viewed the conflicts evidenced in the pages of the New Testament as the result of assaults from without upon the unified apostolic religion. The opponents of Paul were accordingly understood as Jews or pagans. Where conflict emerged between groups manifestly standing within the church, one side could nevertheless be regarded as "heretics," hence not *really* Christians and thus, after all, outsiders. Already the docetists who arose within the Johannine circle in the first century were read out of the church in this fashion: "They went out from us, but they were not of us ..." (1 John 2:19). A dualistic picture of hostile "spirits" in league with Satan was already employed in this document to explain the experience of dissonance within the church. The Christian Apologists from Justin Martyr to Eusebius of Caesarea elaborated the notion of demonic influence into a comprehensive explanation for opposition from Jews, pagans, and Christian heretics alike.

There was one figure in antiquity, however, who anticipated the modern interest in Paul's opponents as indicators of internal conflict in the earliest church itself. This was Marcion, whose radical reinterpretation of Paul in the second century led to his excommunication, followed by his organization of a counter-church so vigorous that it endured for centuries in some places. Marcion became the first student of Paul's letters to make the identification of his opponents the hermeneutical key for unlocking Paul's whole meaning. For example, the "Marcionite prologues," probably produced by one of Marcion's followers, include this statement about Colossians: "... although they also had been led astray by false apostles, the apostle did not personally come to them, but corrects them also by a letter."[2] These opponents, according to Marcion, were the same ones whom Paul faced at every turn: "false, judaizing apostles," whom Marcion found described chiefly in Galatians 1:6-9; 2:4; 2 Corinthians 11:13-14.[3] These apostles, he believed, had created a conspiracy to restore allegiance to the Jewish God of law and justice (whom, Marcion thought, Paul distinguished from the previously unknown, altogether beneficent God who appeared in Jesus). Because of the confusion and weakness of the original Jerusalem apostles (from whom Marcion, reading Galatians more carefully than some modern interpreters, distinguished the opponents), the conspirators succeeded in dominating the church until he, Marcion, exposed their plot. Marcion was a forerunner of many later interpreters in another respect as well. He thoroughly identified his own position with Paul's, as he understood it, and that of Paul's opponents with *his* opponents, the catholic church of the second century.

The experience of disruption in the church at the time of the Reformation, accompanied as it was by the stirrings of a new historical scholarship in renaissance Humanism, quickened sensitivities to the presence of conflict in the apostolic age. For example, in Paul's struggle with his opponents, especially those of Galatia, Luther saw foreshadowed his own battle against the papacy on the one hand and the "fanatics" on the other. To a large degree this was true of the other Reformers as well, but Calvin's characterization of the Colossian opponents sounds surprisingly modern and judicious: they were Jews, he said, of a mystical propensity, heavily influenced by speculations of a neo-Platonic type.[4] The seeds were thus sown for a more rigorously critical picture of early Christianity's evolution, but also for the perennial danger of distorting the past by the projection of one's own situation. The subsequent hardening of positions in Protestant scholasticism and in the Counterreformation, however, had the effect on both sides of reinforcing the image of an original, unified body of apostolic doctrine, opposition to which had to be viewed as qualitatively different and alien in origin.

Only in the wake of English Deism and the continental Enlightenment were the philosophical perspectives finally effective for an altogether fresh approach to the diversity of early Christianity.[5] Ferdinand Christian Baur, who has for good reason been called "the true author of historical-critical theology,"[6] opened the door to the new approach--and new controversy--with his long essay in 1831 on "the Christ-party in the Corinthian Congregation."[7] Baur's New Testament studies and his subsequent adaptations of Hegel's philosophy of history led him to a masterful synthesis in which conflict became the key to all history, and Paul's conflicts the key to the history of early Christianity.

Baur's historical studies of the New Testament probably did more than any other single factor to establish the pattern by which the identification of early Christian factions and the evaluation of their significance have proceeded. He insisted that one must begin by recognizing the actual evidence for conflict and division in the New Testament texts, particularly the undoubted letters of Paul, and then proceed to reconstruct the internal logic of each of the contending positions. He thus developed what he called "tendency criticism," a term taken up by his opponents and used with opprobrium. He meant that for every document in the New Testament it was necessary to ask initially, not how its ideas fit into a whole system of theology, but for what aim was it written? In what situation was it written? For whose benefit? To counter what opposing views? Only by asking questions of this order could one succeed in obtaining a genuinely historical picture of the past, rather than a dogmatic or purely literary abstraction.[8]

Baur also saw quite clearly that such an approach to history was by no means a mere gathering and recital of facts, but involved imaginative, speculative reconstruction: "Without speculation, every historical investigation ... is a mere tarrying on the superfluous and external side of the subject matter."[9] One could not claim to have *understood* a text if he merely paraphrased the fragmentary statements found there. He must draw a plausible outline of the historic context in which those statements functioned. That Baur found in Hegel's philosophy much of the rational structure with which to give expression to that outline meant that he was a man of his own time; it was both a source of his power and a limitation. Nevertheless, his basic perception of the historian's task is brilliantly conceived and remains normative, however much a later historian will wish to modify its idealistic framework: "the striving to place oneself in (*sich hineinstellen*) the objective course of the subject matter itself and to follow it in all the moments in which it moves itself on ...."[10]

The controversy over Baur's models of early Christian evolution raged initially within theological circles and turned on theological questions. Toward the end of the nineteenth century, however, new factors began to intrude themselves into the study of early Christianity, often instigated by classicists, semitists, secular historians, archaeologists, and other scholars outside the theological faculties, lending a new breadth and liveliness to the discussion. There began then the remarkable series of archaeological and literary discoveries which, continuing right down to the present, have transformed our view of Greco-Roman culture and consequently of the Christian sect that took shape within it. Coupled with these discoveries was a growing cosmopolitanism in ways of looking at religious phenomena, leading to the development of self-conscious methods for comparative study of similar or related religions. Evolutionary theories, of both the idealist and the naturalist types, filled the intellectual atmosphere, leading to attempts to trace the development of religious concepts and practices and their transformation as they moved from one cultural context to another, to uncover the influences of one culture on another, and to explain the meaning of religious phenomena in terms of their origins and histories. These manifold factors brought into being the amorphous constellation of trends referred to in Europe as "the history of religions" (*Religionsgeschichte*) and in English-speaking countries usually as "comparative religion."[11]

The effect of the History of Religions movement upon the historical quest for Paul's opponents was profound. Materials were accumulating which made it seem plausible to try to identify the opposition party referred to in a given letter with a particular group or movement in antiquity.

If the identification could be made to stick, then the fragmentary nature of Paul's allusions could be filled in by information about the group in question gleaned from other sources. Yet the identifications were almost always hypothetical, and the delineation of the groups and movements frequently suffered from an understandable tendency to over-generalize from similarities found in the available data, the survival of which was inevitably somewhat accidental. Categories which were useful for sorting and grasping the data frequently took on a life of their own as scholars were tempted to transmute category labels into real, homogeneous entities of history. The most notorious and perplexing examples are "apocalyptic" and "gnosticism," both of which have played enormous roles in modern attempts to understand early Christianity, but the delineation of which remains a subject of intense controversy.

Interest in comparative studies has been greatly enhanced by the numerous discoveries, some dramatic, which brought unexpectedly to light long-hidden evidence from the Mediterranean culture. Among them were innumerable Hellenistic papyri and inscriptions (such as the inscriptions from Claros which play such a large role in the essay by Dibelius below); the publication of Mandaean and Manichaean texts in the 1920's, which so gripped one segment of scholarship that a scoffer once spoke of "Mandaean fever" in German New Testament research; the Qumran manuscripts from the Dead Sea area discovered beginning in 1947, which equally raised theological and anti-theological temperatures for a while; the large Gnostic library discovered near Nag Hammadi, Egypt, around the same time; the massive and provocative collection of Jewish iconography by Erwin Goodenough. Each discovery attracts its partisans, who in their zeal to exploit the new opportunities for gaining insight into the ancient world, frequently treat the new material as a unique key for opening all doors in sight. Such excess is not only understandable, it is perhaps not altogether deplorable. History remains an art, not an exact science, and one of its enduring methods remains trial and error. As Baur saw and stated acutely, the historian must *reconstruct* the past, he cannot avoid speculation in making his reconstruction, and his reconstruction will win credence only to the extent that it is able to withstand the assault of alternative constructs which likewise claim to make sense of as much of the data as possible.

The intellectual character of the reconstruction, however, has led invariably to what is perhaps the gravest weakness in modern critical study of the New Testament. Baur shared with his critics, both among the conservative dogmatic historians and the rationalist theologians, the assumption that the conflicts among the early Christians were basically and determinatively *ideational* and confessional. They were conflicts over doctrine--though not, to be sure, in the narrow and arid fashion of many of the conflicts in post-Reformation scholasticism, with which Baur had little patience. His idealist position itself assured that the debate about dogmas was construed as a debate about the fundamental structure of reality. For him, therefore, the description of the ideational conflicts of early Christianity was as direct a way of attempting to "place oneself into" the actual mode of early Christians' existence as would be, for example, Rudolf Bultmann's existential analysis of Christian myths. Still, the idealist basis, together with the social setting of German New Testament scholarship--in theological faculties of universities--were fated to pro-duce a one-sidedly cerebral view of history. The great liberal critic, Adolf Jülicher, called attention to the limitation:

> It is not mainly from ideas and principles that a new religion draws its life: the decisive influences are emotions, feelings, hopes: Baur's picture of the his-torical development of the Apostolic and post-Apostolic ages is too logical and correct, too deficient in warmth of colour to have probability on its side.[12]

To a degree the History of Religions movement afforded a corrective to the intellectualizing view of religion, by focusing upon institutions, rituals, and symbols. A good example of the corrective is to be seen in Dibelius' essay below, in which he insists that not merely the ideas of the opposing group at Colossae, and not merely their subjective experiences (as Jülicher's romantic protest against Baur could suggest), but also their social organization and ritual procedures must be the object of the historian's quest. Dibelius' voice was in this respect a lonely one, however. Apart from the American "Chicago school" of the 1930's, which undertook a creative but short-lived sociological approach to the history of early Christianity, and a few, mostly quite limited and

tendentious studies by Marxist historians, students of the New Testament
have been content to explore the implications of the writers' doctrines
without regard to their social contexts. The pioneers of religious sociology, Troeltsch, Weber, and Wach, have had only the faintest of echoes in
New Testament historiography, while the functionalist, empirical, and
structural approaches of French and Anglo-American sociology and anthropology have so far had no influence at all in these circles.[13]

    In the past three decades, studies of factions and conflicts in
earliest Christianity have appeared at a constantly accelerating rate.
Among the most important have been the several provocative essays by
Ernst Käsemann,[14] the careful study by Günther Bornkamm reprinted below,
Dieter Georgi's extensive examination of "Paul's Opponents in Second
Corinthians,"[15] Walter Schmithals' brilliantly one-sided pan-Gnosticism,[16]
and a number of redaction-critical studies of the gospels too many even
to list here without inevitably slighting some important works.[17]

    It would require a social history of American and European uni-
versities in this century to explain why these questions have so captured
the imagination particularly of German and American Protestants.[18] It may
be that the aroused sense of the significance and productivity of conflict
was stirred by such experiences as the Church Struggle of the German Confessing Church during the Hitler period, the political and social con-
frontations which shook both American and European society in the sixties,
and the confessional dialogues and negotiations of the ecumenical movement. Whatever the immediate occasions, it is clear that the dialectical
tradition of German theology and the historical models of post-Reformation
Germany have played an inordinate role in shaping the terms of the discussion. Thus the factions, movements, and groups which are reconstructed in
various studies are invariably regarded as gaining their primary identity
through their *confession* or *creed*, and the focal point of that confession
is almost always thought to be *christological*. An uninitiated observer
might be pardoned for wondering just how many religious groups could be
most effectively described in those terms. Yet we only understand the
past by bringing it into relationship with models that are familiar to us,
and if those which have served one school of scholarship seem distorted,
the critic has the obligation to seek more fitting ones.

The essays which follow have been chosen for their inherent quality, their influence on wider scholarship, and the variety of their perspectives. They are intended, of course, not as exhaustive representatives of scholarship on Colossians, but as prolific samples. Other examples are reviewed briefly in the EPILOGUE or listed in the Select Bibliography.

* * *

NOTES

[1]Ernst Käsemann, "The Canon of the New Testament and the Unity of the Church," in *Essays on New Testament Themes*, trans. W. J. Montague (SBT, 41; Naperville, Ill.: Alec R. Allenson, 1964) 100.

[2]Quoted by W. G. Kümmel, *The New Testament: The History of the Investigation of Its Problems*, trans. S. M. Gilmour and H. C. Kee (Nashville: Abingdon, 1972) 14.

[3]See Adolf von Harnack, *Marcion: Das Evangelium vom fremden Gott* (3d ed., Darmstadt: Wissenschaftliche Buchgesellschaft, 1960) 37-38.

[4]Calvin dismisses conjectures that there may have been two classes of errorists opposed by Paul, taking them to be solely Jews. However, he takes Paul's mention of "philosophy" to suggest that the opponents indulged in subtle speculations, "for they contrived a way of access to God through means of angels, and put forth many speculations of that nature, such as are contained in the books of Dionysius on the Celestial Hierarchy, drawn from the school of the Platonists" (*Commentary on the Epistle of the Colossians*, trans. John Pringle [Commentaries of Calvin, vol. 42; Edinburgh: The Calvin Translation Society, 1851] 133).

[5]On this point, and for a valuable and lucid survey of the development of a key period in modern NT scholarship, see Luigi Salvatorelli, "From Locke to Reitzenstein: The Historical Investigation of

the Origins of Christianity," *HTR* 22 (1929) 263-369. For a more comprehensive review, brought down to the 1950's, see the monumental work of
W. G. Kümmel now happily available in English (see n. 2).

[6]Emmanuel Hirsch, *Geschichte der neueren evangelischen Theologie
im Zusammenhang mit den allgemeinen Bewegungen des europäischen Denkens*,
vol. 5 (Gutersloh: C. Bertelmanns Verlag, 1954) 518, cited by Peter C.
Hodgson, *The Formation of Historical Theology* (New York: Harper & Row,
1966) 1.

[7]"Die Christuspartei in der korinthischen Gemeinde, der Gegen-
satz des petrinischen und paulinischen Christenthums in der ältesten
Kirche, der Apostel Petrus in Rom," *Tübinger Zeitschrift für Theologie* 5
(1831) 61-206.

[8]Baur's tentative conclusions about the Colossian situation
illustrate both his boldness and his careful attention to the text. Paul
could not have written either Ephesians or Colossians, he reasoned, because
they contained too many elements proper to later Christian Gnosticism, for
which Baur, unlike many more recent scholars, could find no first-century
evidence. Baur felt that the polemics of Colossians had been exaggerated
by previous scholars. The danger of false teaching was not the occasion
of the letter, but only a means by which the author emphasized his main
themes, chief of which was his cosmic christology. This theme was expounded
in a way so fraught with gnostic language that the opponents could not have
been gnostics, else the polemic would have missed its mark. Rather, Baur
believed the opponents were probably Ebionites, the Jewish-Christian sect
mentioned by second-century writers. They regarded Christ, he thought, as
merely one of the archangels, while the author of Colossians insisted on
his uniqueness and superiority to angels. Baur notes in passing the total
difference between this response to a Judaizing faction and that by Paul
in Galatians. While Paul stressed soteriology, this writer stresses
christology. (*Paul the Apostle of Jesus Christ* ..., trans. A. Menzies
[London and Edinburgh: Williams & Norgate, 1875] II, 26-32.)

[12]Adolf Jülicher, *Einleitung in das Neue Testament* (1st ed., 1894), quoted by Kümmel (see n. 2 above) 175.

[13]At present, numerous voices are heard calling for attempts at an effective social description of early Christianity, and some tentative steps are being taken in that direction by some American scholars, including one of the Editors. It remains to be seen whether such an approach is in fact feasible, and whether it can avoid the dangers of artificiality and one-sidedness in yet a new direction.

[14]Of those available in English, especially his proposal about Col 1:15-20, "A Primitive Christian Baptismal Liturgy," in *Essays on New Testament Themes* (see n. 1 above), 149-68; "The Canon of the New Testament and the Unity of the Church," (see n. 1); "The Beginnings of Christian Theology," in *Apocalypticism*, ed. Robert W. Funk (Journal for Theology and the Church, 6; New York: Herder and Herder, 1969) 17-46; and "On the Topic of Primitive Christian Apocalyptic," *ibid.*, 99-133.

[15]*Die Gegner des Paulus im 2. Korintherbrief* (WMANT, 11; Neukirchener Verlag, 1964).

[16]In English, *Gnosticism in Corinth*, trans. John E. Steely (Nashville: Abingdon, 1971) and *Paul and the Gnostics*, trans. John E. Steely (Nashville: Abingdon, 1972).

[17]For a beginning, see Helmut Koester, "One Jesus and Four Primitive Gospels," in *Trajectories through Early Christianity*, ed. James M. Robinson and Helmut Koester (Philadelphia: Fortress, 1971) 158-204.

[18]A systematic and interpretive history of this kind of research would be invaluable. Several of the works cited above contain sketches of the history of research into their particular areas. The most comprehensive treatment we know concerning the history of attempts to describe Paul's opponents in a particular letter is contained in the first part of a Yale dissertation by John G. Hawkins, *The Opponents of Paul in Galatia* (Ann Arbor:

University Microfilms, 1971) 5-85. There is nothing of like scope on the Colossian question. Among the most careful expositions of the historical issues involved in the whole approach we have been discussing are found in the *Trajectories* essays by Robinson and Koester (see n. 17 above), especially the two articles by Koester, "Gnomai Diaphoroi: The Origin and Nature of Diversification in the History of Early Christianity," 114-57, and "The Structure and Criteria of Early Christian Beliefs," 205-31. Koester and Robinson see themselves in part as following out and expanding the agenda set forth by Walter Bauer in a book published in 1934 but only recently translated into English, *Orthodoxy and Heresy in Earliest Christianity*, translation ed. Robert A. Kraft and Gerhard Krodel (Philadelphia: Fortress, 1971). Appendix 2 is a valuable contribution to the history of scholarship.

* * *

THE COLOSSIAN HERESY

J. B. Lightfoot*

From the language of St Paul, addressed to the Church of
Colossae, we may infer the presence of two disturbing elements which
threatened the purity of Christian faith and practice in this community.
These elements are distinguishable in themselves, though it does not follow
that they present the teaching of two distinct parties.

1.   A mere glance at the epistle suffices to detect the presence of
JUDAISM in the teaching which the Apostle combats. The observance of
sabbaths and new moons is decisive in this respect. The distinction of
meats and drinks points in the same direction.[1] Even the enforcement of
the initiatory rite of Judaism may be inferred from the contrast implied
in St Paul's recommendation of the spiritual circumcision.[2]

2.   On the other hand a closer examination of its language shows
that these Judaic features do not exhaust the portraiture of the heresy
or heresies against which the epistle is directed. We discern an element
of theosophic speculation, which is alien to the spirit of Judaism proper.
We are confronted with a shadowy mysticism, which loses itself in the contemplation of the unseen world. We discover a tendency to interpose certain spiritual agencies, intermediate beings, between God and man, as the
instruments of communication and the objects of worship.[3] Anticipating
the result which will appear more clearly hereafter, we may say that along
with its Judaism there was a GNOSTIC element in the false teaching which
prevailed at Colossae.

Have we then two heresies here, or one only? Were these elements
distinct, or were they fused into the same system? In other words, is St
Paul controverting a phase of Judaism on the one hand, and a phase of
Gnosticism on the other; or did he find himself in conflict with a Judaeo-
Gnostic heresy which combined the two?[4]

*Joseph Barber Lightfoot (1828-1889) was Lady Margaret's Professor
at Cambridge University and, from 1879, Bishop of Durham. This essay is
from his commentary, *St. Paul's Epistles to the Colossians and to Philemon*
(3rd edition, London: Macmillan and Co., 1879).

On closer examination we find ourselves compelled to adopt the
latter alternative. The epistle itself contains no hint that the Apostle
has more than one set of antagonists in view; and the needless multiplica-
tion of persons or events is always to be deprecated in historical criticism. Nor indeed does the hypothesis of a single complex heresy present
any real difficulty. If the two elements seem irreconcilable, or at least
incongruous, at first sight, the incongruity disappears on further examination. It will be shown in the course of this investigation, that some
special tendencies of religious thought among the Jews themselves before
and about this time prepared the way for such a combination in a Christian
community like the Church of Colossae.[5] Moreover we shall find that the
Christian heresies of the next succeeding ages exhibit in a more developed
form the same complex type, which here appears in its nascent state;[6] this
later development not only showing that the combination was historically
possible in itself, but likewise presupposing some earlier stage of its
existence such as confronts us at Colossae.

But in fact the Apostle's language hardly leaves the question
open. The two elements are so closely interwoven in his refutation, that
it is impossible to separate them. He passes backwards and forwards from
one to the other in such a way as to show that they are only parts of one
complex whole. On this point the logical connexion of the sentences is
decisive: 'Beware lest any man make spoil of you through philosophy and
vain deceit after the tradition of men, after the rudiments of the world
...Ye were circumcised with a circumcision not made with hands...And you
...did He quicken,...blotting out the handwriting of ordinances which
was against you...Let no man therefore judge you in meat or drink, or in
respect of a holy day or a new moon or a sabbath...Let no man beguile you
of your prize ·in a self-imposed humility and service of angels...If ye
died with Christ from the rudiments of the world, why...are ye subject to
ordinances...which things have a show of wisdom in self-imposed service
and humility and hard treatment of the body, but are of no value against
indulgence of the flesh.'[7] Here the superior wisdom, the speculative
element which is characteristic of Gnosticism, and the ritual observance,
the practical element which was supplied by Judaism, are regarded not
only as springing from the same stem, but also as intertwined in their

growth. And the more carefully we examine the sequence of the Apostle's
thoughts, the more intimate will the connexion appear.

Having described the speculative element in this complex heresy
provisionally as Gnostic, I purpose enquiring in the first place, how far
Judaism prior to and independently of Christianity had allied itself with
Gnostic modes of thought; and afterwards, whether the description of the
Colossian heresy is such as to justify us in thus classing it as a species
of Gnosticism. But, as a preliminary to these enquiries, some definition
of the word, or at least some conception of the leading ideas which it
involves, will be necessary. With its complex varieties and elaborate
developments we have no concern here: for, if Gnosticism can be found at
all in the records of the Apostolic age, it will obviously appear in a
simple and elementary form. Divested of its accessories and presented in
its barest outline, it is not difficult of delineation.[8]

1.   As the name attests,[9] Gnosticism implies the possession of a
superior wisdom, which is hidden from others. It makes a distinction
between the select few who have this higher gift, and the vulgar many
who are without it. Faith, blind faith, suffices the latter, while knowledge is the exclusive possession of the former. Thus it recognises a
separation of intellectual *caste* in religion, introducing the distinction
of an initiation of some kind or other between the two classes. In short
it is animated by the exclusive *aristocratic* spirit,[10] which distinguishes
the ancient religions, and from which it was a main function of Christianity
to deliver mankind.

2.   This was its spirit; and the intellectual questions, on which
its energies were concentrated and to which it professed to hold the key,
were mainly twofold. How can the work of creation be explained? and,
How are we to account for the existence of evil?[11] To reconcile the
creation of the world and the existence of evil with the conception of
God as the absolute Being, was the problem which all the Gnostic systems
set themselves to solve. It will be seen that the two questions cannot
be treated independently but have a very close and intimate connexion
with each other.

The Gnostic argument ran as follows: Did God create the world

out of nothing, evolve it from Himself? Then, God being perfectly good
and creation having resulted from His sole act without any opposing or
modifying influence, evil would have been impossible; for otherwise we
are driven to the conclusion that God created evil.

This solution being rejected as impossible, the Gnostic was
obliged to postulate some antagonistic principle independent of God, by
which His creative energy was thwarted and limited. This opposing principle, the kingdom of evil, he conceived to be the world of matter. The
precise idea of its mode of operation varies in different Gnostic systems.
It is sometimes regarded as a dead passive resistance, sometimes as a
turbulent active power. But, though the exact point of view may shift,
the object contemplated is always the same. In some way or other evil is
regarded as residing in the material, sensible world. Thus Gnostic
speculation on the existence of evil ends in a dualism.

This point being conceded, the ulterior question arises: How
then is creation possible? How can the Infinite communicate with the
Finite, the Good with the Evil? How can God act upon matter? God is
perfect, absolute, incomprehensible.

This, the Gnostic went on to argue, could only have been
possible by some self-limitation on the part of God. God must express
Himself in some way. There must be some evolution, some effluence, of
Deity. Thus the Divine Being germinates, as it were; and the first ger-
mination again evolves a second from itself in like manner. In this way
we obtain a series of successive emanations, which may be more or fewer,
as the requirements of any particular system demand. In each successive
evolution the Divine element is feebler. They sink gradually lower and
lower in the scale, as they are farther removed from their source; until
at length contact with matter is possible, and creation ensues. These
are the emanations, aeons, spirits, or angels, of Gnosticism, conceived
as more or less concrete and personal according to the different aspects
in which they are regarded in different systems.

3.   Such is the bare outline (and nothing more is needed for my
immediate purpose) of the speculative views of Gnosticism. But it is
obvious that these views must have exerted a powerful influence on the
ethical systems of their advocates, and thus they would involve important

practical consequences. If matter is the principle of evil, it is of
infinite moment for a man to know how he can avoid its baneful influence
and thus keep his higher nature unclogged and unsullied.

To this practical question two directly opposite answers were
given:[12]

(i)   On the one hand, it was contended that the desired end might
best be attained by a rigorous abstinence. Thus communication with
matter, if it could not be entirely avoided, might be reduced to a minimum. Its grosser defilements at all events would be escaped. The material
part of man would be subdued and mortified, if it could not be annihilated;
and the spirit, thus set free, would be sublimated, and rise to its proper
level. Thus the ethics of Gnosticism pointed in the first instance to a
strict *asceticism*.

(ii)   But obviously the results thus attained are very slight and
inadequate. Matter is about us everywhere. We do but touch the skirts
of the evil, when we endeavour to fence ourselves about by prohibitive
ordinances, as, for instance, when we enjoin a spare diet or forbid
marriage. Some more comprehensive rule is wanted, which shall apply to
every contingency and every moment of our lives. Arguing in this way,
other Gnostic teachers arrived at an ethical rule directly opposed to the
former. 'Cultivate an entire indifference,' they said, 'to the world of
sense. Do not give it a thought one way or the other, but follow your own
impulses. The ascetic principle assigns a certain importance to matter.
The ascetic fails in consequence to assert his own independence. The true
rule of life is to treat matter as something alien to you, towards which
you have no duties or obligations and which you can use or leave unused
as you like.'[13] In this way the reaction from rigid asceticism led to
the opposite extreme of unrestrained *licentiousness*, both alike springing
from the same false conception of matter as the principle of evil.

Gnosticism, as defined by these characteristic features, has
obviously no necessary connexion with Christianity.[14] Christianity would
naturally arouse it to unwonted activity, by leading men to dwell more
earnestly on the nature and power of evil, and thus stimulating more systematic thought on the theological questions which had already arrested
attention. After no long time Gnosticism would absorb into its system

more or fewer Christian elements, or Christianity in some of its forms
would receive a tinge from Gnosticism. But the thing itself had an independent root, and seems to have been prior in time. The probabilities
of the case, and the scanty traditions of history, alike point to this
independence of the two.[15] If so, it is a matter of little moment at
what precise time the name 'Gnostic' was adopted, whether before or after
contact with Christianity; for we are concerned only with the growth and
direction of thought which the name represents.[16]

        If then Gnosticism was not an offspring of Christianity, but a
direction of religious speculation which existed independently, we are at
liberty to entertain the question whether it did not form an alliance with
Judaism, contemporaneously with or prior to its alliance with Christianity.
There is at least no obstacle which bars such an investigation at the outset. If this should prove to be the case, then we have a combination
which prepares the way for the otherwise strange phenomena presented in
the Epistle to the Colossians.
        Those, who have sought analogies to the three Jewish sects
among the philosophical schools of Greece and Rome, have compared the
Sadducees to the Epicureans, the Pharisees to the Stoics, and the Essenes
to the Pythagoreans. Like all historical parallels, this comparison is
open to misapprehension: but, carefully guarded, the illustration is pertinent and instructive.
        With the Sadducees we have no concern here. Whatever respect
may be due to their attitude in the earlier stages of their history, at
the Christian era at least they have ceased to deserve our sympathy; for
their position has become mainly *negative*. They take their stand on
denials--the denial of the existence of angels, the denial of the resurrection of the dead, the denial of a progressive development in the Jewish
Church. In these negative tendencies, in the materialistic teaching of
the sect, and in the moral consequences to which it led, a very rough
resemblance to the Epicureans will appear.[17]
        The two *positive* sects were the Pharisees and the Essenes.
Both alike were strict observers of the ritual law; but, while the
Pharisee was essentially *practical*, the tendency of the Essene was to

mysticism; while the Pharisee was a man of the world, the Essene was a
member of a brotherhood. In this respect the Stoic and the Pythagorean
were the nearest counterparts which the history of Greek philosophy and
social life could offer. These analogies indeed are suggested by Josephus
himself.[18]

   While the portrait of the Pharisee is distinctly traced and
easily recognised, this is not the case with the Essene. The Essene is
the great enigma of Hebrew history. Admired alike by Jew, by Heathen,
and by Christian, he yet remains a dim vague outline, on which the highest
subtlety of successive critics has been employed to supply a substantial
form and an adequate colouring. An ascetic mystical dreamy recluse, he
seems too far removed from the hard experience of life to be capable of
realisation.

   And yet by careful use of the existing materials the portrait
of this sect may be so far restored, as to establish with a reasonable
amount of probability the point with which alone we are here concerned.
It will appear from the delineations of ancient writers, more especially
of Philo and Josephus, that the characteristic feature of Essenism was a
particular direction of mystic speculation, involving a rigid asceticism
as its practical consequence. Following the definition of Gnosticism
which has been already given, we may not unfitly call this tendency *Gnostic*.

   Having in this statement anticipated the results, I shall now
endeavour to develope the main features of Essenism; and, while doing so,
I will ask my readers to bear in mind the portrait of the Colossian heresy
in St Paul, and to mark the resemblances, as the enquiry proceeds.[19]

   The Judaic element is especially prominent in the life and teaching of the sect. The Essene was exceptionally rigorous in his observance
of the Mosaic ritual. In his strict abstinence from work on the sabbath
he far surpassed all the other Jews. He would not light a fire, would not
move a vessel, would not perform even the most ordinary functions of life.[20]
The whole day was given up to religious exercises and to exposition of the
Scriptures.[21] His respect for the law extended also the the lawgiver.
After God, the name of Moses was held in the highest reverence. He who
blasphemed his name was punished with death.[22] In all these points the
Essene was an exaggeration, almost a caricature, of the Pharisee.

So far the Essene has not departed from the principles of normal
Judaism; but here the divergence begins. In three main points we trace
the working of influences which must have been derived from external
sources.

1.   To the legalism of the Pharisee, the Essene added an asceticism,
which was peculiarly his own, and which in many respects contradicted the
tenets of the other sect. The honourable, and even exaggerated, estimate
of marriage, which was characteristic of the Jew, and of the Pharisee as
the typical Jew, found no favour with the Essene.[23] Marriage was to him
an abomination. Those Essenes who lived together as members of an order,
and in whom the principles of the sect were carried to their logical consequences, eschewed it altogether. To secure the continuance of their
brotherhood they adopted children, whom they brought up in the doctrines
and practices of the community. There were others however who took a
different view. They accepted marriage, as necessary for the preservation
of the race. Yet even with them it seems to have been regarded only as an
inevitable evil. They fenced it off by stringent rules, demanding a three
years' probation and enjoining various purificatory rites.[24] The conception of marriage, as quickening and educating the affections and thus
exalting and refining human life, was wholly foreign to their minds.
Woman was a mere instrument of temptation in their eyes, deceitful, faith-
less, selfish, jealous, misled and misleading by her passions.

But their ascetic tendencies did not stop here. The Pharisee
was very careful to observe the distinction of meats lawful and unlawful,
as laid down by the Mosaic code, and even rendered these ordinances vexa-
tious by minute definitions of his own. But the Essene went far beyond
him. He drank no wine, he did not touch animal food. His meal consisted
of a piece of bread and a single mess of vegetables. Even this simple
fare was prepared for him by special officers consecrated for the purpose,
that it might be free from all contamination.[25] Nay, so stringent were
the rules of the order on this point, that when an Essene was excommunicated,
he often died of starvation, being bound by his oath not to take food prepared by defiled hands, and thus being reduced to eat the very grass of
the field.[26]

Again, in hot climates oil for anointing the body is almost a

necessary of life. From this too the Essenes strictly abstained. Even if
they were accidentally smeared, they were careful at once to wash themselves, holding the mere touch to be a contamination.[27]

From these facts it seems clear that Essene abstinence was something more than the mere exaggeration of Pharisaic principles. The rigour
of the Pharisee was based on his obligation of obedience to an absolute
external law. The Essene introduced a new principle. He condemned in any
form the gratification of the natural cravings, nor would he consent to
regard it as moral or immoral only according to the motive which suggested
it or the consequences which flowed from it. It was in itself an absolute
evil. He sought to disengage himself, as far as possible, from the conditions of physical life. In short, in the asceticism of the Essene we seem
to see the germ of that Gnostic dualism which regards matter as the principle, or at least the abode, of evil.

2.   And, when we come to investigate the speculative tenets of the
sect, we shall find that the Essenes have diverged appreciably from the
common type of Jewish orthodoxy.

(i)   Attention was directed above to their respect for Moses and the
Mosaic law, which they shared in common with the Pharisee. But there was
another side to their theological teaching. Though our information is
somewhat defective, still in the scanty notices which are preserved we
find sufficient indications that they had absorbed some foreign elements
of religious thought into their system. Thus at day-break they addressed
certain prayers, which had been handed down from their forefathers, to the
Sun, 'as if entreating him to rise.'[28] They were careful also to conceal
and bury all polluting substances, so as not 'to insult the rays of the
god.'[29] We cannot indeed suppose that they regarded the sun as more than
a symbol of the unseen power who gives light and life; but their outward
demonstrations of reverence were sufficiently prominent to attach to
them, or to a sect derived from them, the epithet of 'Sun-worshippers,'[30]
and some connexion with the characteristic feature of Parsee devotion at
once suggests itself. The practice at all events stands in strong contrast to the denunciations of worship paid to the 'hosts of heaven' in the
Hebrew prophets.

(ii)   Nor again is it an insignificant fact that, while the Pharisee

maintained the resurrection of the body as a cardinal article of his
faith, the Essene restricted himself to a belief in the immortality of
the soul. The soul, he maintained, was confined in the flesh, as in a
prison-house. Only when disengaged from these fetters would it be truly
free. Then it would soar aloft, rejoicing in its newly attained liberty.[31]
This doctrine accords with the fundamental conception of the malignity of
matter. To those who held this conception a resurrection of the body
would be repulsive, as involving a perpetuation of evil.

(iii)   But they also separated themselves from the religious belief
of the orthodox Jew in another respect, which would provoke more notice.
While they sent gifts to the temple at Jerusalem, they refused to offer
sacrifices there.[32] It would appear that the slaughter of animals was
altogether forbidden by their creed.[33] It is certain that they were
afraid of contracting some ceremonial impurity by offering victims in
the temple. Meanwhile they had sacrifices, bloodless sacrifices, of their
own. They regarded their simple meals with their accompanying prayers
and thanksgiving, not only as devotional but even as sacrificial rites.
Those who prepared and presided over these meals were their consecrated
priests.[34]

(iv)   In what other respects they may have departed from, or added
to, the normal creed of Judaism, we do not know. But it is expressly
stated that, when a novice after passing through the probationary stages
was admitted to the full privileges of the order, the oath of admission
bound him 'to conceal nothing from the members of the sect, and to report
nothing concerning them to others, even though threatened with death; not
to communicate any of their doctrines to anyone otherwise than as he himself had received them; but to abstain from robbery, and in like manner
to guard carefully the books of their sect, and *the names of the angels.*'[35]
It may be reasonably supposed that more lurks under this last expression
than meets the ear. This esoteric doctrine, relating to angelic beings,
may have been another link which attached Essenism to the religion of
Zoroaster. At all events we seem to be justified in connecting it with
the self-imposed service and worshipping of angels at Colossae: and we
may well suspect that we have here a germ which was developed into the
Gnostic doctrine of aeons or emanations.

(v)   If so, it is not unconnected with another notice relating to
Essene peculiarities. The Gnostic doctrine of intermediate beings between
God and the world, as we have seen, was intimately connected with speculations respecting creation. Now we are specially informed that the Essenes,
while leaving physical studies in general to speculative idlers (μετεωρολέσχαις), as being beyond the reach of human nature, yet excepted from
their general condemnation that philosophy which treats of the existence
of God and the generation of the universe.[36]

(vi)   Mention has been made incidentally of certain secret books
peculiar to the sect. The existence of such an apocryphal literature was
a sure token of some abnormal development in doctrine.[37] In the passage
quoted it is mentioned in relation to some form of angelology. Elsewhere
their skill in prediction, for which they were especially famous, is connected with the perusal of certain 'sacred books,' which however are not
described.[38] But more especially, we are told that the Essenes studied
with extraordinary diligence the writings of the ancients, selecting those
especially which could be turned to profit for soul and body, and that
from these they learnt the qualities of roots and the properties of
stones.[39] This expression, as illustrated by other notices, points clearly
to the study of occult sciences, and recalls the alliance with the practice
of magical arts, which was a distinguishing feature of Gnosticism, and is
condemned by Christian teachers even in the heresies of the Apostolic age.

3.   But the notice to which I have just alluded suggests a broader
affinity with Gnosticism. Not only did the theological speculations of
the Essenes take a Gnostic turn, but they guarded their peculiar tenets
with Gnostic reserve. They too had their esoteric doctrine which they
looked upon as the exclusive possession of the privileged few; their
'mysteries' which it was a grievous offence to communicate to the uninitiated. This doctrine was contained, as we have seen, in an apocryphal
literature. Their whole organisation was arranged so as to prevent the
divulgence of its secrets to those without. The long period of noviciate,
the careful rites of initiation, the distinction of the several orders[40]
in the community, the solemn oaths by which they bound their members, were
so many safeguards against a betrayal of this precious deposit, which they
held to be restricted to the inmost circle of the brotherhood.

In selecting these details I have not attempted to give a
finished portrait of Essenism. From this point of view the delineation
would be imperfect and misleading: for I have left out of sight the nobler
features of the sect, their courageous endurance, their simple piety, their
brotherly love. My object was solely to call attention to those features
which distinguish it from the normal type of Judaism, and seem to justify
the attribution of Gnostic influences. And here it has been seen that the
three characteristics, which were singled out above as distinctive of
Gnosticism, reappear in the Essenes; though it has been convenient to consider them in the reversed order. This Jewish sect exhibits the same exclusiveness in the communication of its doctrines. Its theological speculations take the same direction, dwelling on the mysteries of creation,
regarding matter as the abode of evil, and postulating certain intermediate spiritual agencies as necessary links of communication between
heaven and earth. And lastly, its speculative opinions involve the same
ethical conclusions, and lead in like manner to a rigid asceticism. If
the notices relating to these points do not always explain themselves, yet
read in the light of the heresies of the Apostolic age and in that of subsequent Judaeo-Gnostic Christianity, their bearing seems to be distinct
enough; so that we should not be far wrong, if we were to designate Essenism
as Gnostic Judaism.[41]

But the Essenes of whom historical notices are preserved were
inhabitants of the Holy Land. Their monasteries were situated on the shores
of the Dead Sea. We are told indeed, that the sect was not confined to any
one place, and that members of the order were found in great numbers in
divers cities and villages.[42] But Judaea in one notice, Palestine and
Syria in another, are especially named as the localities of the Essene
settlements.[43] Have we any reason to suppose that they were represented
among the Jews of the Dispersion? In Egypt indeed we find ourselves confronted with a similar ascetic sect, the Therapeutes, who may perhaps have
had an independent origin, but who nevertheless exhibit substantially the
same type of Jewish thought and practice.[44] But the Dispersion of Egypt,
it may be argued, was exceptional; and we might expect to find here organi-
sations and developments of Judaism hardly less marked and various than
in the mother country. What ground have we for assuming the existence of

this type in Asia Minor? Do we meet with any traces of it in the cities
of the Lycus, or in proconsular Asia generally, which would justify the
opinion that it might make its influence felt in the Christian communities
of that district?

Now it has been shown that the colonies of the Jews in this
neighbourhood were populous and influential;[45] and it might be argued
with great probability that among these large numbers Essene Judaism could
not be unrepresented. But indeed throughout this investigation, when I
speak of the Judaism in the Colossian Church as Essene, I do not assume a
precise identity of origin, but only an essential affinity of type, with
the Essenes of the mother country. As a matter of history, it may or may
not have sprung from the colonies on the shores of the Dead Sea; but as
this can neither be proved nor disproved, so also it is immaterial to my
main purpose. All along its frontier, wherever Judaism became enamoured
of and was wedded to Oriental mysticism, the same union would produce substantially the same results. In a country where Phrygia, Persia, Syria,
all in turn had moulded religious thought, it would be strange indeed if
Judaism entirely escaped these influences. Nor, as a matter of fact, are
indications wanting to show that it was not unaffected by them. If the
traces are few, they are at least as numerous and as clear as with our
defective information on the whole subject we have any right to expect in
this particular instance.

When St Paul visits Ephesus, he comes in contact with certain
strolling Jews, exorcists, who attempt to cast out evil spirits.[46] Connecting this fact with the notices of Josephus, from which we infer that exorcisms of this kind were especially practised by the Essenes,[47] we seem to
have an indication of their presence in the capital of proconsular Asia.
If so, it is a significant fact that in their exorcisms they employed the
name of our Lord: for then we must regard this as the earliest notice of
those overtures of alliance on the part of Essenism, which involved such
important consequences in the subsequent history of the Church. It is
also worth observing, that the next incident in St Luke's narrative is the
burning of their magical books by those whom St Paul converted on this
occasion.[48] As Jews are especially mentioned among these converts, and
as books of charms are ascribed to the Essenes by Josephus, the two

incidents, standing in this close connexion, throw great light on the type of Judaism which thus appears at Ephesus.[49]

Somewhat later we have another notice which bears in the same direction. The Sibylline Oracle, which forms the fourth book in the existing collection, is discovered by internal evidence to have been written about A.D. 80.[50] It is plainly a product of Judaism, but its Judaism does not belong to the normal Pharisaic type. With Essenism it rejects sacrifices, even regarding the shedding of blood as a pollution,[51] and with Essenism also it inculcates the duty of frequent washings.[52] Yet from other indications we are led to the conclusion, that this poem was not written in the interests of Essenism properly so called, but represents some allied though independent development of Judaism. In some respects at all events its language seems quite inconsistent with the purer type of Essenism.[53] But its general tendency is clear: and of its locality there can hardly be a doubt. The affairs of Asia Minor occupy a disproportionate space in the poet's description of the past and vision of the future. The cities of the Maeander and its neighbourhood, among these Laodicea, are mentioned with emphasis.[54]

And certainly the moral and intellectual atmosphere would not be unfavourable to the growth of such a plant. The same district, which in speculative philosophy had produced a Thales and a Heraclitus,[55] had developed in popular religion the worship of the Phrygian Cybele and Sabazius and of the Ephesian Artemis.[56] Cosmological speculation, mystic theosophy, religious fanaticism, all had their home here. Associated with Judaism or with Christianity the natural temperament and the intellectual bias of the people would take a new direction; but the old type would not be altogether obliterated. Phrygia reared the hybrid monstrosities of Ophitism.[57] She was the mother of Montanist enthusiasm,[58] and the foster-mother of Novatian rigorism.[59] The syncretist, the mystic, the devotee, the puritan, would find a congenial climate in these regions of Asia Minor.

It has thus been shown *first*, that Essene Judaism was Gnostic in its character; and *secondly*, that this type of Jewish thought and practice had established itself in the Apostolic age in those parts of Asia Minor with which we are more directly concerned. It now remains to examine the

heresy of the Colossian Church more nearly, and to see whether it deserves
the name, which provisionally was given to it, of Gnostic Judaism. Its
Judaism all will allow. Its claim to be regarded as Gnostic will require
a closer scrutiny. And in conducting this examination, it will be convenient to take the three notes of Gnosticism which have been already laid
down, and to enquire how far it satisfies these tests.

1.   It has been pointed out that Gnosticism strove to establish, or
rather to preserve, an *intellectual oligarchy* in religion. It had its
hidden wisdom, its exclusive mysteries, its privileged class.

Now I think it will be evident, that St Paul in this epistle
feels himself challenged to contend for the *universality* of the Gospel.
This indeed is a characteristic feature of the Apostle's teaching at all
times, and holds an equally prominent place in the epistles of an earlier
date. But the point to be observed is, that the Apostle, in maintaining
this doctrine, has changed the mode of his defence; and this fact suggests
that there has been a change in the direction of the attack. It is no
longer against national exclusiveness, but against intellectual exclusiveness, that he contends. His adversaries do not now plead ceremonial
restrictions, or at least do not plead these alone: but they erect an arti-
ficial barrier of spiritual privilege, even more fatal to the universal
claims of the Gospel, because more specious and more insidious. It is not
now against the Jew as such, but against the Jew become Gnostic, that he
fights the battle of liberty. In other words; it is not against Christian
Pharisaism but against Christian Essenism that he defends his position.
Only in the light of such an antagonism can we understand the emphatic
iteration with which he claims to 'warn *every* man and teach *every* man in
every wisdom, that he may present *every* man perfect in Christ Jesus.[60] It
will be remembered that 'wisdom' in Gnostic teaching was the exclusive possession of the few; it will not be forgotten that 'perfection' was the term
especially applied in their language to this privileged minority, as con-
tradistinguished from the common herd of believers; and thus it will be
readily understood why St Paul should go on to say that this universality
of the Gospel is the one object of his contention, to which all the energies
of his life are directed, and having done so, should express his intense
anxiety for the Churches of Colossae and the neighbourhood, lest they should

be led astray by a spurious wisdom to desert the true knowledge.[61] This
danger also will enable us to appreciate a novel feature in another passage
of the epistle. While dwelling on the obliteration of all distinctions in
Christ, he repeats his earlier contrasts, 'Greek and Jew,' 'circumcision
and uncircumcision,' 'bondslave and free'; but to these he adds new words
which at once give a wider scope and a more immediate application to the
lesson. In Christ the existence of 'barbarian' and even 'Scythian,' the
lowest type of barbarian, is extinguished.[62] As culture, civilisation,
philosophy, knowledge, are no conditions of acceptance, so neither is
their absence any disqualification in the believer. The aristocracy of
intellectual discernment, which Gnosticism upheld in religion, is abhor-
rent to the first principles of the Gospel.

        Hence also must be explained the frequent occurrence of the
words 'wisdom' (σοφία), 'intelligence' (σύνεσις), 'knowledge' (γνῶσις),
'perfect knowledge' (ἐπίγνωσις), in this epistle.[63] St Paul takes up the
language of his opponents, and translates it into a higher sphere. The
false teachers put forward a 'philosophy,' but it was only an empty deceit,
only a plausible display of false reasoning.[64] They pretended 'wisdom,'
but it was merely the profession, not the reality.[65] Against these pre-
tentions the Apostle sets the true wisdom of the Gospel. On its wealth,
its fulness, its perfection, he is never tired of dwelling.[66] The true
wisdom, he would argue, is essentially spiritual and yet essentially
definite; while the false is argumentative, is speculative, is vague and
dreamy.[67] Again they had their rites of initiation. St Paul contrasts
with these the one universal, comprehensive mystery,[68] the knowledge of
God in Christ. This mystery is complete in itself: it contains 'all the
treasures of wisdom and of knowledge hidden' in it.[69] Moreover it is
offered to all without distinction: though once hidden, its revelation is
unrestricted, except by the waywardness and disobedience of men. The
esoteric spirit of Gnosticism finds no countenance in the Apostle's
teaching.

        2.   From the informing spirit of Gnosticism we turn to the specula-
tive tenets--the cosmogony and the theology of the Gnostic.

        And here too the affinities to Gnosticism reveal themselves in
the Colossian heresy. We cannot fail to observe that the Apostle has in

view the doctrine of intermediate agencies, regarded as instruments in
the creation and government of the world. Though this tenet is not distinctly mentioned, it is tacitly assumed in the teaching which St Paul
opposes to it. Against the philosophy of successive evolutions from the
Divine nature, angelic mediators forming the successive links in the chain
which binds the finite to the Infinite, he sets the doctrine of the one
Eternal Son, the Word of God begotten before the worlds.[70] The angelology
of the heretics had a twofold bearing; it was intimately connected at once
with cosmogony and with religion. Correspondingly St Paul represents the
mediatorial function of Christ as twofold: it is exercised in the natural
creation, and it is exercised in the spiritual creation. In both these
spheres His initiative is absolute, His control is universal, His action
is complete. By His agency the world of matter was created and is sus-
tained. He is at once the beginning and the end of the material universe;
'All things have been created through Him and unto Him.' Nor is His
office in the spiritual world less complete. In the Church, as in the
Universe, He is sole, absolute, supreme; the primary source from which all
life proceeds and the ultimate arbiter in whom all feuds are reconciled.

On the one hand, in relation to Deity, He is the visible image
of the invisible God. He is not only the chief manifestation of the
Divine nature: He exhausts the Godhead manifested. In Him resides the
totality of the Divine powers and attributes. For this totality Gnostic
teachers had a technical term, the *pleroma* or *plentitude*.[71] From the
pleroma they supposed that all those agencies issued, through which God
has at any time exerted His power in creation, or manifested His will
through revelation. These mediatorial beings would retain more or less
of its influence, according as they claimed direct parentage from it or
traced their descent through successive evolutions. But in all cases this
pleroma was distributed, diluted, transformed and darkened by foreign admixture. They were only partial and blurred images, often deceptive carica-
tures, of their original, broken lights of the great central Light. It is
not improbable that, like later speculators of the same school, they found
a place somewhere or other in their genealogy of spiritual beings for the
Christ. If so, St Paul's language becomes doubly significant. But this
hypothesis is not needed to explain its reference. In contrast to their

doctrine, he asserts and repeats the assertion, that the pleroma abides
absolutely and wholly in Christ as the Word of God. The entire light is
concentrated in Him.

Hence it follows that, as regards created things, His supremacy
must be absolute. In heaven as in earth, over things immaterial as over
things material, He is king. Speculations on the nature of intermediate
spiritual agencies--their names, their ranks, their offices--were rife in
the schools of Judaeo-Gnostic thought. 'Thrones, dominations, princedoms,
virtues, powers'--these formed part of the spiritual nomenclature which
they had invented to describe different grades of angelic mediators. Without entering into these speculations, the Apostle asserts that Christ is
Lord of all, the highest and the lowest, whatever rank they may hold and
by whatever name they are called,[72] for they are parts of creation and He
is the source of creation. Through Him they became, and unto Him they tend.

Hence the worship of angels, which the false teachers inculcated,
was utterly wrong in principle. The motive of this angelolatry it is not
difficult to imagine. There was a show of humility,[73] for there was a confession of weakness, in this subservience to inferior mediatorial agencies.
It was held feasible to grasp at the lower links of the chain which bound
earth to heaven, when heaven itself seemed far beyond the reach of man.
The successive grades of intermediate beings were as successive steps, by
which man might mount the ladder leading up to the throne of God. This
carefully woven web of sophistry the Apostle tears to shreds. The doctrine
of the false teachers was based on confident assumptions respecting angelic
beings of whom they could know nothing. It was moreover a denial of
Christ's twofold personality and His mediatorial office. It follows from
the true conception of Christ's Person, that He and He alone can bridge
over the chasm between earth and heaven; for He is at once the lowest and
the highest. He raises up man to God, for He brings down God to man. Thus
the chain is reduced to a single link, this link being the Word made flesh.
As the *pleroma* resides in Him, so is it communicated to us through Him.[74]
To substitute allegiance to any other spiritual mediator is to sever the
connexion of the limbs with the Head, which is the centre of life and the
mainspring of all energy throughout the body.[75]

Hence follows the practical conclusion, that, whatever is done,

must be done in the name of the Lord.[76] Wives must submit to their hus-
bands 'in the Lord': children must obey their parents 'in the Lord': servants must work for their masters as working 'unto the Lord.'[77] This
iteration, 'in the Lord,' 'unto the Lord,' is not an irrelevant form of
words; but arises as an immediate inference from the main idea which under-
lies the doctrinal portion of the epistle.

3.   It has been shown that the speculative tenets of Gnosticism might
lead (and as a matter of fact we know that they did lead) to either of two
practical extremes, to rigid asceticism or to unbridled license. The latter alternative appears to some extent in the heresy of the Pastoral
Epistles[78] and still more plainly in those of the Catholic Epistles[79] and
the Apocalypse.[80] It is constantly urged by Catholic writers as a reproach
against later Gnostic sects.

But the former and nobler extreme was the first impulse of the
Gnostic. To escape from the infection of evil by escaping from the domination of matter was his chief anxiety. This appears very plainly in the
Colossian heresy. Though the prohibitions to which the Apostle alludes
might be explained in part by the ordinances of the Mosaic ritual, this
explanation will not cover all the facts. Thus for instance drinks are
mentioned as well as meats,[81] though on the former the law of Moses is
silent. Thus again the rigorous denunciation, 'Touch not, taste not,
handle not,'[82] seems to go very far beyond the Levitical enactments. And
moreover the *motive* of these prohibitions is Essene rather than Pharisaic,
Gnostic rather than Jewish. These severities of discipline were intended
'to check indulgence of the flesh.'[83] They professed to treat the body
with entire disregard, to ignore its cravings and to deny its wants. In
short they betray a strong *ascetic* tendency,[84] of which normal Judaism,
as represented by the Pharisee, offers no explanation.

And St Paul's answer points to the same inference. The difference will appear more plainly, if we compare it with his treatment of
Pharisaic Judaism in the Galatian Church. This epistle offers nothing at
all corresponding to his language on that occasion; 'If righteousness be
by law, then Christ died in vain'; 'If ye be circumcised, Christ shall
profit you nothing'; 'Christ is nullified for you, whosoever are justified
by law; ye are fallen from grace.'[85] The point of view in fact is wholly

changed. With these Essene or Gnostic Judaizers the Mosaic law was neither
the motive nor the standard, it was only the starting point, of their aus-
terities. Hence in replying the Apostle no longer deals with law, as law;
he no longer points the contrast of grace and works; but he enters upon
the *moral* aspects of these ascetic practices. He denounces them, as con-
centrating the thoughts on earthly and perishable things.[86] He points out
that they fail in their purpose, and are found valueless against carnal
indulgences.[87] In their place he offers the true and only remedy against
sin--the elevation of the inner life in Christ, the transference of the
affections into a higher sphere,[88] where the temptations of the flesh are
powerless. Thus dying with Christ, they will kill *all* their earthly members.[89] Thus rising with Christ, they will be renewed in the image of
God their Creator.[90]

In attempting to draw a complete portrait of the Colossian
heresy from a few features accidentally exhibited in St Paul's epistle, it
has been necessary to supply certain links; and some assurance may not un-
reasonably be required that this has not been done arbitrarily. Nor is
this security wanting. In all such cases the test will be twofold. The
result must be consistent with itself: and it must do no violence to the
historical conditions under which the phenomena arose.

1.   In the present instance the former of these tests is fully
satisfied. The consistency and the symmetry of the result is its great
recommendation. The postulate of a Gnostic type brings the separate
parts of the representation into direct connexion. The speculative opinions and the practical tendencies of the heresy thus explain, and are explained by, each other. It is analogous to the hypothesis of the comparative anatomist, who by referring the fossil remains to their proper type
restores the whole skeleton of some unknown animal from a few bones belonging to different extremities of the body, and without the intermediate and
connecting parts. In the one case, as in the other, the result is the
justification of the postulate.

2.   And again; the historical conditions of the problem are carefully
observed. It has been shown already, that Judaism in the preceding age
had in one of its developments assumed a form which was the natural pre-
cursor of the Colossian heresy. In order to complete the argument it will

be necessary to show that Christianity in the generation next succeeding exhibited a perverted type, which was its natural outgrowth. If this can be done, the Colossian heresy will take its proper place in a regular historical sequence.

I have already pointed out that the language of St John in the Apocalypse, which was probably written within a few years of this epistle, seems to imply the continuance in this district of the same type of heresy which is here denounced by St Paul. But the notices in this book are not more definite than those of the Epistle to the Colossians itself; and we are led to look outside the Canonical writings for some more explicit evidence. Has early Christian history then preserved any record of a distinctly Gnostic school existing on the confines of the Apostolic age, which may be considered a legitimate development of the phase of religious speculation that confronts us here?

We find exactly the phenomenon which we are seeking in the heresy of Cerinthus.[91] The time, the place, the circumstances, all agree. This heresiarch is said to have been originally a native of Alexandria;[92] but proconsular Asia is allowed on all hands to have been the scene of his activity as a teacher.[93] He lived and taught at the close of the Apostolic age, that is, in the latest decade of the first century. Some writers indeed make him an antagonist of St Peter and St Paul,[94] but their authority is not trustworthy, nor is this very early date at all probable. But there can be no reasonable doubt that he was a contemporary of St John, who was related by Polycarp to have denounced him face to face on one memorable occasion,[95] and is moreover said by Irenaeus to have written his Gospel with the direct object of confuting his errors.[96]

'Cerinthus,' writes Neander, 'is best entitled to be considered as the intermediate link between the Judaizing and the Gnostic sects.' 'Even among the ancients,' he adds, 'opposite reports respecting his doctrines have been given from opposite points of view, according as the Gnostic or the Judaizing element was exclusively insisted upon: and the dispute on this point has been kept up even to modern times. In point of chronology too Cerinthus may be regarded as representing the principle in its transition from Judaism to Gnosticism.'[97]

Of his Judaism no doubt has been or can be entertained. The
gross Chiliastic doctrine ascribed to him,[98] even though it may have been
exaggerated in the representations of adverse writers, can only be explained
by a Jewish origin. His conception of the Person of Christ was Ebionite,
that is Judaic, in its main features.[99] He is said moreover to have en-
forced the rite of circumcision and to have inculcated the observance of
sabbaths.[100] It is related also that the Cerinthians, like the Ebionites,
accepted the Gospel of St Matthew alone.[101]

At the same time, it is said by an ancient writer that his ad-
herence to Judaism was only partial.[102] This limitation is doubtless correct. As Gnostic principles asserted themselves more distinctly, pure
Judaism necessarily suffered. All or nearly all the early Gnostic heresies
were Judaic; and for a time a compromise was effected which involved more
or less concession on either side. But the ultimate incompatibility of
the two at length became evident, and a precarious alliance was exchanged
for an open antagonism. This final result however was not reached till
the middle of the second century: and meanwhile it was a question to what
extent Judaism was prepared to make concessions for the sake of this new
ally. Even the Jewish Essenes, as we have seen, departed from the orthodox
position in the matter of sacrifices; and if we possessed fuller information, we should probably find that they made still larger concessions than
this. Of the Colossian heretics we can only form a conjecture, but the
angelology and angelolatry attributed to them point to a further step in
the same direction. As we pass from them to Cerinthus we are no longer
left in doubt; for the Gnostic element has clearly gained the ascendant,
though it has not yet driven its rival out of the field. Two characteristic features in his teaching especially deserve consideration, both as
evincing the tendency of his speculations and as throwing back light on
the notices in the Colossian Epistle.

1.   His cosmogony is essentially Gnostic. The great problem of
creation presented itself to him in the same aspect; and the solution
which he offered was generically the same. The world, he asserted, was
not made by the highest God, but by an angel or power far removed from,
and ignorant of, this Supreme Being.[103] Other authorities describing his
system speak not of a single power, but of powers, as creating the

universe:[104] but all alike represent this demiurge, or these demiurges,
as ignorant of the absolute God. It is moreover stated that he held the
Mosaic law to have been given not by the supreme God Himself, but by this
angel, or one of these angels, who created the world.[105]

From these notices it is plain that angelology had an important
place in his speculations; and that he employed it to explain the existence
of evil supposed to be inherent in the physical world, as well as to
account for the imperfections of the old dispensation. The 'remote distance' of his angelic demiurge from the supreme God can hardly be explained
except on the hypothesis of *successive* generations of these intermediate
agencies. Thus his solution is thoroughly Gnostic. At the same time, as
contrasted with later and more sharply defined Gnostic systems, the Judaic
origin and complexion of his cosmogony is obvious. His intermediate
agencies still retain the name and the personality of angels, and have not
yet given way to those vague idealities which, as emanations or aeons,
took their place in later speculations. Thus his theory is linked on to
the angelology of later Judaism founded on the angelic appearances recorded
in the Old Testament narrative. And again: while later Gnostics represent
the demiurge and giver of the law as antagonistic to the supreme and good
God, Cerinthus does not go beyond postulating his ignorance. He went as
far as he could without breaking entirely with the Old Testament and
abandoning his Judaic standing-ground.

In these respects Cerinthus is the proper link between the inci-
pient gnosis of the Colossian heretics and the mature gnosis of the second
century. In the Colossian epistle we still breathe the atmosphere of
Jewish angelology, nor is there any trace of the *aeon* of later Gnosticism;[106]
while yet speculation is so far advanced that the angels have an important
function in explaining the mysteries of the creation and government of the
world. On the other hand it has not reached the point at which we find it
in Cerinthus. Gnostic conceptions respecting the relation of the demiurgic
agency to the supreme God would appear to have passed through three stages.
This relation was represented first, as imperfect appreciation; next, as
entire ignorance; lastly, as direct antagonism. The second and third are
the standing points of Cerinthus and of the later Gnostic teachers respectively. The first was probably the position of the Colossian false

teachers. The imperfections of the natural world, they would urge, were
due to the limited capacities of these angels to whom the demiurgic work
was committed, and to their imperfect sympathy with the Supreme God; but
at the same time they might fitly receive worship as mediators between God
and man; and indeed humanity seemed in its weakness to need the intervention of some such beings less remote from itself than the highest heaven.

2.   Again the Christology of Cerinthus deserves attention from this
point of view. Here all our authorities are agreed. As a Judaizer
Cerinthus held with the Ebionites that Jesus was only the son of Joseph
and Mary, born in the natural way. As a Gnostic he maintained that the
Christ first descended in the form of a dove on the carpenter's son at his
baptism; that He revealed to him the unknown Father, and worked miracles
through him: and that at length He took His flight and left him, so that
Jesus alone suffered and rose, while the Christ remained impassible.[107]
It would appear also, though this is not certain, that he described this
re-ascension of the Christ as a return 'to His own *pleroma*.'[108]

Now it is not clear from St Paul's language what opinions the
Colossian heretics held respecting the person of our Lord; but we may
safely assume that he regarded them as inadequate and derogatory. The
emphasis, with which he asserts the eternal being and absolute sovereignty
of Christ, can hardly be explained in any other way. But individual expressions tempt us to conjecture that the same ideas were already floating
in the air, which ultimately took form and consistency in the tenets of
Cerinthus. Thus, when he reiterates the statement that the *whole* pleroma
abides *permanently* in Christ,[109] he would appear to be tacitly refuting
some opinion which maintained only mutable and imperfect relations between
the two. When again he speaks of the true gospel first taught to the
Colossians as the doctrine of 'the Christ, *even* Jesus the Lord,'[110] his
language might seem to be directed against the tendency to separate the
heavenly Christ from the earthly Jesus, as though the connexion were only
transient. When lastly he dwells on the work of reconciliation, as wrought
'through the blood of Christ's cross,' 'in the body of His flesh through
death,'[111] we may perhaps infer that he already discerned a disposition to
put aside Christ's passion as a stumbling-block in the way of philosophical
religion. Thus regarded, the Apostle's language gains force and point;

though no stress can be laid on explanations which are so largely conjectural.

But if so, the very generality of his language shows that these
speculations were still vague and fluctuating. The difference which
separates these heretics from Cerinthus may be measured by the greater
precision and directness in the Apostolic counter-statement, as we turn
from the Epistle to the Colossians to the Gospel of St John. In this
interval, extending over nearly a quarter of a century, speculation has
taken a definite shape. The elements of Gnostic theory, which were before
held in solution, had meanwhile crystallized around the facts of the Gospel.
Yet still we seem justified, even at the earlier date, in speaking of these
general ideas as Gnostic, guarding ourselves at the same time against misunderstanding with the twofold caution, that we here employ the term to
express the simplest and most elementary conceptions of this tendency of
thought, and that we do not postulate its use as a distinct designation of
any sect or sects at this early date. Thus limited, the view that the
writer of this epistle is combating a Gnostic heresy seems free from all
objections, while it appears necessary to explain his language; and certainly it does not, as is sometimes imagined, place any weapon in the
hands of those who would assail the early date and Apostolic authorship
of the epistle.

* * *

NOTES

[1]Col. 2:16, 17, 21 ff.

[2]2:11.

[3]2:4, 8, 18, 23.

[4]The Colossian heresy has been made the subject of special
dissertations by SCHNECKENBURGER *Beiträge zur Einleitung ins N. T.*
(Stuttgart 1832), and *Ueber das Alter der jüdischen Proselyten-Taufe,
nebst einer Beilage über die Irrlehrer zu Colossä* (Berlin 1828); by

OSIANDER "Ueber die Colossischen Irrlehrer" *Tübinger Zeitschrift* 3
(1834) 96 ff.; and by RHEINWALD *De Pseudodoctoribus Colossensibus* (Bonn
1834). But more valuable contributions to the subject will often be found
in introductions to the commentaries on the epistle. Those of BLEEK,
DAVIES, MEYER, OLSHAUSEN, STEIGER, and DE WETTE may be mentioned. Among
other works which may be consulted are BAUR *Der Apostel Paulus* 417 ff.;
BOEHMER *Isagoge in Epistolam ad Colossenses* (Berlin 1829) 56 ff., 277 ff.;
BURTON *Inquiry into the Heresies of the Apostolic Age*, Lectures 4, 5;
EWALD *Die Sendschreiben des Apostels Paulus* 462 ff.; HILGENFELD "Der
Gnosticismus u. das Neue Testament," *ZWT* 13 (1870) 233 ff.; R. A. LIPSIUS
in *Schenkels Bibel-Lexicon*, s.v. Gnosis; MAYERHOFF *Der Brief an die
Colosser* 107 ff.; NEANDER *Planting of the Christian Church* 1. 319 ff.;
PRESSENSE *Trois Premiers Siècles* 2. 194 ff.; STORR *Opuscula* 2. 149 ff.;
THIERSCH *Die Kirche im Apostolischen Zeitalter* 146 ff. Of all the accounts
of these Colossian false teachers, I have found none more satisfactory than
that of Neander, whose opinions are followed in the main by the most sober
of later writers.

       In the investigation which follows I have assumed that the Colos-
sian false teachers were Christians in some sense. The views maintained
by some earlier critics, who regarded them as (1) Jews, or (2) Greek philosophers, or (3) Chaldean magi, have found no favour and do not need serious
consideration. See Meyer's introduction for an enumeration of such views.
A refutation of them will be found in Bleek's *Vorlesungen* 12 ff.

[5]See below.

[6]See below.

[7]Col. 2:8-23. Hilgenfeld (*Der Gnosticismus* 250 ff.) contends
strenuously for the separation of the two elements. He argues that 'these
two tendencies are related to one another as fire and water, and nothing
stands in the way of allowing the author after the first side-glance at
the Gnostics to pass over with vs. 11 to the Judaizers, with whom Col. 2:16
ff. is exclusively concerned.' He supposes therefore that 2:8-10 refers to
'pure Gnostics,' and 2:16-23 to 'pure Judaizers.' To this it is sufficient

to answer (1) That, if the two elements be so antagonistic, they managed nevertheless to reconcile their differences; for we find them united in several Judaeo-Gnostic heresies in the first half of the second century, ξυνώμοσαν γάρ, ὄντες ἔχθιστοι τὸ πρίν, πῦρ καὶ θάλασσα, καὶ τὰ πίστ᾽ ἐδειξάτην; (2) That the two passages are directly connected together by τὰ στοιχεῖα τοῦ κόσμου, which occurs in both vss. 8, 20; (3) That it is not a simple transition once for all from the Gnostic to the Judaic element, but the epistle passes to and fro several times from the one to the other; while no hint is given that two separate heresies are attacked, but on the contrary the sentences are connected in a logical sequence (e.g. vs. 9 ὅτι, 10 ὅς, 11 ἐν ᾧ, 12 ἐν ᾧ, 13 καὶ, 16 οὖν). I hope to make this point clear in my notes on the passage.

The hypothesis of more than one heresy is maintained also by Heinrichs (Koppe *N. T.* 7. Part 2, 1803). At an earlier date it seems to be favoured by Grotius (notes on 2:16, 21); but his language is not very explicit. And earlier still Calvin in his argument to the epistle writes, 'Putant aliqui duo fuisse hominum genera, qui abducere tentarent Colossenses ab evangelii puritate,' but rejects this view as uncalled for.

The same question is raised with regard to the heretical teachers of the Pastoral Epistles, and should probably be answered in the same way.

[8]The chief authorities for the history of Gnosticism are NEANDER *Church History* 2. 1 ff.; BAUR *Die Christliche Gnosis* (Tübingen, 1835); MATTER *Histoire Critique du Gnosticisme* (2nd ed., Strasbourg and Paris, 1834); R. A. LIPSIUS *Gnosticismus* in Ersch u. Gruber *s. v.* (Leipzig, 1860); MANSEL *Gnostic Heresies of the First and Second Centuries* (London, 1875); and for Gnostic art, KING *Gnostics and their Remains* (London 1864).

[9]See esp. Iren. 1. 6. 1 ff., Clement Alex. *Strom.* 2. p. 433 ff. (Potter)....

[10]See Neander 1 ff., from whom the epithet is borrowed.

[11]The fathers speak of this as the main question about which the Gnostics busy themselves; *Unde malum?* πόθεν ἡ κακία; Tertullian *de Praescr.*

7, *adv. Marc.* 1. 2, Eusebius *H. E.* 5. 27; passages quoted by Baur
Christliche Gnosis 19. On the leading conceptions of Gnosticism see
especially Neander, 9 ff.

[12]On this point see Clement *Strom.* 3. 5 (p. 529) εἰς δύο διελόντες
πράγματα ἁπάσας τὰς αἱρέσεις ἀποκρινώμεθα αὐτοῖς· ἢ γάρ τοι ἀδιαφόρως
ζῆν διδάσκουσιν, ἢ τὸ ὑπέρτονον ἄγουσαι ἐγκράτειαν διὰ δυσσεβείας καὶ
φιλαπεχθημοσύνης καταγγέλλουσι, with the whole passage which follows.
As examples of the one extreme may be instanced the Carpocratians and
Cainites: of the other the Encratites.

[13]See for instance the description of the Carpocratians in
Irenaeus 1. 25. 3 ff., 2. 32. 1 ff., Hippolytus *Haer.* 7. 32, Epiphanius
Haer. 27. 2 ff.; from which passages it appears that they justified their
moral profligacy on the principle that the highest perfection consists in
the most complete contempt of mundane things.

[14]It will be seen from the description in the text, that
Gnosticism (as I have defined it) presupposes only a belief in one God,
the absolute Being, as against the vulgar polytheism. All its *essential*
features, as a speculative system, may be explained from this simple element of belief, without any intervention of specially Christian or even
Jewish doctrine. Christianity added two new elements to it; (1) the idea
of *Redemption*, (2) the person of *Christ*. To explain the former, and to
find a place for the latter, henceforth become prominent questions which
press for solution; and Gnosticism in its several developments undergoes
various modifications in the endeavour to solve them. Redemption must be
set in some relation to the fundamental Gnostic conception of the antagonism
between God and matter; and Christ must have some place found for Him in
the fundamental Gnostic doctrine of emanations.

If it be urged that there is no authority for the name 'Gnostic'
as applied to these pre-Christian theosophists, I am not concerned to prove
the contrary, as my main position is not affected thereby. The term
'Gnostic' is here used, only because no other is so convenient or so appropriate. See note 16 below.

[15]This question will require closer investigation ... [in a discussion of] the genuineness of the Epistle to the Colossians. Meanwhile I content myself with referring to Baur *Christliche Gnosis* 29 ff. and Lipsius *Gnosticismus* 230 ff. Both these writers concede, and indeed insist upon, the non-Christian basis of Gnosticism, at least so far as I have maintained it in the text. Thus for instance Baur says (p. 52), 'Though Christian gnosis is the completion of gnosis, yet the Christian element in gnosis is not so essential as that gnosis cannot still be gnosis even without this element. But just as we can abstract it from the Christian element, so can we also go still further and regard even the Jewish as not strictly an essential element of gnosis.' In another work (*Die drei ersten Jahrhunderte* p. 167, 1st ed.) he expresses himself still more strongly to the same effect, but the expressions are modified in the second edition.

[16]We may perhaps gather from the notices which are preserved that, though the substantive γνῶσις was used with more or less precision even before contact with Christianity to designate the superior illumination of these opinions, the adjective γνωστικοί was not distinctly applied to those who maintained them till somewhat later. Still it is possible that pre-Christian Gnostics already so designated themselves. Hippolytus speaks of the Naassenes or Ophites as giving themselves this name; *Haer.* 5. 6 μετὰ δὲ ταῦτα ἐπεκάλεσαν ἑαυτοὺς γνωστικούς, φάσκοντες μόνοι τὰ βάθη γινώσκειν; cf. §§ 8, 11. His language seems to imply (though it is not explicit) that they were the first to adopt the name. The Ophites were plainly among the earliest Gnostic sects, as the heathen element is still predominant in their teaching, and their Christianity seems to have been a later graft on their pagan theosophy; but at what stage in their development they adopted the name γνωστικοί does not appear. Irenaeus (*Haer.* 1. 25. 6) peaks of the name as affected especially by the Carpocratians. For the use of the substantive γνῶσις see I Cor 8:1, 13:2, 8, I Tim 6:20, ... comp. Rev 2:24 οὕτινες οὐκ ἔγνωσαν τὰ βαθέα τοῦ Σατανᾶ, ὡς λέγουσιν (as explained by the passage already quoted from Hippolytus. *Haer.* 5. 6....)

[17]The name *Epicureans* seems to be applied to them even in the Talmud; see Eisenmenger's *Entdecktes Judenthum* 1. 95, 694 ff.; cf. Keim

Geschichte Jesu von Nazara 1. 281.

[18]For the Pharisees see *Life* 2 παραπλήσιός ἐστι τῇ παρ' Ἕλλησι
Στωϊκῇ λεγομένῃ: for the Essenes, *Ant.* 15. 10. 4 διαίτῃ χρώμενον τῇ παρ'
Ἕλλησιν ὑπὸ Πυθαγόρου καταδεδειγμένῃ.

[19]The really important contemporary sources of information
respecting the Essenes are JOSEPHUS, *JW* 2. 8. 2-13, *Ant.* 13. 5. 9; 18. 1. 5;
Life 2 (with notices of individual Essenes *JW* 1. 3. 5; 2. 7. 3; 2. 20. 4;
3. 2. 1, *Ant.* 13. 2. 2; 15. 10. 4, 5); and PHILO, *Quod omnis probus liber*
§ 12 ff., *Apol. pro Jud.* [= *Hypothetica* 11] a fragment quoted by Eusebius
Praep. Evang. 8. 11). The account of the Therapeutes by the latter writer,
de Vita Contemplativa . . . , must also be consulted, as describing a
closely allied sect. To these should be added the short notice of PLINY,
N. H. 5. 15. 17, as expressing the views of a Roman writer. His account,
we may conjecture, was taken from Alexander Polyhistor, a contemporary of
Sulla, whom he mentions in his prefatory elenchus as one of his authorities
for this 5th book, and who wrote a work *On the Jews* (Clement Alex. *Strom.*
1. 21, p. 396, Eusebius *Praep. Ev.* 9. 17). Significant mention of the
Essenes is found also in the Christian HEGESIPPUS (Eusebius *H. E.* 4. 22)
and in the heathen DION CHRYSOSTOM (Synesius *Dion* 3, p. 39). EPIPHANIUS
(*Haer.* pp. 28 ff., 40 ff.) discusses two separate sects, which he calls
Essenes and *Ossaeans* respectively. These are doubtless different names
of the same persons. His account is, as usual, confused and inaccurate,
but has a certain value. All other authorities are secondary. HIPPOLYTUS,
Haer. 9. 18-28, follows Josephus (*JW* 2. 8. 2 ff.) almost exclusively.
PORPHYRY also (*de Abstinentia*, 4. 11 ff.) copies this same passage of
Josephus, with a few unimportant exceptions probably taken from a lost
work by the same author, πρὸς τοὺς Ἕλληνας, which he mentions by name.
EUSEBIUS (*Praep. Evang.* 8. 11 ff., 9. 3) contents himself with quoting
Philo and Porphyry. SOLINUS (*Polyh.* 35. 9 ff.) merely abstracts Pliny.
TALMUDICAL and RABBINICAL passages, supposed to contain references to the
Essenes, are collected by Frankel in the articles mentioned in a later
paragraph; but the allusions are most uncertain (see the second disserta-
tion on the Essenes). The authorities for the history of the Essenes are

the subject of an article by W. Clemens in the *ZWT* 12 (1869) 328 ff.

The attack on the genuineness of Philo's treatise *De Vita Contemplativa* made by Grätz (3. 463 ff.) has been met by Zeller (*Philosophie*, 3. 2. 255 ff.), whose refutation is complete. The attack of the same writer (3. 464) on the genuineness of the treatise *Quod omnis probus liber* Zeller considers too frivolous to need refuting (p. 235). A refutation will be found in the above-mentioned article of W. Clemens (pp. 340 ff.).

Of modern writings relating to the Essenes the following may be especially mentioned; BELLERMANN *Ueber Essäer u. Therapeuten*, Berlin 1821; GFRÖRER *Philo* 2. 299 ff.; DAHNE *Ersch u. Gruber's Encyklopädie* s.v.; FRANKEL *Zeitschrift für die religiösen Interessen des Judenthums* 1846, 441 ff., *Monatsschrift für Geschichte u. Wissenschaft des Judenthums* 1853, 1. 30 ff., 61 ff.; BÖTTGER *Ueber den Orden der Essäer*, Dresden 1849; EWALD *Geschichte des Volkes Israel* 4. 420 ff., 7. 153 ff; RITSCHL *Entstehung der Altkatholischen Kirche* 179 ff. (2 ed., 1857), and *Theologische Jahrbücher* 1855, 315 ff.; JOST *Geschichte des Judenthums* 1. 207 ff.; GRAETZ *Geschichte der Juden* 3. 79 ff., 463 ff. (2 ed., 1863); HILGENFELD *Jüdische Apocalyptik* 245 ff., and *ZWT* 10. 97 ff., 11. 343 ff., 14 30 ff.; WESTCOTT *Smith's Dictionary of the Bible* s.v.; GINSBURG *The Essenes* (London 1864), and in *Kitto's Cyclopaedia* s.v.; DERENBOURG *L'Histoire et la Géographie de la Palestine* 166 ff., 460 ff.; KEIM *Geschichte Jesu von Nazara* 1. 282 ff.; HAUSRATH *Neutestamentliche Zeitgeschichte* 1. 133 ff.; LIPSIUS *Schenkel's Bibel Lexicon* s.v.; HERZFELD *Geschichte des Volkes Israel* 2. 368 ff., 388 ff., 509 ff. (2 ed., 1863); ZELLER *Philosophie der Griechen* 3. 2, 234 ff. (2 ed., 1868); LANGEN *Judenthum in Palästina* 190 ff.; LÖWY *Kritisch-talmudisches Lexicon* s.v. (Wien 1863); WEISS *Zur Geschichte der jüdischen Tradition* 120 ff. (Wien).

[20] *JW* 2. 8. 9 φυλάσσονται ... ταῖς ἑβδόμασιν ἔργων ἐφάπτεσθαι διαφορώτατα ᾿Ιουδαίων ἁπάντων· οὐ μόνον γὰρ τροφὰς ἑαυτοῖς πρὸ ἡμέρας μιᾶς παρασκευάζουσιν, ὡς μηδὲ πῦρ ἐναύοιεν ἐκείνῃ τῇ ἡμέρᾳ, ἀλλ' οὐδὲ σκεῦός τι μετακινῆσαι θαρροῦσιν κ.τ.λ. Hippolytus (*Haer.* 9. 25) adds that some of them do not so much as leave their beds on this day.

[21]Philo *Quod omn. prob. lib.* § 12.   Of the Therapeutes see Philo
Vit. Cont. § 3, 4.

[22]*JW* 2.8., 9 [§ 145] σέβας δὲ μέγιστον παρ' αὐτοῖς μετὰ τὸν θεὸν
τὸ ὄνομα τοῦ νομοθέτου, κἂν βλασφημήσῃ τις εἰς τοῦτον (i.e. τὸν νομοθέτην),
κολάζεσθαι θανάτῳ: cf. 2. 8, 10 [§ 152].

[23]*JW* 2. 8., 2 [§ 120] γάμου μὲν ὑπεροψία παρ' αὐτοῖς ... τὰς
τῶν γυναικῶν ἀσελγείας φυλασσόμενοι καὶ μηδεμίαν τηρεῖν πεπεισμένοι τὴν
πρὸς ἕνα πίστιν, *Ant.* 18. 1. 5; Philo *Fragm.* p. 633 γάμον παρῃτήσαντο μετὰ
τοῦ διαφερόντως ἀσκεῖν ἐγκράτειαν· Ἐσσαίων γὰρ οὐδεὶς ἄγεται γυναῖκα,
διότι φίλαυτον ἡ γυνὴ καὶ ζηλότυπον οὐ μετρίως καὶ δεινὸν ἀνδρὸς ἤθη
παρασαλεῦσαι, with more to the same purpose.   This peculiarity astonished
the heathen Pliny, *N. H.* 5. 15, 'gens sola et in toto orbe praeter ceteros
mira, sine ulla femina, venere abdicata ... In diem ex aequo convenarum
turba renascitur large frequentantibus ... Ita per saeculorum millia
(incredibile dictu) gens aeterna est, in qua nemo nascitur.   Tam foecunda
illis aliorum vitae poenitentia est.'

[24]*JW* 2. 8, 13 [§ 160] Josephus speaks of these as ἕτερον Ἐσσηνῶν
τάγμα, ὃ δίαιταν μὲν καὶ ἔθη καὶ νόμιμα τοῖς ἄλλοις ὁμοφρονοῦν, διεστὸς
δὲ τῇ κατὰ γάμον δόξῃ. We may suppose that they corresponded to the third
order of a Benedictine or Franciscan brotherhood; so that, living in the
world, they would observe the rule up to a certain point, but would not be
bound by vows of celibacy or subject to the more rigorous discipline of
the sect.

[25]*JW* 2. 8, 5 [§ 130]; see Philo's account of the Therapeutes,
Vit. Cont. § 4 σιτοῦνται δὲ πολυτελὲς οὐδέν, ἀλλὰ ἄρτον εὐτελῆ· καὶ ὄψον
ἅλες, οὓς οἱ ἀβροδιαιτότατοι παραρτύουσιν ὑσσώπῳ· ποτὸν ὕδωρ ναματιαῖον
αὐτοῖς ἐστιν; and again more to the same effect in § 9: and compare the
Essene story of St James in Hegesippus (Eusebius *H. E.* 2. 23) οἶνον καὶ
σίκερα οὐκ ἔπιεν, οὐδὲ ἔμψυχον ἔφαγε.   Their abstention from animal food
accounts for Porphyry's giving them so prominent a place in his treatise:
see Zeller, p. 243.

[26]*JW* 2. 8, 8 [§ 143].

[27]*JW* 2. 8, 3 [§ 123]. κηλῖδα δὲ ὑπολαμβάνουσι τὸ ἔλαιον κ.τ.λ.; Hegesippus *loc. cit.* ἔλαιον οὐκ ἠλείφατο.

[28]*JW* 2. 8, 5 [§ 128] πρός γε μὴν τὸ θεῖον ἰδίως εὐσεβεῖς· πρὶν γὰρ ἀνασχεῖν τὸν ἥλιον οὐδὲν φθέγγονται τῶν βεβήλων, πατρίους δέ τινας εἰς αὐτὸν εὐχάς, ὥσπερ ἱκετεύοντες ἀνατεῖλαι. Compare what Philo says of the Therapeutes, *Vit. Cont.* § 3 ἡλίου μὲν ἀνίσχοντος εὐημερίαν αἰτούμενοι τὴν ὄντως εὐημερίαν, φωτὸς οὐρανίου τὴν διάνοιαν αὐτῶν ἀναπλησθῆναι, and § 11. On the attempt of Frankel (458) to resolve this worship, which Josephus states to be offered to the sun (εἰς αὐτόν), into the ordinary prayers of the Pharisaic Jew at day-break, see the second dissertation on the Essenes.

[29]*JW* 2. 8, 9 [§ 148] ὡς μὴ τὰς αὐγὰς ὑβρίζοιεν τοῦ θεοῦ. There can be no doubt, I think, that by τοῦ θεοῦ is meant the 'sun-god'; comp. Euripides *Heracl.* 749 θεοῦ φαεσίμβροτοι αὐγαί, *Alc.* 722 τὸ φέγγος τοῦτο τοῦ θεοῦ, Appian *Praef.* 9 δυομένου τοῦ θεοῦ, *Lib.* 113 τοῦ θεοῦ περὶ δείλην ἑσπέραν ὄντος, *Civ.* 4. 79 δύνοντος ἄρτι τοῦ θεοῦ: cf. Herodas 2. 24. Dr. Ginsburg has obliterated this very important touch by translating τὰς αὐγὰς τοῦ θεοῦ 'the Divine rays' (*Essenes* 47). It is a significant fact that Hippolytus (*Haer.* 9. 25) omits the words τοῦ θεοῦ, evidently regarding them as a stumbling-block. How Josephus expressed himself in the original Hebrew of the *Bellum Judaicum*, it is vain to speculate: but the Greek translation was authorised, if not made, by him.

[30]Epiphanius *Haer.* 19. 2; 20. 3 Ὀσσηνοὶ δὲ μετέστησαν ἀπὸ Ἰουδαϊσμοῦ εἰς τὴν τῶν Σαμψαίων αἵρεσιν, 53. 1, 2 Σαμψαῖοι γὰρ ἑρμηνεύονται Ἡλιακοί, from the Hebrew שמש 'the sun.' The historical connexion of the Sampsaeans with the Essenes is evident from these passages: though it is difficult to say what their precise relations to each other were.

[31]*JW* 2. 8, 11 [§ 154] καὶ γὰρ ἔρρωται παρ' αὐτοῖς ἥδε ἡ δόξα, φθαρτὰ μὲν εἶναι τὰ σώματα καὶ τὴν ὕλην οὐ μόνιμον αὐτοῖς, τὰς δὲ ψυχὰς ἀθανάτους ἀεὶ διαμένειν ... ἐπειδὰν δὲ ἀνεθῶσι τῶν κατὰ σάρκα δεσμῶν, οἷα δὴ μακρᾶς δουλείας ἀπηλλαγμένας, τότε χαίρειν καὶ μετεώρους φέρεσθαι

κ.τ.λ. To this doctrine the teaching of the Pharisees stands in direct
contrast; 2. 8, 13 [sic, § 163]: cf. also *Ant.* 18. 1. 3, 5.

Nothing can be more explicit than the language of Josephus. On
the other hand Hippolytus (*Haer.* 9. 27) says of them ὁμολογοῦσι γὰρ καὶ
τὴν σάρκα ἀναστήσεσθαι καὶ ἔσεσθαι ἀθάνατον ὃν τρόπον ἤδη ἀθάνατός ἐστιν
ἡ ψυχή κ.τ.λ.; but his authority is worthless on this point, as he can have
had no personal knowledge of the facts: see Zeller p. 251, note 2. Hilgenfeld takes a different view; *ZWT* 14, 49.

[32]*Ant.* 18. 1. 5 εἰς δὲ τὸ ἱερὸν ἀναθήματά τε στέλλοντες θυσίας
οὐκ ἐπιτελοῦσι διαφορότητι ἁγνειῶν, ἃς νομίζοιεν, καὶ δι᾿ αὐτὸ εἰργόμενοι
τοῦ κοινοῦ τεμενίσματος ἐφ᾿ αὑτῶν τὰς θυσίας ἐπιτελοῦσι. So Philo *Quod
omn. prob. lib.* § 12 describes them as οὐ ζῷα καταθύοντες ἀλλ᾿ ἱεροπρεπεῖς·
τὰς ἑαυτῶν διανοίας κατασκευάζειν ἀξιοῦντες.

[33]The following considerations show that their abstention should
probably be explained in this way: (1) Though the language of Josephus
may be ambiguous, that of Philo is unequivocal on this point; (2) Their
abstention from the temple-sacrifices cannot be considered apart from the
fact that they ate no animal food: see above note 25. (3) The Christianised
Essenes, or Ebionites, though strong Judaizers in many respects, yet distinctly protested against the sacrifice of animals; see [pseudo-] Clement
Hom. 3. 45, 52, and cf. Ritschl 224. On this subject see also Zeller
244 ff.

[34]*Ant.* 18. 1. 5 ἱερεῖς τε [χειροτονοῦσι] διὰ ποίησιν σίτου τε καὶ
βρωμάτων, *JW* 2. 8, 5 [§ 131] προκατεύχεται δὲ ὁ ἱερεὺς τῆς τροφῆς κ.τ.λ.;
see Ritschl 181.

[35]*JW* 2. 8, 7 [§ 139] ὅρκους αὐτοῖς ὄμνυσι φρικώδεις...μήτε
κρύψειν τι τοὺς αἱρετιστὰς μήτε ἑτέροις αὐτῶν τι μηνύσειν, καὶ ἂν μέχρι
θανάτου τις βιάζηται. πρὸς τούτοις ὀμνύουσι μηδενὶ μὲν μεταδοῦναι τῶν
δογμάτων ἑτέρως ἢ ὡς αὐτὸς μετέλαβεν· ἀφέξεσθαι δὲ λῃστείας καὶ συντηρήσειν
ὁμοίως τά τε τῆς αἱρέσεως αὐτῶν βιβλία καὶ τὰ τῶν ἀγγέλων ὀνόματα. With
this notice should be compared the Ebionite διαμαρτυρία, or protest of

initiation, prefixed to the *Clementine Homilies*, which shows how closely
the Christian Essenes followed the practice of their Jewish predecessors
in this respect. See Zeller 254.

[36]Philo *Omn. prob. lib.* § 12 (p. 458) τὸ δὲ φυσικὸν ὡς μεῖζον
ἢ κατὰ ἀνθρωπίνην φύσιν μετεωρολέσχαις ἀπολιπόντες, πλὴν ὅσον αὐτοῦ περὶ
ὑπάρξεως θεοῦ καὶ τῆς τοῦ παντὸς γενέσεως φιλοσοφεῖται.

[37]The word *Apocrypha* was used originally to designate the secret
books which contained the esoteric doctrine of a sect. The secondary
sense 'spurious' was derived from the general character of these writings,
which were heretical, mostly Gnostic, forgeries. See Prof. Plumptre's
article *Apocrypha* in Smith's *Dictionary of the Bible.*...

[38]*JW* 2. 8, 12 [§ 159] εἰσὶ δὲ ἐν αὐτοῖς οἳ καὶ τὰ μέλλοντα
προγινώσκειν ὑπισχνοῦνται, βίβλοις ἱεραῖς καὶ διαφόροις ἁγνείαις καὶ
προφητῶν ἀποφθέγμασιν ἐμπαιδοτριβούμενοι· σπάνιον δέ, εἴποτε, ἐν ταῖς
προαγορεύσεσιν ἀστοχήσουσιν. Dr. Ginsburg (p. 49) translates βίβλοις
ἱεραῖς '*the* sacred Scripture,' and προφητῶν ἀποφθέγμασιν '*the* sayings of
the prophets'; but as the definite articles are wanting, the expressions
cannot be so rendered, nor does there seem to be any reference to the
Canonical writings.
        We learn from an anecdote in *Ant.* 13. 11. 2, that the teachers
of this sect communicated the art of prediction to their disciples by
instruction. We may therefore conjecture that with the Essenes this
acquisition was connected with magic or astrology. At all events it is
not treated as a direct inspiration.

[39]*JW* 2. 8, 6 [§ 136] σπουδάζουσι δὲ ἐκτόπως περὶ τὰ τῶν παλαιῶν
συγγράμματα, μάλιστα τὰ πρὸς ὠφέλειαν ψυχῆς καὶ σώματος ἐκλέγοντες· ἔνθεν
αὐτοῖς πρὸς θεραπείαν παθῶν ῥίζαι τε ἀλεξιτήριοι καὶ λίθων ἰδιότητες
ἀνερευνῶνται. This passage might seem at first sight to refer simply to
the *medicinal* qualities of vegetable and mineral substances; but a comparison with another notice in Josephus invests it with a different meaning.
In *Ant.* 8. 2, 5 he states that Solomon, having received by divine inspiration

the art of defeating demons for the advantage and healing of man (εἰς
ὠφέλειαν καὶ θεραπείαν τοῖς ἀνθρώποις), composed and left behind him
charms (ἐπῳδάς) by which diseases were allayed, and diverse kinds of
exorcisms (τρόπους ἐξορκώσεων) by which demons were cast out. 'This mode
of healing,' he adds, 'is very powerful even to the present day'; and he
then relates how, as he was credibly informed (ἱστόρησα), one of his
countrymen, Eleazar by name, had healed several persons possessed by demons
in the presence of Vespasian and his sons and a number of officers and
common soldiers. This he did by applying to the nose of the possessed
his ring, which had concealed in it one of the *roots* which Solomon had
directed to be used, and thus drawing out the demon through the nostrils
of the person smelling it. At the same time he adjured the evil spirit not
to return, 'making mention of Solomon and repeating the charms composed by
him.' On one occasion this Eleazar gave ocular proof that the demon was
exorcized; and thus, adds Josephus, σαφὴς ἡ Σολομῶνος καθίστατο σύνεσις
καὶ σοφία. On these books relating to the occult arts and ascribed to
Solomon see Fabricius *Cod. Pseud. Vet. Test.* 1. p. 1036 ff., where many
curious notices are gathered together. See especially Origen *In Matth.
Comm.* 35. § 110 (3. 910), Pseudo-Justin *Quaest.* 55.

          This interpretation explains all the expressions in the passage.
The λίθων ἰδιότητες naturally points to the use of charms or amulets, as
may be seen e.g. from the treatise, Damigeron *de Lapidibus*, printed in the
Spicil. Solemn. 3. 324 ff.: comp. King *Antique Gems* Sect. 4, *Gnostics and
their Remains*. The reference to 'the books of the ancients' thus finds
an adequate explanation. On the other hand the only expression which
seemed to militate against this view, ἀλεξιτήριοι ῥίζαι, is justified by
the story in the *Antiquities*; comp. also [pseudo-] Clement *Hom.* 8. 14.
It should be added also that Hippolytus (*Haer.* 9. 22) paraphrases the
language of Josephus so as to give it this sense; πάνυ δὲ περιέργως
ἔχουσι περὶ βοτάνας καὶ λίθους, περιεργότεροι ὄντες πρὸς τὰς τούτων
ἐνεργείας, φάσκοντες μὴ μάτην ταῦτα γενονέναι. The sense which περίεργος
('curiosus') bears in Acts 19:19 and elsewhere, referring to magical arts,
illustrates its use here.

          Thus these Essenes were dealers in charms, rather than physicians.
And yet it is quite possible that along with this practice of the occult

sciences they studied the healing art in its nobler forms. The works of
Alexander of Tralles, an eminent ancient physician, constantly recommend
the use of such charms, of which some obviously come from a Jewish source
and not improbably may have been taken from these Solomonian books to
which Josephus refers. A number of passages from this and other writers,
specifying charms of various kinds, are given in Becker and Marquardt
Rom. Alterth. 4. 116 ff. See also Spencer's note on Origen *c. Cels.* 17 ff.

[40]See especially *JW* 2. 8, 7, 10 [§§ 137-42, 150].

[41]I have said nothing of the Kabbala, as a development of Jewish
thought illustrating the Colossian heresy: because the books containing
the Kabbalistic speculations are comparatively recent, and if they contain
ancient elements, it seems impossible to separate these from later additions or to assign to them even an approximate date. The Kabbalistic
doctrine however will serve to show to what extent Judaism may be developed in the direction of speculative mysticism.

[42]Philo *Fragm.* p. 632 οἰκοῦσι δὲ πολλὰς μὲν πόλεις τῆς ᾽Ιουδαίας,
πολλὰς δὲ κώμας, καὶ μεγάλους καὶ πολυανθρώπους ὁμίλους; Josephus, *JW* 2.
8. 4 μία δὲ οὐκ ἔστιν αὐτῶν πόλις, ἀλλ᾽ ἐν ἑκάστῃ κατοικοῦσι πολλοί. On
the notices of the settlements and dispersion of the Essenes see Zeller 239.

[43]Philo names *Judaea* in *Fragm.* p. 632; *Palestine* and *Syria* in
Quod omn. prob. lib. 12, p. 457. Their chief settlements were in the neigh-
bourhood of the Dead Sea. This fact is mentioned by the heathen writers
Pliny (*N. H.* 5. 15) and Dion Chrysostom (Synesius *Dio* 3). The name of the
'Essene gate' at Jerusalem (*JW* 5. 4, 2 [§ 145]) seems to point to some
establishment of the order close to the walls of that city.

[44]They are only known to us from Philo's treatise *de Vita Contemplativa*. Their settlements were on the shores of the Mareotic lake
near Alexandria. Unlike the Essenes, they were not gathered together in
convents as members of a fraternity, but lived apart as anchorites, though
in the same neighbourhood. In other respects their tenets and practices

were very similar to those of the Essenes.

[45]The Epistle to the Colossians supposes a powerful Jewish colony
in Laodicea and the neighbourhood. We are not however left to draw this
inference from the epistle alone, but the fact is established by ample
independent testimony. When, with the insolent licence characteristic of
Oriental kings, Antiochus the Great transplanted two thousand Jewish
families from Babylonia and Mesopotamia into Lydia and Phrygia (*Ant.* 12.
3, 4), we can hardly doubt that among the principal stations of these new
colonists would be the two most thriving cities of Phrygia, which were also
the two most important settlements of the Syrian kings; Apamea and Laodicea,
the one founded by his grandfather Antiochus the First, the other by his
father Antiochus the Second. If the commercial importance of Apamea at
this time was greater (for somewhat later it was reckoned second only to
Ephesus among the cities of Asia Minor as a centre of trade), the political
rank of Laodicea stood higher. When mention is made of Lydia and Phrygia,
this latter city especially is pointed out by its position, for it stood
near the frontier of the two countries. A Jewish settlement once established, the influx of their fellow-countrymen would be rapid and continuous.
Accordingly under the Roman domination we find them gathered here in very
large numbers. When Flaccus the propraetor of Asia (B.C. 62), who was
afterwards accused of maladministration in his province and defended by
Cicero, forbade the contributions of the Jews to the temple-worship and
the consequent exportation of money to Palestine, he seized as contraband
not less than twenty pounds weight in gold in the single district of which
Laodicea was the capital (Cicero *pro Flacc.* 28; *Ant.* 14. 7, 2). Calculated
at the rate of a half-shekel for each man, this sum represents a population
of more than eleven thousand adult freemen: for women, children, and slaves
were exempted. It must be remembered, however, that this is only the sum
which the Roman officers succeeded in detecting and confiscating; and that
therefore the whole Jewish population would probably be much larger than
this partial estimate implies. The amount seized at Apamea, the other
great Phrygian centre, was five times as large as this. Somewhat later we
have a document purporting to be a decree of the Laodiceans, in which they
thank the Roman Consul for a measure granting to Jews the liberty of

observing their sabbaths and practising other rites of their religion
(*Ant.* 14. 10, 21); and though this decree is probably spurious, yet it
serves equally well to show that at this time Laodicea was regarded as an
important centre of the dispersion in Asia Minor. To the same effect
may be quoted the extravagant hyperbole in the Talmud (bT Moed Katon 26a),
that when on a certain occasion an insurrection of the Jews broke out in
Caesarea the metropolis of Cappadocia, which brought down upon their heads
the cruel vengeance of king Sapor and led to a massacre of 12,000, 'the
wall of Laodicea was cloven with the sound of the harpstrings' in the fatal
and premature merriment of the insurgents. This place was doubtless singled
out, because it had a peculiar interest for the Jews, as one of their chief
settlements. It will be remembered also, that Phrygia is especially mentioned among those countries which furnished their quota of worshippers at
Jerusalem, and were thus represented at the baptism of the Christian Church
on the great day of Pentecost. [This note is excerpted from pp. 19-22 of
the introduction. -Ed.]

[46]Acts 19:13 τῶν περιερχομένων 'Ιουδαίων ἐξορκιστῶν.

[47]See above, note 39.

[48]There is doubtless a reference to the charms called 'Εφέσια
γράμματα in this passage: see Wetstein ad loc., and the references in
Becker and Marquardt *Rom. Alterth.* 4. 123 ff. But this supposition does
not exclude the Jews from a share in these magical arts, while the context
points to some such participation.

[49]I can only regard it as an accidental coincidence that the
epulones of the Ephesian Artemis were called *Essenes*, Pausanius 8. 13. 1
τοὺς τῇ 'Αρτέμιδι ἱστιάτορας τῇ 'Εφεσίᾳ γινομένους, καλουμένους δὲ ὑπὸ
τῶν πολιτῶν 'Εσσῆνας: see Guhl *Ephesiaca* 106 ff. The *Etymol. Magn.* has
'Εσσήν· ὁ βασιλεὺς κατὰ 'Εφεσίους, and adds several absurd derivations of
the word. In the sense of 'a king' it is used by Callimachus *Hymn. Jov.*
66 οὖ σε θεῶν ἐσσῆνα πάλιν θέσαν. It is probably not a Greek word, as
other terms connected with the worship of the Ephesian Artemis (e.g.

μεγάβυζος, a Persian word) point to an oriental or at least a non-Greek
origin; and some have derived it from the Aramaic חסין *chasin* 'strong' or
'powerful.' But there is no sufficient ground for connecting it directly
with the name of the sect 'Εσσηνοί or 'Εσσαῖοι, as some writers are disposed
to do (e.g. Spanheim on *Callim*. 1. c., Creuzer *Symbolik* 4. 347, 349); though
this view is favoured by the fact that certain ascetic practices were enjoined on these pagan 'Essenes.'

[50]Its date is fixed by the following allusions. The temple at
Jerusalem has been destroyed by Titus (vss. 122 ff.), and the cities of
Campania have been overwhelmed in fire and ashes (vss. 127 ff.). Nero has
disappeared and his disappearance has been followed by bloody contests in
Rome (vss. 116 ff.); but his return is still expected (vss. 134 ff.).

[51]See vss. 27-30 οἳ νηοὺς μὲν ἅπαντας ἀποστρέφουσιν ἰδόντες, καὶ
βωμοὺς, εἰκαῖα λίθων ἱδρύματα κωφῶν αἵμασιν ἐμψύχων μεμιασμένα καὶ θυσίῃσι
τετραπόδων κ.τ.λ. In an earlier passage vss. 8 ff. it is said of God,
οὔτε γὰρ οἶκον ἔχει ναῷ λίθον ἱδρυθέντα κωφότατον νωδόν τε, βροτῶν
πολυαλγέα λώβην.

[52]Verse 160 ἐν ποταμοῖς λούσασθε ὅλον δέμας ἀενάοισι. Another
point of contact with the Essenes is the great stress on prayers before
meals, vs. 26 εὐλογέοντες πρὶν πιέειν φαγέειν τε. Ewald (*Sibyll. Bücher*
46) points also to the prominence of the words εὐσεβεῖν, εὐσεβής, εὐσεβία
(vss. 26, 35, 42, 45, 133, 148, 151, 162, 165, 181, 183) to designate the
elect of God, as tending in the same direction. The force of this latter
argument will depend mainly on the derivation which is given to the name
Essene. ...

[53]Thus for instance, Ewald (47) points to the tacit approval of
marriage in vs. 33. I hardly think however that this passage, which merely
condemns adultery, can be taken to imply so much. More irreconcilable with
pure Essenism is the belief in the resurrection of the body and the future
life on earth, which is maintained in vss. 176 ff.; though Hilgenfeld (*ZWT*
14. 49) does not recognise the difficulty. See above. This Sibylline

writer was perhaps rather a Hemerobaptist than an Essene....Alexandre, *Orac. Sibyll.* (2. 323), says of this Sibylline Oracle, 'Ipse liber haud dubie Christianus est,' but there is nothing distinctly Christian in its teaching.

[54]vss. 106 ff., 145 ff. It begins κλῦθι λεὼς 'Ασίης μεγαλαυχέος Εὐρώπης τε.

[55]The exceptional activity of the forces of nature in these districts of Asia Minor may have directed the speculations of the Ionic school towards physics, and more especially towards cosmogony. In Heraclitus there is also a strong mystical element. But besides such broader affinities, I venture to call attention to special dicta of the two philosophers mentioned in the text, which curiously recall the tenets of the Judaeo-Gnostic teachers. Thales declared (Diogenes Laertius, 1. 27) τὸν κόσμον ἔμψυχον καὶ δαιμόνων πλήρη, or, as reported by Aristotle (*de An.* 1. 5, p. 411), πάντα πλήρη θεῶν εἶναι. In a recorded saying of Heraclitus we have the very language of a Gnostic teacher; Clement Alex. *Strom.* 5. 13, p. 699, τὰ μὲν τῆς γνώσιος βάθη κρύπτειν ἀπιστίη ἀγαθή, καθ' 'Ηράκλειτον· ἀπιστίη γὰρ διαφυγγάνει τὸ μὴ γινώσκεσθαι. See above.

[56]For the characteristic features of Phrygian religious worship see Steiger *Kolosser* 70 ff.

[57]The prominence, which the Phrygian mysteries and Phrygian rites held in the syncretism of the Ophites, is clear from the account of Hippolytus *Haer.* 5. 7 ff. Indeed Phrygia appears to have been the proper home of Ophitism. Yet the admixture of Judaic elements is not less obvious, as the name *Naassene*, derived from the Hebrew word for a serpent, shows.

[58]The name, by which the Montanists were commonly known in the early ages, was the sect of the 'Phrygians'; Clement *Strom.* 7. 17, p. 900 αἱ δὲ [τῶν αἰρέσεων] ἀπὸ ἔθνους [προσαγορεύονται], ὡς ἡ τῶν Φρυγῶν (cf. Eusebius *H. E.* 4. 27; 5. 16, Hippolytus, *Haer.* 8. 19; 10. 25). From οἱ (or ἡ) κατὰ Φρυγάς (Eusebius *H. E.* 2. 25; 5. 16, 18; 6. 20) comes the

soloecistic Latin name *Cataphryges*.

[59]Socrates (4. 28) accounts for the spread of Novatianism in
Phrygia by the σωφροσύνη of the Phrygian temper. If so, it is a striking
testimony to the power of Christianity, that under its influence the
religious enthusiasm of the Phrygians should have taken this direction,
and that they should have exchanged the fanatical orgiasm of their heathen
worship for the rigid puritanism of the Novatianist.

[60]1. 28 νουθετοῦντες πάντα ἄνθρωπον καὶ διδάσκοντες πάντα
ἄνθρωπον ἐν πάσῃ σοφίᾳ ἵνα παραστήσωμεν πάντα ἄνθρωπον τέλειον ἐν Χριστῷ
κ.τ.λ. The reiteration has offended the scribes; and the first πάντα
ἄνθρωπον is omitted in some copies, the second in others.

[61]The connexion of the sentences should be carefully observed.
After the passage quoted in the last note comes the asseveration that this
is the one object of the Apostle's preaching (1:29) εἰς ὃ καὶ κοπιῶ κ.τ.λ.;
then the expression of concern on behalf of the Colossians (2:1) θέλω γὰρ
ὑμᾶς εἰδέναι ἡλίκον ἀγῶνα ἔχω ὑπὲρ ὑμῶν κ.τ.λ.; then the desire that they
may be brought (2:2) εἰς πᾶν πλοῦτος τῆς πληροφορίας τῆς συνέσεως, εἰς
ἐπίγνωσιν τοῦ μυστηρίου τοῦ θεοῦ; then the definition of this mystery
(2:2, 3), Χριστοῦ ἐν ᾧ εἰσὶν πάντες οἱ θησαυροὶ κ.τ.λ.; then the warning
against the false teachers (2:4) τοῦτο λέγω ἵνα μηδεὶς ὑμᾶς παραλογίζηται
κ.τ.λ.

[62]Col. 3:11 after περιτομὴ καὶ ἀκροβυστία the Apostle adds
βάρβαρος, Σκύθης. There is nothing corresponding to this in the parallel
passage, Gal. 3:28.

[63]For σοφία see 1:9, 28; 2:3; 3:16; 4:5; for σύνεσις 1:9; 2:2;
for γνῶσις 2:3; for ἐπίγνωσις 1:9, 10; 2:2, 3:10.

[64]2:4 πιθανολογία, 2:8 κενὴ ἀπάτη.

[65]2:23 λόγον μὲν ἔχοντα σοφίας, where the μὲν suggests the contrast of the suppressed clause.

[66]e.g. 1:9, 28; 3:16 ἐν πάσῃ σοφίᾳ; 2:2 τῆς πληροφορίας. For
the 'wealth' of this knowledge compare 1:27, 2:2, 3:16.

[67]2:4, 18.

[68]1:26, 27; 2:2; 4:3.

[69]2:2 ἐν ᾧ εἰσὶν πάντες οἱ θησαυροὶ τῆς σοφίας καὶ τῆς γνώσεως
ἀπόκρυφοι.

[70]The two great Christological passages are 1:15-20, 2:9-15.
They will be found to justify the statements in this and the following
paragraphs of the text.

[71]1:19 ἐν αὐτῷ εὐδόκησεν πᾶν τὸ πλήρωμα κατοικῆσαι, 2:9 ἐν
αὐτῷ κατοικεῖ πᾶν τὸ πλήρωμα τῆς θεότητος σωματικῶς.

[72]See especially 1:16 εἴτε θρόνοι εἴτε κυριότητες εἴτε ἀρχαὶ
εἴτε ἐξουσίαι κ.τ.λ., compared with the parallel passage in Eph 1:21
ὑπεράνω πάσης ἀρχῆς καὶ ἐξουσίας καὶ δυνάμεως καὶ κυριότητος καὶ παντὸς
ὀνόματος ὀνομαζομένου κ.τ.λ. Compare also 2:10 ἡ κεφαλὴ πάσης ἀρχῆς καὶ
ἐξουσίας, and 2:15 ἀπεκδυσάμενος τὰς ἀρχὰς καὶ τὰς ἐξουσίας κ.τ.λ.

[73]2:18 θέλων ἐν ταπεινοφροσύνῃ καὶ θρησκείᾳ τῶν ἀγγέλων κ.τ.λ.

[74]2:10; cf. 1:9.

[75]2:18

[76]3:17

[77]3:18, 20, 23.

[78]At least in 2 Tim. 3:1-7, where, though the most monstrous
developments of the evil were still future, the Apostle's language implies

that it had already begun. On the other hand in the picture of the heresy in 1 Tim. 4:2 the ascetic tendency still predominates.

[79] 2 Pet. 2:10 ff., Jude 8.

[80] Rev. 2:14, 20-22.

[81] 2:16.

[82] 2:21.

[83] 2:23.

[84] Asceticism is of two kinds. There is the asceticism of dualism (whether conscious or unconscious), which springs from a false principle; and there is the asceticism of self-discipline, which is the training of the Christian athlete (1 Cor. 9:27). I need not say that the remarks in the text apply only to the former.

[85] Gal. 2:21; 5:2, 4.

[86] 2:8, 20-22.

[87] 2:23 οὐκ ἐν τιμῇ τινι πρὸς πλησμονὴν τῆς σαρκός.

[88] 3:1, 2.

[89] 3:3, 5.

[90] 3:10.

[91] The relation of Cerinthus to the Colossian heresy is briefly indicated by Neander Planting of Christianity 1. 325 ff. It has been remarked by other writers also, both earlier and later. The subject appears to me to deserve a fuller investigation than it has yet received.

[92]Hippolytus *Haer.* 7. 33 Αἰγυπτίων παιδεύᾳ ἀσκηθεύς, 9. 21 ὁ ἐν
Αἰγύπτῳ ἀσκηθεύς, Theodoret. *Haer. Fab.* 2. 3 ἐν Αἰγύπτῳ πλεῖστοῦ διατρύψας
χρόνον.

[93]Irenaeus 1. 26. 1 'et Cerinthus autem quidam...in Asia docuit,'
Epiphanius *Haer.* 28. 1 ἐγένετο δὲ οὗτος ὁ Κήρινθος ἐν τῇ 'Ασύᾳ διατρίβων,
κάκεῖσε τοῦ κηρύγματος τὴν ἀρχὴν πεποιημένος, Theodoret. loc. cit. ὕστερον
εἰς τὴν 'Ασύαν ἀφίκετο. The scene of his encounter with St John in the
bath is placed at Ephesus: see below, note 95.

[94]Epiphanius (28. 2 ff.) represents him as the ringleader of the
Judaizing opponents of the Apostles in the Acts and Epistles to the
Corinthians and Galatians. Philastrius (*Haer.* 36) takes the same line.

[95]The well-known story of the encounter between St John and
Cerinthus in the bath is related by Irenaeus (3. 3. 4) on the authority
of Polycarp, who appears from the sequence of Irenaeus' narrative to have
told it at Rome, when he paid his visit to Anicetus; ὃς καὶ ἐπὶ 'Ανικήτου
ἐπιδημήσας τῇ 'Ρώμῃ πολλοὺς ἀπὸ τῶν προειρημένων αἱρετικῶν ἐπέστρεφεν...καὶ
εἰσὶν οἱ ἀκηκοότες αὐτοῦ ὅτι 'Ιωάννης κ.τ.λ.

[96]Irenaeus 3. 11. 1.

[97]*Church History* 2. 42 (Bohn's Trans.).

[98]See the *Dialogue of Gaius and Proclus* in Eusebius, *H. E.* 3. 28,
Dionysius of Alexandria, ibid. 7. 25, Theodoret loc. cit., Augustine
Haer. 8.

[99]See below.

[100]Epiphanius *Haer.* 28. 4, 5, Philastrius *Haer.* 36, Augustine
loc. cit. The statements of these writers would not carry much weight in
themselves; but in this instance they are rendered highly probable by the
known Judaism of Cerinthus.

[101]Epiphanius, *Haer.* 28. 5; 30. 14, Philastrius *Haer.* 36.

[102]Epiphanius, *Haer.* 28. 1 προσέχειν τῷ ᾽Ιουδαϊσμῷ ἀπὸ μέρους.

[103]Irenaeus, 1. 26. 1 'Non a primo Deo factum esse mundum docuit, sed a virtute quadam valde separata et distante ab ea principalitate quae est super universa, et ignorante eum qui est super omnia Deum'; Hippolytus, *Haer.* 7. 33 ἔλεγεν οὐχ ὑπὸ τοῦ πρώτου θεοῦ γεγονέναι τὸν κόσμον, ἀλλ' ὑπὸ δυνάμεώς τινος κεχωρισμένης τῆς ὑπὲρ τὰ ὅλα ἐξουσίας καὶ ἀγνοούσης τὸν ὑπὲρ πάντα θεόν, 10. 21 ὑπὸ δυνάμεώς τινος ἀγγελικῆς, πολὺ κεχωρισμένης καὶ διεστώσης τῆς ὑπὲρ τὰ ὅλα αὐθεντίας καὶ ἀγνοούσης τὸν ὑπὲρ πάντα θεόν.

[104]Pseudo-Tertullian, *Haer.* 3 'Carpocrates praeterea hanc tulit sectam: Unam esse dicit virtutem in superioribus principalem, ex hac prolatos angelos atque virtutes, quos distantes longe a superioribus virtutibus mundum istum in inferioribus partibus condidisse...Post hunc Cerinthus haereticus erupit, similia docens. Nam et ipse mundum institutum esse ab illis dicit'; Epiphanius, *Haer.* 28. 1 ἕνα εἶναι τῶν ἀγγέλων τῶν τὸν κόσμον πεποιηκότων; Theodoret. *H. F.* 2. 3 ἕνα μὲν εἶναι τὸν τῶν ὅλων θεόν, οὐκ αὐτὸν δὲ εἶναι τοῦ κόσμου δημιουργόν, ἀλλὰ δυνάμεις τινὰς κεχωρισμένας καὶ παντελῶς αὐτὸν ἀγνοούσας; Augustine *Haer.* 8. The one statement is quite reconcilable with the other. Among those angels by whose instrumentality the world was created, Cerinthus appears to have assigned a position of preeminence to one, whom he regarded as the demiurge in a special sense and under whom the others worked; see Neander *Church History* 2, 43.

[105]Pseudo-Tertullian, loc. cit.; Epiphanius, *Haer.* 28. 4 τὸν δεδωκότα νόμον ἕνα εἶναι τῶν ἀγγέλων τῶν τὸν κόσμον πεποιηκότων.

[106]I am quite unable to see any reference to the Gnostic conception of an *aeon* in the passages of the New Testament, which are sometimes quoted in support of this view, e.g., by Baur *Paulus* 428, Burton *Lectures* 111 ff.

[107]Irenaeus 1. 26. 1, Hippolytus, *Haer*. 7. 33; 10. 21, Epiphanius, *Haer*. 28. 1, Theodoret. *H. F*. 2. 3. The arguments by which Lipsius (*Gnosticismus* 245, 258, in Ersch u. Gruber; *Quellenkritik des Epiphanios* 118 ff.) attempts to show that Cerinthus did not separate the Christ from Jesus, and that Irenaeus (and subsequent authors copying him) have wrongly attributed to this heretic the theories of later Gnostics, seem insufficient to outweigh these direct statements. It is more probable that the system of Cerinthus should have admitted some foreign elements not very consistent with his Judaic standing point, than that these writers should have been misinformed. Inconsistency was a necessary condition of Judaic Gnosticism. The point however is comparatively unimportant as affecting my main purpose.

[108]Irenaeus (3. 11. 1), after speaking of Cerinthus, the Nicolaitans, and others, proceeds 'non, quemadmodum illi dicunt, alterum quidem fabricatorem (i.e. demiurgum), alium autem Patrem Domini: et alium quidem fabricatoris filium, alterum vero de superioribus Christum, quem et impassibilem perseverasse, descendentem in Jesum filium fabricatoris, et iterum *revolasse in suum pleroma*.' The doctrine is precisely that which he has before ascribed to Cerinthus (1. 26. 1), but the mode of statement may have been borrowed from the Nicolaitans or the Valentinians or some other later Gnostics. There is however no improbability in the supposition that Cerinthus used the word *pleroma* in this way.

[109]1:19, 2:9. See above, note 71.

[110]2:6 παρελάβετε τὸν Χριστον, Ἰησοῦν τὸν Κύριον.

[111]1:20, 22.

THE ISIS INITIATION IN APULEIUS
AND RELATED INITIATORY RITES

Martin Dibelius[*]

Just in the last decade or so the portrayal of the Isis mysteries which Apuleius sketches in the eleventh book of the *Metamorphoses* has again engaged the attention of scholars to a heightened degree. The primary point of the inquiry, in keeping with the newly revived interest in Hellenistic cultural and religious history, has been to see what information about the spiritual influences of the epoch and its religious situation could be gained from Apuleius' presentation. Indeed, the lines which lead from East to West seem to be clear: an Egyptian cult, transplanted to Greek soil, depicted in Latin language. Further, an ancient national religion, spiritualized by mysticism, expanded by a syncretistic universalism--one sees how the major tendencies of the age come together here.

More than anything else the works of Reitzenstein have advanced our understanding of the Isis mysteries in this sense.[1] He juxtaposes the ritual of the ancient religion, the usage of the mystery cults, finally the terminology of the mysticism which we meet in the Hermetic writings, but also in Philo and Paul as well as in various effusions and transformations in literature and magic. The results are equally informative for recognizing the influences as for judging the mood and temper. Still, because this scholar's interest is fixed on the continuous lines of connection, the individual structure does not always emerge into clarity. That is especially true of the cultic actions of the mysteries, as they

*Martin Dibelius (1883-1947) was Professor of New Testament in Heidelberg. His pioneer work in the form criticism of the Gospels, the stylistic criticism of the Acts and Letters, and the use of archaeological and comparative studies to place early Christian documents within a more realistic picture of their cultural milieu, has earned him an enduring place in historical scholarship. The essay translated here, "Die Isisweihe bei Apuleius und verwandte Initiations-Riten," first appeared in the *Sitzungsberichte der Heidelberger Akademie der Wissenschaften, Philosophisch-historische Klasse,* Band 8 (1917, 4. Abhandlung). It was reprinted in Dibelius' collected essays, *Botschaft und Geschichte,* ed. Günther Bornkamm with Heinz Kraft, vol. 2, © J. C. B. Mohr (Paul Siebeck), Tübingen, 1956, and is translated by permission of the publisher.

are more alluded to than described by Apuleius. The family resemblance of
the Hermetic literature, which Reitzenstein connects with the Apuleius text,
forcefully shows the relationship between the two as far as inner meaning
and the mood of the religious experience are concerned, but in the process
questions about the material content of the cultic procedures recede into
the background. Moreover, it is disputed what cultic meaning the Hermetic
texts have, especially the so-called "prophet's initiation," and thus the
cultic side of the mysteries, and particularly all the detailed questions
connected with them, receive less attention from Reitzenstein, who wants
to exhibit the continuous development.

       Two works by de Jong have minutely investigated the question,
what actually happened in the initiatory ceremony of the Isis mysteries.[2]
He has performed the indubitable service of freeing the study of the Isis
mysteries from the weight of hypotheses about the Eleusinian mysteries.
He was led in his dissertation to the connection between magic and the
mysteries. Then, in a larger monograph, he undertook not only to investigate the ancient reports about this connection, but also to adduce modern
reports of spiritualist and other "occult" phenomena, and to weigh the
question how far these phenomena may be comparable to the experience of
Apuleius' Isis initiate. However, as one can readily understand, the investigation and evaluation of this material attracted so much attention,
becoming virtually an end in itself, that the fruits of the discussion for
our understanding of the Isis mysteries consists mainly in general conjectures. But most important, the subjective element--visionary experience--
and the objective side--cultic action--are in no way balanced off against
one another. Indeed the latter recedes completely into the background.
Yet for the history of religions it is at least as important to know what
one undertook to do in following the sacred ritual in the initiatory celebration of Isis as it is to know what the individual or perhaps all the
initiates--under the influence of a contagious mass suggestion--experienced
in terms of hallucinations or felt as an emotional temper.

       I shall try to come closer to a solution to these questions by
an interpretation of the pertinent passages in Apuleius. The resulting
observations about the terminology of the mysteries will then permit, in
conclusion, a glimpse beyond the Isis mysteries to broader contexts in the
history of religions.

I

Naturally the investigation must take as its starting point the famous passage in which Apuleius describes the chief element of the initiatory celebration at Cenchreae, the nocturnal consecration: 11. 23 (at the end). The detailed analysis of the words of that description is as problematic as is its meaning as a whole: *accessi confinium mortis et calcato Proserpinae limine per omnia vectus elementa remeavi, nocte media vidi solem candido coruscantem lumine, deos inferos et deos superos accessi coram et adoravi de proxumo.* [Adlington-Gaselee (Loeb) translate: "I approached near unto hell, even to the gates of Proserpine, and after that I was ravished throughout all the elements, I returned to my proper place: about midnight I saw the sun brightly shine, I saw likewise the gods celestial and the gods infernal, before whom I presented myself and worshipped them."]

The only clue which the author himself gives for the interpretation is found in 11. 21: *ipsamque traditionem ad instar voluntariae mortis et precariae salutis celebrari* ... Initiation—for that is what *traditio* refers to[3]—as an image of death and of gracious salvation from death: that must guide our interpretation. In view of the scene depicted in 11. 24, in which the new initiate is presented to the entering throng as a god, we may immediately add that this newly bestowed life is of divine character. The whole event is an ἀπαθανατισμός [immortalization]. The salvation from death, *precaria salus*, is expressed in the passage with which we began by the word *remeavi*: from the threshold of Proserpine the initiate returns safely, after a journey through the elements.[5] Thus the sentence, *accessi confinium mortis* [I approached the bounds of death] cannot describe simply grave mortal danger. It does not serve merely to express the notion that "the soul is attached to the body by the slenderest of threads," as De Jong (p. 230) puts it, in the words of a medium. Rather, an entrance must have taken place, in order for one to speak of a return.

Thus there emerges from the depiction we are examining a first part: from *accessi* to *remeavi* describes the entrance of the initiate into the realm of the dead and his return. The following sentence relates that the initiate sees the sun; we may at once assume that this act also belongs somehow under the rubric *ad instar precariae salutis* ["resembling a precarious salvation"]. Perhaps the next words help: *deos inferos et deos superos accessi coram et adoravi de proxumo* ["I approached the lower gods and the upper gods and worshipped them from near at hand"]. The position of the *inferi* before the *superi* is striking,[6] especially if one compares the prayer in 11. 25: *te superi colunt, observant inferi* [The (gods) above revere you, those below honor you]. But this problem is solved without remainder if the sentence is taken as a summary of the previously depicted actions: the initiate has encountered the *inferi* in Proserpine's realm; he has seen the *superi* in the place where he confronted the dazzling white light of the sun. It is a priori plausible that this vision of the sun is in fact a vision of God, and this can be confirmed from other witnesses (see below). Here, where we want to limit ourselves to Apuleius' text, it suffices to refer to 11. 24. There Lucius is presented as a god, *in vicem simulacri*, adorned *ad instar Solis*. That makes the equation, vision of the sun = vision of god, sufficiently probable that we may venture the above explanation. Then the content of the whole section would be as follows: entry into the realm of the dead, vision of the *dii inferi*, happy return connected with a journey through all elements, an epiphany of light and vision of the *dii superi*.

        This interpretation at the same time opens up the structure of the passage for us. The words do not portray a series of sequential acts, but an allusive presentation of the proceedings is followed by a sentence that emphasizes anew their religious significance: "I beheld the gods of the underworld and the gods of the upper world, face to face." There are two possible explanations for this concluding sentence: either the author wants to proclaim once again the nature of the salvation he has received, or the official language of his cultus impells him to add this concluding explanation to the description.

        No doubt the latter is the case. Lucius (=Apuleius) is not speaking freely of his personal impressions, but is reproducing that which the cultic language is able to say about the initiatory experience. Quite possibly the obligation of silence would itself prevent his making personal confessions about this act. In any case he would certainly not bracket such a confession with the words which he writes before and after the passage we have lifted out: he may not impart, he says, *quid deinde dictum,*

quid factum [what then was said, what done]. Nevertheless, he did not want
to frustrate for long the reader's pious curiosity. Then he introduces our
passage with the words: *igitur audi, sed crede, quae vera sunt* [Therefore
listen, but believe it to be true]. What follows then is not an actual
report of the *dictum* and *factum* of the initiation, for *dicerem, si dicere
liceret* ["I would tell, if it were permitted to tell"]! It seems rather
to be a fixed text, which deserves reverence: *crede quae vera sunt*! And
this impression is confirmed by the remark which the author appends immediately after the text in question: *ecce tibi rettuli, quae, quamvis audita,
ignores tamen necesse est* "see, I have told you things of which, however
much you have heard, you must remain ignorant" . Thus he is persuaded
that the reader cannot deduce the proceedings of the initiation from the
information he has given. Are we to believe that Apuleius himself assembled
the enigmatic allusions in order to satisfy the reader's curiosity and at
the same time the obligation of silence? If such an individual exegesis
of the secrecy mandate is a priori unlikely, it becomes completely incredible if we pay attention to the solemn introduction of the words: "Believe
what is true." Rather, everything points to the conclusion that the text
from *accessi* to *proxumo* is a fixed text, and that our author--in order
neither to disappoint his reader at this highpoint of his narrative nor
to spill the secrets--has communicated a formula of his cult.

II.

  Also the style of the sentences we are concerned with can rein-
force this conjecture, though it cannot prove it.[7] Once our passage is
recognized as a formula, it recalls immediately certain συνθήματα [pass-
words] of ancient mysteries divulged by Clement of Alexandria and Firmicus
Maternus, the one from Eueusis, the other from the Attis mysteries. They
have in common with our formula the fact that they report a sacramental
action carried out with the believer. The form is also common: short
clauses in the historical tense. The purpose of such a formulation and
the manner of its stylization requires closer investigation.

  The symbol of Eleusis, which Clement reproduces in the *Protrepticus* (ed. Stählin, II, 21, p. 16; in the Latin text of Arnobius, *Adv.
nat.* 5, 26), tells of the sacramental procedure in the manner described:

ἐνήστευσα, ἔπιον τὸν κυκεῶνα, ἔλαβον ἐκ κίστης, ἐργασάμενος ἀπεθέμην εἰς
κάλαθον καὶ ἐκ καλάθου εἰς κίστην ["I fasted, I drank the *kukeon*, I took
from the hamper, after manipulating (the object) I replaced (it) in the
basket and from the basket into the hamper"]. Similar form and similar,
i.e. sacramental content also characterize the Attis formula whose third
element is extant in three versions. Clement reproduces it in the *Pro-*
trepticus II, 15, p. 13 (Stählin) in this form (A): ἐκ τυμπάνου ἔφαγον,
ἐκ κυμβάλου ἔπιον, ἐκερνοφόρησα, ὑπὸ τὸν παστὸν ὑπέδυν ["I ate from the
drum, I drank from the cymbal, I carried the *kernos*, I entered (?) the
bridal chamber"]. Firmicus Maternus, *De errore profanarum religionum* 18,
1 (ed. Ziegler, p. 43 [in the new ed. 1953, p. 62]) presents a related
Greek text: ἐκ τυμπάνου βέβρωκα, ἐκ κυμβάλου πέπωκα, γέγονα μύστης Ἄττεως
["I have eaten from the drum, I have drunk from the cymbal, I have become
an initiate of Attis"] (B). But before that he gives the formula in Latin:
de tympano manducavi, de cymbalo bibi, et religionis secreta perdidici
["I have eaten from the drum, I have drunk from the cymbal, and I have
memorized the secrets of the cult"] (C). Form A seems to imply that the
speaker has already received the highest degree of initiation, for the
last clause of the saying probably means, "I have entered the bridal
chamber," and is to be understood to refer to sexual union with the deity.[8]
Form C sounds much more colorless: *religionis secreta perdidici*. Anyone
could say that who had received the preliminary instructions, like Lucius
in Apuleius 11, 22: *profert (sacerdos) quosdam libros litteris ignorabilibus*
praenotatos ... indidem mihi praedicat, quae forent ad usum teletae neces-
sario praeparanda ... 23 secretoque mandatis quibusdam, quae voce meliora
sunt ... ["(The priest) brought certain books written in unknown characters
... From there he announced to me that which would be necessary in prepar-
ing for the rites of initiation....entrusted me with secrets not to be
uttered..."]. --and that ten days before the initiation! Form B could in
a pinch be understood in the same way: "I have by means of the eating and
drinking become a member of the mystery-family of the Phrygian deities,"[9]
while the unbiased reader, if he ignores the Latin form, would refer Text
B, like Text A, to the acquisition of full initiation.

Anyone who considers the mutual relationship among the three
versions must not overlook Firmicus Maternus' statement about the use of

the saying: *habent enim propria signa propria responsa, quae illis in istorum sacrilegiorum coetibus diaboli tradidit disciplina. In quodam templo ut in interioribus partibus homo moriturus possit admitti, dicit* (formula C follows), *quod Graeco sermone dicitur* (formula B) [Indeed they have certain signs, certain passwords which the Devil's doctrine has transmitted to them in the assemblies of this sacreligious cult. In a certain temple a man condemned to death, in order to be admitted to the inner rooms, says: (formula C), which in Greek is: (formula B)]. The half-initiated novice, if he is to be admitted to the interior of the temple for the highest initiation, the *voluntaria mors*, must recite the saying. That fits formula C in any case, but it would only suit B if we had to interpret this text, especially the final words (γέγονα μυστὴς "Αττεως) [I have become the initiate of Attis] according to C and not according to A. But I cannot rid myself of the suspicion that the striking difference between Text B and its putative translation is not accidental and that it is somehow connected with the introductory remark of the author quoted above. There are two possible explanations. (1) Firmicus composed a summary statement from his knowledge of the Attis mysteries and other, analogous mysteries. In that case this testimony by the knowledgable reporter would certainly not be worthless in itself,[10] but it would tell us nothing at all about the use of our formula. For then he would perhaps have adapted Form C to fit that summary statement, without having made a corresponding correction of the Greek original (B). Perhaps also his own bias influenced the formation of version C and the summary that agrees with it. The admonitions of his eighteenth chapter, in the extant text, relate only to the eating and drinking of the initiates, in order to refer to "bread of Christ, cup of Christ." Consequently the lacuna which is to be assumed at the end of 18 may quite possibly have contained an allusion to the false *religionis secreta* and a reference to the true divine secrets.[11] In either case Form C, if composed by the author from either of these motives, would be excluded as an independent witness. (2) The other possibility for explaining the lack of agreement between B and C is that C was an origional text known to Firmicus only in Latin--in chapters 19-22 he always cites the original Greek texts, without offering a Latin translation-- and that the summary is appropriate to C. In that case, B would be another

recension of the saying known to the author, about whose recitation he
knew nothing to report. Thus he inserted it here as an ostensibly equivalent Greek text. Then C would be evidence for a rather interesting development in the Attis mysteries: an indoctrination in the *secreta religionis*,
which perhaps originally consisted of instruction about the impending initiation (cf. Apuleius 11, 22 *quae forent ad usum teletae necessario praeparanda*), would have achieved greater and greater importance, until
finally the person to be initiated had to give a testimony of his participation in this indoctrination before the initiation could be performed.
This would be the same development as Reitzenstein has demonstrated in the
Asclepius of Ps.-Apuleius: while in the thirteenth chapter of the Hermetic
Corpus a mystical rebirth, though to be sure in a spiritual re-interpreta-
tion in which doctrine is also involved, is portrayed, in the Asclepius
text mysticism has by and large been banished, and "only the simple
instruction remains" (*ARW* 7, 410). We shall have to reckon with a
growth of doctrinal elements in the later period of development also within
the mysteries, and Firmicus Maternus would be a witness for this later
period.

Of the two possible causes for the disharmony between B and C
considered here, in neither case does the Christian author's summary remark
have any applicability to version B, and still less, naturally, for Text A
from Clement.[12] The actual function of the sayings must rather be uncovered
by other means.

The other sacred texts which Firmicus reproduces in chapters 19-22
of his work as *signa* and *symbola* do not help us, since their function is not
clear in every case. The fact that Firmicus treats them one after another
by no means justifies the deduction that these sayings are all used for the
same purpose, though in different mysteries.[13] The word *symbolum* does not
justify such an assumption, for the usage of Clement of Alexandria, well-
acquainted with mystical terminology, shows that σύμβολον can designate
the sacred formula but also the sacred object.[14] Our investigation of
Firmicus' summary note on the Attis symbol has shown how little weight is
to be given to his testimony in this question. That his knowledge is not
especially trustworthy is proved by a striking imprecision in the statements of this very passage. The same chapter 18 explains the Attis saying

as a password at the entry into the *interiores partes* is opened with the
following words (ed. Ziegler, p. 43 [1953 ed., p. 62]): *libet nunc
explanare quibus se signis vel quibus symbolis in ipsis superstitionibus
miseranda hominum turba cognoscat* [Now I want to explain by which sign
or which symbol the miserable mob of men in this superstition recognize
one another]. According to that, the following sayings would be signs
for mutual recognition of the initiates, but according to Firmicus the
Attis symbol was a response during the initiation. And one will hardly
believe that the following saying (19, 1, p. 47) ...δὲ νυμφίε χαῖρε νέον
φῶς ["rejoice, bridegroom, at the new light"] was originally a recognition
sign.[15] Certainly the well-known θαρρεῖτε μύσται κτλ ["be of good courage,
initiates"] (Firmicus Maternus 22, 1, p. 57 [69]) and probably also the
cry in chap. 21, p. 55 [68] αἰαῖ δίκερως δίμορφε ["Ho, two-horned, double-
formed one!"], are parts of the liturgy. Naturally there could have been
a development in the usage of sacred formulae. A liturgical response at
the reception of a higher initiation could have become a recognition sign
or, vice versa, a *signum* could have become a *responsum*.[16] A secret watch-
word could by means of frequent use have become public[17] and thus lose its
value for its actual function, secret agreement among the initiates, but
nevertheless retain its sanctity and validity--of course from then on only
as an insignia, no longer as a secret sign of recognition. After all we
shall do well, when we make conjectures about the meaning of our three
mystery sayings, to fix our attention not on the author's comments, but
on the testimony of content and style of the formulas.

Considered from that perspective, the sacred texts of the Isis
mysteries reported by Apuleius prove to be close relatives of both the
Elusinian and the Attis symbols. All three sayings consist of a few short
clauses in the aorist or perfect tense, juxtaposed without syntactic connections, and elaborated, if at all, only by participial constructions.
In each case the initiate recounts, in the first person and in words that
allude rather than describe, sacred actions which he has carried out.
The similarity between Text B of the Attis symbol and our Isis text is
especially clear, for each is concluded with a clause that proclaims what
sort of salvation the initiate has attained: "I have become a *mystēs* of
Attis" in the former, and from *accessi coram et adoravi de proxumo* in the

Isis formula anyone who knows the religious language of the time will
recognize the thought, "I have become the God."[18]

The tense permits the inference that the sayings were not formulated for use during the sacred action itself. The situation is different with texts which are related in content, in which the present or the
perfect with a present sense dominates, as in the saying of the Marcosians
in Irenaeus I. 21. 3: ἐστήριγμαι καὶ λελύτρωμαι, καὶ λυτροῦμαι τὴν ψυχήν
μου ἀπὸ τοῦ αἰῶνος τούτου καὶ πάντων τῶν παρ' αὐτοῦ ἐν τῷ ὀνόματι τοῦ 'Ιαώ,
ὃς ἐλυτρώσατο τὴν ψυχὴν αὐτοῦ εἰς ἀπολύτρωσιν ἐν Χριστῷ τῷ ζῶντι ["I have
been established and I have been redeemed, and I redeem my soul from this
aeon and from all those beyond it, in the name of Iao, who redeemed his
soul for redemption in Christ the living"]. Here one can infer from the
words themselves just what Irenaeus says about them: that they form a
liturgical response. With this text, but not with the sayings we have been
considering, we could also classify the conclusion of the so-called Mithra
Liturgy, in case it has any cultic meaning at all.[19]   In tense the Sabazios
saying reported by Demosthenes, *De cor.* § 259, is related to our texts:
ἔφυγον κακόν, εὗρον ἄμεινον ["I fled from evil; I found the better"] --How-
ever, here again only the religious gain is lauded, more or less as in the
last clause of the Isis text, but the allusions to the particular actions
are lacking. Again, the testimony of the author agrees: this saying also
is said to be a response after the initiation. Such delimitations by contrast with other texts facilitate the understanding of our texts. We have
to see in them not liturgical formulas to be spoken in the initiation (note
the tenses), nor, probably, parts of the liturgy at all (note the recount-
ing of the particular actions), but most likely sayings with which the
initiate of the Eleusinian, the Attis, or the Isis mysteries confesses
himself outside in the world as a member of his cultic community.

        Thus one would have to conjecture as the purpose of such formula-
tions[20] first of all the mutual recognition of initiates, regardless of
whether they occurred secretly or openly. The Aberkios inscription allows
one to infer for the Attis cult--if indeed the inscription is related to
the Attis mysteries[21]--how an initiate could come to desire an affiliation
by some such means in a foreign environment. For the Isis worship, the
story of Lucius' journey to Rome (Apuleius, *Metam.* 11, 26) attests something

similar. Still other thoughts and intentions which were linked with such
sayings are indicated by one of the familiar gold tablets from a lower-
Italian mystery circle (*IG* 14, 641). At the conclusion of the inscription
words are used which doubtless belong to a formula; with them the initiate
attests the fact of his initiation: ἔριφος ἐς γάλ' ἔπετον ["a kid, I fell
into milk"]. In any case it is a fixed formulation, attested also by
inscription no. 642, which applies the same clause to the initiate in the
second person. Perhaps it is only part of a *symbolum*; the whole text in
that case might be considered a parallel to the sayings we are concerned
with, since the extant words evidently relate to a sacramental action
which guarantees immortal life in the beyond.[22] Now if the deceased who
was provided with this tablet arrived in the underworld armed with such a
saying, then he might hope to find there the promised salvation. Such a
notion could also be connected with the sayings we have been concerned
with, especially with the Isis text, since the goddess expressly proclaims
to Lucius (Apuleius, *Metam.* 11.6) that he will be favored even in Hades
as her initiate: *vives autem beatus, vives in mea tutela gloriosus, et cum
spatium saeculi tui permensus ad inferos demearis, ibi quoque in ipso sub-
terraneo semirotundo me, quam vides, Acherontis tenebris interlucentem
Stygiisque penetralibus regnantem, campos Elysios incolens ipse, tibi
propitiam frequens adorabis* ["Moreover your life will be blessed; under
my protection your life will be glorious. And when after your allotted
span of life you descend to the underworld, even there in that subterranean
vault, as you see me shining in the darkness of Acheron, ruling the inmost
part of the Styx, you, dwelling in the Elysian fields, shall worship me,
your patron"].

The most important objection which can be raised against the
evaluation of the Isis texts put forth here consists in a reference to
the *fides silentii* [vow of silence].[23] Is it credible that Apuleius,
himself an initiate in the mysteries, would have exposed a sacred cultic
formula to the public? The argument is probably not so strong as it
appears. If the author had felt himself obligated, by vows or piety, to
an unconditional silence about the initiation, then he would have left
the entire eleventh book of the Metamorphoses unwritten, because then as
now it could become a most important source for the curiosity and

inquisitiveness of "profane" people. In reality the rule of silence had
limited application. A brief account of the cultic saga was permitted
even in the presence of uninitiated persons; only the details, especially
sacred objects and actions shown in the mysteries, were to be protected
from profane eyes.[24] Of the formulas of the cultus, naturally the liturgical
versicles, which would accompany the action and could explain it, would be
guarded with equal care.[25] Also in the case of *symbola* which serve as signs
of recognition, the duty of discretion is at first mandated by their purpose. But just in this last instance it is probable that frequent use let
the secret come into the possession of uninitiated persons, and it may be
doubted whether sayings which were written down for the benefit of the
dead in their graves remained completely secret.

Even these general considerations about the duty of silence in
the mysteries make it seem not impossible that Apuleius could with good
conscience communicate a formula of the Isis worship. However, we have in
addition his own statement about the duty of silence, which illuminates
the difference between the concealment of sacred objects and keeping silent
about sacred formulas. In the Apology, chaps. 53 ff., he defends himself
against the accusation that he secretly keeps magical apparatus. The com-
plaint is based on the fact that Apuleius kept concealed in the house of
Pontianus certain objects wrapped in a cloth, which no one had ever seen.
His defense seeks to prove that these are *signa* and *monumenta* of mysteries--
an exceedingly difficult proof, since the duty of silence permits him
neither to mention the things by name nor to demonstrate the harmlessness
of their use. Apuleius is aware of this difficulty; therefore he appeals
to the knowledge of some initiates who happen to be present. They can confirm that one does keep such things: *sacrorum pleraque initia in Graecia
participavi. eorum quaedam signa et monumenta tradita mihi a sacerdotibus
sedulo conservo. nihil insolitum, nihil incognitum dico* ["I have been
initiated into various of the Greek mysteries, and preserve with the utmost
care certain emblems and mementoes of my initiation with which the priests
presented me. There is nothing abnormal or unheard of in this."--trans.
H. E. Butler, 1909]; (that much is known about the mysteries despite the
duty of silence; one who is initiated knows still more:) *vel unius Liberi
patris mystae*[26] *qui adestis scitis, quid domi conditum celetis et absque*

omnibus profanis tacite veneremini ["Those of you here present who have
been initiated into the mysteries of father Liber alone, know what you
keep hidden at home, safe from all profane touch and the object of your
silent veneration."--trans. Butler] (*Apol.* 55, p. 62 Helm). The not
altogether clear passage at the end of chap. 56 (p. 64) must also be understood as a similar appeal.[27] Only here, where the issue is not the fact
of keeping the objects but the content of the cloth, the speaker turns to
fellow members of his *own* cult. If one of them is present, he is to prove
himself an initiate (*si qui forte adest eorundem sollemnium mihi particeps,
s i g n u m   d a t o)* ["If any of you that are here present had any part
with me in these same solemn ceremonies, give the sign"--trans. Butler,
modified] and then the opponent may obtain an explanation from him.
Apuleius does not say what it is he has in mind. After the cited words,
these follow: *et audias licet quae ego adservem* ["And you shall hear what
it is I keep thus"]. That sounds as if the other is to name the objects,
but it cannot mean that, for Apuleius affirms for his part: *nam equidem
nullo unquam periculo compellar, quae reticenda accepi, haec ad profanos
enuntiare* ["For no thought of personal safety shall induce me to reveal to
the uninitiated the secrets that I have received and sworn to conceal"--
trans. Butler]. Since he cannot demand of his cult-brother the violation
of the mandate of silence which he so solemnly rejects for himself, then
his intention is probably only that the disinterested third party should
testify to the opponent of the harmlessness of the sacred objects, or at
least corroborate that what Apuleius keeps is no *magicum*. Whether this
intention was actually carried out in the trial is doubtful. While in
chap. 55 it is expressly stated that a similar appeal to those present
was answered,[28] naturally by someone whom the accused had engaged in ad-
vance, here there is no such indication. Possibly the passage belongs
therefore to the redaction of the speech[29] and is thus nothing more than
a rhetorical transition. Besides, if the reading *et audiat licet quae ego
adservem* were correct,[30] according to which Apuleius would permit himself
to name the secret things only to the third party, then we would certainly
have a case of pure rhetoric, since this concession could serve neither
the judge nor the plaintiff. We are interested only in the presupposition,
that the cult-brother of the speaker could prove himself in the presence

of the assembly as *eorundem sollemnium mihi particeps*. *Signum dato*--in
the given situation that is not "he should give *a* sign";[31] it can only
mean, he should give *the* sign recognized among the members of the cult.
And for good reason scholars have long thought of a sacred formula in that
connection.[32] Then Apuleius would provide an instance in which such a
saying would be used in the presence of uninitiated persons.

　　　　Finally, even the formulation of these symbols gives evidence
that such a thing would be possible. They are so restrained that the profane person cannot discover anything essential from them. That this is
true of the ἔριφος-line of the lower-Italian initiates requires no proof.
The Attis symbol from Firmicus and Clement lacks the main item, the object,
and thus the answer to the question what one ate and drank. The Eleusinian
formula betrays neither what was in the κίστη nor what one did with it
(ἐργασάμενος[33]). And our Isis text affords manifold puzzles not only for
the present-day reader; the author who reveals it confidently depends himself on its opacity: *quae, quamvis audita, ignores tamen necesse est* ["of
which, however much you have heard, you must remain ignorant"]. Whoever
considers carefully that the reader becomes acquainted with the saying
only in translation, thus in a form which is in no way suited for any mis-
use by laymen, will hardly accuse the author on account of this revelation
of betrayal of the mysteries. But in that case the mandate of silence
affords no evidence contrary to the supposition that Apuleius has here
taken up in translation a sacred formula of the Isis worship into his presentation of the initiation.

                                    III

　　　　We return to the Apuleius text. Now, since it has turned out to
be a fixed formulation, an enhanced significance may be ascribed to it.
The text reproduces not merely individual moods, but so to speak official
interpretations. Whoever wants to investigate what the procedures are
which are alluded to and explained in the text, has to face the question,
raised especially by de Jong's work, whether real actions are to be considered at all, or whether the entire initiation may not rather consist
in inward events which the person to be initiated would experience in a
dreaming or trance state.[34]

With this question we approach the first act of the initiation, the descent to the realm of the dead. We have already shown that the *accessi* has to be interpreted in accord with the *remeavi*, so that one may speak of entry into the realm of the dead and return. But the reference of both, *accedere* and *remeare*, to a solely inward experience of contemplative, dreaming, or ecstatic type seems to me to be excluded by the following consideration: Lucius already received various revelations of the goddess in circumstances of that sort. The first epiphany of the goddess, together with the revelation of her name[35] and the proclamation of his salvation, occurred in a dream (11.3-6). In similar fashion the believer, waiting eagerly for the day of initiation, hears nightly directives of the goddess (11.19). He hears a dream-oracle (11.20) and finally is summoned in the same manner to the initiation (11.22). And now should the so passionately awaited initiation be in its essence a psychological event? The climax after so much suspense merely a repetition? That seems incredible, especially since Apuleius' account immediately before this passage provides another obvious explanation.

Tunc semotis procul profanis omnibus ["Then, all uninitiated persons having been dismissed"], the author relates there, *lenteo rudique me contectum amicimine arrepta manu sacerdos d e d u c i t ad ipsius sacrarii penetralia* ["a new linen robe was placed on me; the priest took my hand and *led* me down to the inmost part of the sanctuary."] The verb seems here only to state the obvious. However, if one observes that 11.21 says, *quo rectius ad arcana purissimae religionis secreta p e r v a d e r e m* ["that I might *enter* more correctly the mysteries of the most holy religion"] and that in 11.28, before the Isiris initiation, is said, *tantas caerimonias a d i t u r u s,* [to *approach* such ceremonies], then the conjecture is not to be dismissed that such verbs of leading and going--more precisely, their Greek equivalents--were used in a technical sense.[36] Not only is it said that one is led into the *penetralia* of the sanctuary, but also "approaching" and "entering" apply to *caerimoniae* and *secreta*. The initiation itself is an "entering," sanctioned by the goddess, into the sanctuary, its secrets, and its celebrations. Thus everything points to the literal meaning of the verbs and excludes the assumption of a merely subjective experience. The entry into the sacred place, led by

the mystagogue, is part of the initiation; the space itself is full of the
miraculous--to see this, to take part in it, is a divinely granted experience. To be sure it is perfectly plausible that, besides this experience
shared by every initiate, individuals may have had special experiences.
But what is constitutive for the nature and force of the action is not the
subjective but the objective procedure, as it is alluded to in the formula
reproduced by Apuleius.[37]

On account of the term *deducit* in Apuleius, one would probably
do best to think in terms of an underground room.[38] Here was the realm
of Proserpine. What happened there to the person who entered, we do not
know. As mentioned above, the words *accessi confinium mortis* cannot refer
to an ordeal, because they do not describe the degree of mortal danger at
all, but the entry into the realm of the dead. But these ordeals are not
alluded to elsewhere in our text either, and the fact that such things
existed in the Mithras mysteries, where the differing degrees of the
initiates, the military character, and the moral and practical cast of
the whole make ordeals understandable, does not entail a corresponding
presupposition in the contemplative Isis religion.

Another reference of this first act of the initiation is
suggested by the author himself: Isis is ruler of the underworld. Thus
she depicts herself in 11.6 (cf. also 11.5, *Siculi trilingues Stygiam
Proserpinam* [the trilingual Sicilians call me Stygian Proserpine], and the
mention of the name Proserpine in the prayer 11.2); as such she is pro-
claimed by the priest (11.21); thus she is praised also in the prayer
11.25: *te superi colunt, observant inferi, tu ... regis mundum, calcas
Tartarum* [the (gods) above revere you, those below honor you; you ... rule
the world, tread down hell]. The person to be initiated ventures into her
domain when he "approaches the threshold of Proserpine"; she alone can
grant him salvation from this place of death, but she can also punish by
death anyone who enters there against her will. The warning words of the
priest (11.21: *noxamque letalem contrahere* [he would commit a mortal
offense]) can now be explained without resort to special conjectures not
indicated in the text. It is not mortally dangerous ordeals that make the
initiation a *voluntaria mors*, but the belief, cultivated in the circle of
initiates and communicated to the novice, in the sanctity of the place and

of the action, in the nearness of the goddess and in her power as ruler
of the underworld. The *regina manium* [queen of the dead] is present,
so the sacred room conceals the *inferum deplorata silentia* [lamentable
silences of the underworld] (11.5). The initiate approaches it with the
permission of the goddess; thus he experiences death, anticipating pro-
leptically his own fate. Here we may also finally take into account the
contribution of psychic factors; only they did not create the action out
of nothing, but merely imparted a mood to the cultic act. Asceticism and
the period of waiting aroused the fantasy of the initiate; visions and
dreams, priestly instructions, and sacred texts let him anticipate what
awaited him; fear and hope, reverence and faith obliterate for him, in the
darkness of the sacred room, the border between reality and unreality.
And while the priest murmurs prayers and performs rites, displays symbols
or unveils pictures, the novice feels and sees what the sacred text attests:
that he may approach Proserpine's realm and behold the *dii inferi* face to
face.[39]

      We seek in vain in Apuleius a foundation of this ritual in the
myth. Never is there a suggestion that the initiate suffers the same fate
as Osiris,[40] for example; one would have to look for such an indication
in the final exhibition of the initiate *ad instar solis exornatus* [adorned
as the sun] (11.24). But this possibility cannot be proved; one could
more readily suppose that the Osiris initiation, which Lucius undergoes
in Rome (11.27) would have had reference to the myth. It is expressly
stated that the latter ritual was different from that of Isis: *quanquam
enim conexa, immo vero unita ratio numinis religionisque esset, tamen
teletae discrimen interesse maximum* [Although they are connected, even
united in religious spirit, yet there is a great difference between the
rites].[41] If one may seek at all an explanation of the Isis initiation,
then one is reminded by the sequence of the acts--descent to the realm of
the dead, journey through the elements, vision of the sun and of the *dii
superi*--less of the mythical experiences of the deity than of her cosmic
domain. That "sun," "world," and "Tartarus" belong to her, that *numina*
and *elementa, superi* and *inferi* depend on her, is clearly stated in the
prayer 11.25. But the initiate is permitted that which would cost the
life of another man not summoned by the goddess: he may cross the threshold

of her realm and behold unharmed *inferi, elementa,* and *superi.* Thus, penetrating all the cosmic spheres, he becomes like the cosmic, all-ruling Isis; he becomes deified. In this context it is not strange that both in the sacred text 11.23 and in the prayer 11.25 *inferi* and *superi* are named: they are representatives of the underworld and the celestial world, but in both spheres Isis reigns, in the one as *regina manium* [queen of the dead] (11.5), in the other as *regina caeli* [queen of heaven] (11.2).

The question arises whether and to what extent the second act of the initiation, the journey through the elements, corresponds with a cosmic interpretation of the entire initiation. Also in this instance De Jong at first tested the hypotheses of Du Prel (water and fire ordeals, levitations), but finally corrected them by the opinion that, while occult phenomena were involved, it was more a cast of a visionary appearance of elemental spirits, "through whose swarm he (the initiate) passed in that mystical ecstasy."[42] That the elements should be presented as deities in this Isis cult is indeed not only credible from the outset,[43] but is also suggested by the words of the prayer in 11.25: *gaudent numina, serviunt elementa* [the gods rejoice, the elements serve]. Verb and parallelism here attest the personal conception. On the other hand, nothing in our text points to ordeal by fire or trial by water; what was said about similar conjectures on *accessi confinium mortis* applies in equal measure to the journey through the elements. But in both places the idea of a purely inner experience is to be rejected, although in the latter more than in the former instance we must reckon with the possibility that ecstasy or a similar psychic condition may have given the sacred action a deeper meaning, for example, made the simple walking about of the initiate appear to him a *vehi*, so that with Parsifal he could say, "I scarcely take a step, yet fancy I have come so far." But the connection of *per omnia vectus elementa* with *remeavi* makes it certain that it is a matter here of a cultic act and not only of a subjective event. The return from Proserpine's realm takes place on the way *per omnia elementa.* Thus something like: ascending from the underground area past altars or pictures of the elemental gods or through rooms which are consecrated to them. With that was connected the feeling of being in the elements, able to pass without danger--thanks to the call of the goddess--through their spheres.[44]

Since this way *per omnia elementa* led the initiate from the *dii inferi* at last to the *dii superi*, the meaning of the action is indubitable: the elements represent the world that lies between below and above. I have tried to show in various works[45] that these cosmic deities were conceived of as tyrants of man, who is at their mercy because he stems from them. Ἐξ ἡμῶν παγέντες, ὅτε ἐγένεσθε, πάλιν εἰς ἡμᾶς ἀναλυθήσεσθε, ὅταν δέῃ θνῄσκειν [From us you were put together when you came into being; into us you will again be dissolved when you must die]. --thus the elements call to man (Philo, *Spec. Leg.* i, 266). And this rule condemns mankind to ever-lasting dependence in the sense of Goethe's Ἀνάγκη: "Bedingung und Gesetz; und aller Wille ist nur ein Wollen, weil wir eben sollten."[46] In such dependence, man found two means by which to make his existence bearable: either he must worship the elements, in order not to be harmed by them,[47] or he must entrust himself to a deity that governs the elements and secures his protégé against any threat by the στοιχεῖα. The latter is our case: the grace of Isis has charmed the initiate, and he can ascend unmolested from the realm of the dead through the regions of the elements, thanks to the same goddess who appears in 11.5 as *rerum naturae parens, elementorum omnium domina* [mother of nature, ruler of all the elements].

It cannot be certainly decided, but it is also not of particular importance, whether the four Empedoclean elements are meant or other cosmic στοιχεῖα. It is tempting to think of twelve elements, since Lucius appears the next morning with twelve garments (11.24), which indeed might refer to twelve zones through which he passed,[48] but they would probably be regions of the sky, into which the initiate arrives only after his journey through the elements. Whatever στοιχεῖα may be meant, the cosmic significance of this act also may be affirmed.[49]

It is scarcely necessary to demonstrate the same for the final act of the sacred drama: now the initiate attains to the realm of heaven and beholds the sun. This meaning of the ritual is clearer than its action. It is virtually certain that a ritual was enacted; the sacramental proce-dures would not have followed one another up to this point only to leave the final act up to the inner imaginative power of the visionary. Thus something like this must have occurred: the initiate enters a room which displays the *dii superi* and whose brilliant illumination--perhaps kindled

suddenly--appeared to him all the more dazzling as previously his eyes
were accustomed to darkness. That such lighting effects could be produced
is known from testimony about other mysteries,[50] and Firmicus Maternus
confirms them also for the Isis celebrations.[51] But just because the
solemnities reach their climax here, one will also have to reckon with
the highest intensification of the initiate's state of psychic arousal.
That applies especially to the epiphany of the "upper gods," which has
its place in this phase of the drama, as shown above and confirmed here.
It must remain open to question whether the believer--setting aside the
difference between heavenly and earthly here as elsewhere during the
initiation--takes priests or pictures for gods,[52] or whether by the power
of his belief in light phenomena in theophanies he hallucinates the divine
epiphanies in the gleam of the "white flaring light."[53]

        This final act also of the drama leads the initiate into a domain
of Isis (11.2, *regina caeli*; 11.5, *prima caelitum* and *quae caeli luminosa
culmina ... nutibus meis dispenso*; 11.25, *te superi colunt, ... tu ...
luminas solem*). But here as in the regions he has left behind it is not
his part to see Isis herself; in both places he sees face to face the
deities who rule the universe and direct the destiny of man under the
supreme rule of the goddess. The luminous appearance of the sun is connected with an epiphany of other (astral?) deities. How this connection
was understood is shown most clearly by the directive in the so-called
Mithras liturgy (ed. Dieterich, pp. 10, 27): τοῦτο εἰπόντος στραφήσονται
ἐπί σε αἱ ἀκτῖνες, ἔσει δὲ αὐτῶν μέσον. ὅταν οὖν τοῦτο ποιήσῃς, ὄψει
θεὸν νεώτερον ... ἔχοντα πύρινον στέφανον ["When you have said this, the
rays will turn to you, and you will be in their midst. When you have done
this then, you will see a young god ... wearing a fiery crown."]. He who
sees the divine light absorbs enough of it to enable him to see the god
himself. The apostle Paul has also suggested, in a passage that depicts
the Christ-vision at Damascus, how light phenomena and theophany belong
together: ὅτι ὁ θεὸς ὁ εἰπών· ἐκ σκότος φῶς λάμψει, ὃς ἔλαμψεν ἐν ταῖς
καρδίαις ἡμῶν πρὸς φωτισμὸν τῆς γνώσεως τῆς δόξης τοῦ θεοῦ ἐν προσώπῳ
Χριστοῦ (2 Cor 4:6). If God had not caused his light to shine even into
the inner man, then man would not have obtained the Christ-gnosis. Only
to the "sun-like eye" is the sun visible.

The same is true for our mystery. To him who is illuminated by
the light of the "sun" in the sanctuary appear the "upper gods," especially
the giver of the light, the sun god himself. He must be thought of as
belonging to the circle of the *superi* or at their head, even though his
name is not expressly mentioned again.[54] But then Lucius appears, in the
scene portrayed in 11:24, transformed into his image. This transformation
by means of vision also has its best parallel in Paul: ἡμεῖς δὲ πάντες
ἀνακεκαλυμμένῳ προσώπῳ τὴν δόξαν κυρίου κατοπτριζόμενοι τὴν αὐτὴν εἰκόνα
μεταμορφούμεθα ἀπὸ δόξης εἰς δόξαν (2 Cor 3:18).

Thus the vision of God and deification are the final goal of
this cosmic migration. By grace Lucius is permitted to undertake this
migration; for everyone not elected it would be dangerous--the descent
into Proserpine's realm would bring death to him; the journey through the
elements, destruction; the vision of the gods in the realm of the *dii
superi*, sudden annihilation. But Isis is ruler in all these regions;
under her protection the initiate bestrides "the whole circle of creation,"
in the opposite direction but in the same cosmic breadth as the Faust drama,
that leads "from heaven through the world to Hell." Insofar as Lucius
traverses this way unharmed, he proves himself charmed against chthonic,
earthly, and heavenly powers. The deification at the end of the ceremony
imparts confirmation and duration to this superiority. Thus the union
with Isis--insofar as one can speak of such union[55]--takes place in this
ritual, not in the sacramental meal used elsewhere,[56] not in the ἱερὸς
γάμος [sacral marriage], not in adoption, but in the migration through the
cosmos. The otherwise dangerous encounter with the powers of death and
fate is anticipated and cancelled by the voluntary entry into their sphere
of power. Thus the initiate becomes a participant in the cosmic rule of
his goddess, a member of a protective union whose members have nothing
further to fear from those cosmic powers, but receive everything from the
hand of Isis: happy life (11.6, *vives autem beatus*), longevity (11.21, *ad
novae reponere rursus salutis curricula*, 11.6, *vitam quoque tibi prorogare*),
and life after death (11.6, *cum ... ad inferos demearis*, ... *me ... tibi
propitiam frequens adorabis*).

This freedom from the rule of the cosmic powers means freedom
also from the coercion of fate. That is not only attested by these

allusions and made probable by the beliefs of the time,[57] but also proved
by the words of the priest that greet Lucius, just transformed from beast
to man again, as the future initiate of the goddess (11.15). With rhetorical irony the priest speaks of Fortuna who, really blind, with all her
blows has driven the tormented man at last to a secure harbor. She may
now seek out someone else to persecute, *nam in eos, quorum sibi vitas ⟨in⟩
servitium deae nostrae maiestas vindicavit, non habet locum casus infestus*
[She has no power over those who dedicate their lives to serve the majesty
of our goddess]. But to the saved man he cries, *in tutelam iam receptus
es Fortunae, sed videntis, quae suae lucis splendore ceteros etiam deos
illuminat* [You are safe under the protection of Fortune, but one who sees,
whose clear light enlightens all the gods]. One sees what significance is
here attributed to the Isis mystery: the rule of the cosmic powers and the
blind Fortuna represented by them is replaced by the rule of the gracious
Fortuna videns [Fortune who sees], whom all those powers obey, Isis.

IV

         Both the role played by the elements in the Apuleius text which
has just been investigated and the importance accorded the entry into the
sacred room in the initiatory ceremony may call to mind a cultus which
seems to have been propagated in Asia Minor at the time when the first
missionaries of Christianity were founding their congregations there. To
be sure we have information about it only at third hand; nevertheless, our
Apuleius text itself permits us to know a little about it.
         In his letter to the Colossians, the apostle Paul combats a
movement that wants to secure a place within the Christian congregation
for a cult of the "elements" and an asceticism connected therewith. It is
not apostasy from Christ that he has to chastise--in such a case he would
attack more vigorously--but a juxtaposition of Christ and the elemental
gods or spirits. What he rightly fears is a peril to the Christ cult and
the Christian message, whose exclusivity is incompatible with such a juxtaposition. For that reason Paul emphasizes again and again that Christ has
brought the All, i.e. these very cosmic powers, under his power and has
rendered them harmless: 1:20; 2:15; 2:19.[58] So far as I can see, this is
all widely recognized and requires no extended proof.

What I want to investigate in connection with Apuleius is something else. What was happening in Colossae was not the repristination of
a cult that had been supplanted, for then Paul would not have failed to
stigmatize the doctrine he attacked as "paganism." Also we do not get
the impression that this cult was already established in Colossae when a
disciple of Paul arrived there with the Christian proclamation.[59] Evidently the propaganda for the στοιχεῖα-worship had first appeared in the
place after the Christian congregation was already in existence. The
element-worshippers apparently had nothing whatever to do with the Christ
cult; the syncretic cult of the στοιχεῖα alongside Christ was not their
doing. Rather the melange first arose when members of the Christian group
entered the cultic fellowship of the στοιχεῖα without renouncing their
Christianity. Thus the doublesidedness--usually overlooked--of the polemic
in Colossians is to be explained. When Paul is talking to these Christians,
the adherents to that theocrasy in the literal sense of the word, he is
showing them that Christ is more than the elements. The Christian has
nothing further to fear from those cosmic powers, for he is, in the words
of the Isis priest in Apuleius, *in tutelam receptus Fortunae sed videntis*.
But where Paul combats that propaganda which comes from outside, he says
(2:8): βλέπετε μή τις ὑμᾶς ἔσται ὁ συλαγωγῶν διὰ τῆς φιλοσοφίας καὶ κενῆς
ἀπάτης (as has already happened with the representatives of the theocrasy)
κατὰ τὴν παράδοσιν τῶν ἀνθρώπων, κατὰ τὰ στοιχεῖα τοῦ κόσμου καὶ οὐ κατὰ
Χριστόν. These people thus do not proclaim any juxtaposition; with their
παράδοσις [tradition] they want to surpass every other preaching. They
know no way of salvation κατὰ Χριστόν [according to Christ], but only κατὰ
τὰ στοιχεῖα [according to the elements]. Paul addresses directly only the
Christians who want to unite the two, but behind them stand the representatives of the new παράδοσις.

Although we receive information about this really only at third
hand, yet this limitation of our knowledge is counterbalanced somewhat by
the fact that Paul quite obviously employs technical terms of the combated
doctrine in 2:18. Because these derive not from the Christian στοιχεῖα-
worshippers but from their non-Christian teachers, the tertiary source is
here transformed into a primary one. Paul writes: μηδεὶς ὑμᾶς καταβραβευέτω
θέλων ἐν ταπεινοφροσύῃ (that must be a technical term) καὶ θρησκείᾳ τῶν

ἀγγέλων (= τῶν στοιχείων τοῦ κόσμου), ἃ ἑώρακεν ἐμβατεύων, εἰκῇ φυσιούμενος
ὑπὸ τοῦ νοὸς τῆς σαρκὸς αὐτοῦ. From εἰκῇ on these words naturally contain
a critique, but what precedes is put together from phrases of the polemi-
cized φιλοσοφία. Since the ancient church it has been questioned whether
ἃ ἑώρακεν ἐμβατεύων belongs to these quotations or to the criticism. The
originators of the widely attested variant reading ἃ μὴ ἑώρακεν [which he
has *not* seen],[60] as well as the singular text forms ἃ οὐκ ἑώρακεν or
ἑωράκαμεν [1st person plur.] or ἑωράκατε [2d person plur.], read out of
the phrase a censure of the alien cult, and so did those who corrected the
text to ἀέρα or αἰώρᾳ or ἄμετρα κενεμβατεύων ["treading the empty air," or
"balancing aloft," or "treading the limitless void"]. These conjectures
all rest upon the metaphorical meaning of ἐμβατεύω = investigate (cf.
2 Macc 2:30). Earlier I attempted, while keeping the better attested
reading (without μή), to interpret the words as Paul's polemic, and
translated, "he who boasts of visions."[61] But even so it is not really
apparent why Paul chooses the ambiguous word ἐμβατεύειν. Every doubt
would be removed if this expression were understood as a technical term of
the alien cult. I took that position in my commentary in 1912 and appealed
to an inscription discovered at Giaur-Kui, which seemed to confirm some
sort of cultic meaning for ἐμβατεύω. Without being acquainted with my
exposition, Ramsay employed the same parallel in *Athenaeum* 1913 (I, 106f.).
By then he could refer also to new results of the excavation in late 1912
at Giaur-Kui, at the site of the ancient Notion, published by Macridy-Bey
in the *Österreichische Jahreshefte* (15, 36 ff.). Now these seem indeed to
support my hypothesis, stated at first with caution, to allay possible
suspicions, and to enrich our knowledge of the terminology of the mysteries.[62]

        The inscriptions relate to the oracle of Apollo of Claros, which
one had been inclinded to look for, on the basis of reports by ancient
writers[63] and earlier discoveries in the vicinity of the ruins of ancient
Notion, near the village Giaur-Kui (officially Christian-Kui).[64]
Th. Macridy, in repeated visits to the regionand an archaeological cam-
paign undertaken under the direction of the Imperial Ottoman Museum, sought
and found information about the site and nature of the sanctuary.

        The village Giaur-Kui wanted to build a new church, since its
population, as a result of wine and tobacco culture, had grown considerably.

Stones for the building were sought, at the direction of the priest Papa
Dimitri, from the ruins of Notion, called Kastro by the natives, which lay
three kilometers to the South. They began transporting them to the
village, until in due course the government called a halt. When Macridy
visited the site for the third time in 1904, evidently no damage had yet
occurred which could not be repaired. The priest's information pointed
principally to a single location in the site. The first investigation of
this place and the preliminary excavation undertaken in 1907 then unearthed
the remains of an early Byzantine church. But the walls of this church
contained a number of inscriptions, of which some were related to the
sanctuary of Apollo of Claros. In part these inscriptions were still *in
situ*, in part already dragged into the village, in part still further
removed, as was the important stone 1905, V,[65] which came to light when a
well was being dug and had long since been published.

It is an engaging story how Macridy, starting with these data,
now seeks to identify the location of the Apollo sanctuary.[66] The stones
with the inscriptions are of considerable size, so the temple to which
they doubtless once belonged cannot be too far away. In addition, information from V. J. Arundell[67] points to the same area; in 1826 he found here
remains of two pillars. Yet no living informant has any recollection of
those pillars, and Macridy is at the point of despair. Then a peasant
leads him to a stone, almost totally concealed in brush and earth, on
which his plowshare had often struck in his field. He digs and finds
the remains of two pillars and also of the pediment, on which are inscriptions which leave no room for doubt: the sanctuary of Apollo is found.
A cave to the west from there, very difficult of access, which according
to the statement of Papa Dimitri contains a small pool of water, must then,
as Schuchhardt had already conjectured, be regarded as the oracle-grotto.

Among the inscriptions (approximately second century A.D.) which
report consultations of the oracle god, some yield information about certain ceremonies which many of the inquirers (the so-called θεοπρόποι[68]) had
to undertake.

The texts, insofar as they are of interest to us, follow. The
dates and the names of temple officials are omitted; I have underlined the
expressions which are important for us.

1905, II 2 concerns envoys from Neocaesarea (Pontus). Lines
8ff.: θεοπρόποι ᾽Αντώνιος Νεικήτης ἰατρὸς καὶ Φλαβουλήιος Βᾶσσο[ς]
μυηθέντες καὶ ἐνβατεύσαντες ἐχρήσαντο ἄρχοντος Νεοκαισαρειας ᾽Αντωνίου
Βλάνδου κτλ.[69]

1905, IV 4 concerns envoys from Amisos (Pontus). Lines 12ff.:
Θεοπρόποι ἦλθο[ν] Κρίσπος Τρύφωνος καὶ Π(όπλιος) Πούπιος Καλλικλῆς οὕτινες
μυηθέντες ἐνεβάτευσαν.[70]

1912, 2 concerns an envoy from Lappa (Crete). Lines 5ff.:
Θεοπρόπος ᾽Ανδρικὸς ᾽Αλεξάνδρου παραλ[αβ]ὼν τὰ μυστήρι[α] ἐνεβάτευσεν.[71]

1912, 15 concerns an envoy from Dionysopolis (Moesia inferior).
Lines 9ff.: Θεοπρόπος [θ]εόδωρος ᾽Απήμονος ἀρχι[ερε]ὺς τῆς πατρίδος·
ἐπετέλε[σε] καὶ μυστήρια.[72]

1912, 16 concerns an envoy from Odessus (Moesia inferior).
Lines 9ff.: Θεοπρόπος [θεοφ?]άνης ᾽Αριστοκλέους [...]του γένους ἀρχι-
ερατικός· [ἐπρέ]σβευεν ἐκ τῶν ἰδίων, [ἐπε]τέλεσε καὶ μυστήρια.[73]

1912, 20 concerns an envoy from Stobi (Macedonia). Lines 9ff.:
[θεο]πρόπος Λ(ούκιος) Κορνήλιος [Μου?]δικιανὸς Κρόκος [γέ]νους
Φιλοπαππιδῶν· [ἐπ]ετέλεσε καὶ μυστήρια.[74]

Of these six inscriptions the second (1905, V 4) was already
known, and I had used it in my interpretation of the passage in Colossians.
But it admitted of another interpretation which, if it did not exclude
this use, did make it difficult. One could refer ἐμβατεύειν to the
entrance into the oracle cave. In that case, μυηθέντες [being initiated]
would refer to a ceremony customary prior to the entry of the cave.[75] The
reports of Tacitus (cf. n. 63 above), to be sure, count against the assumption that the θεοπρόποι were led into the sacred grotto. General considerations also incline one to be skeptical toward this assumption: would they
really have unveiled the essential secret, the manner in which the answer
was obtained, to the inquirers? But now the three last named inscriptions
show that there was in Claros an actual cultus, the mysteries of which one
"accomplished." A comparison of the first three inscriptions reveals that
μυηθέντες and παραλαβὼν τὰ μυστήρια [receiving the mysteries] are equivalent expressions. The third technical term, ἐπιτελεῖν μυστήρια [to complete the mysteries], is naturally not identical with παραλαβὼν τὰ μυστήεια,

but seems more likely to sum up the entire action, the παραλαμβάνειν and the ἐμβατεύειν[76]--perhaps with special emphasis on one's own activity?

Then we obtain the following picture of that which these θεοπρόποι experienced in Claros. First they underwent the μύησις, which consisted in παραλαμβάνειν τὰ μυστήρια. One might think of the *mandata quae voce meliora sunt* which Lucius receives, according to Apuleius, *Metam.* 11. 23, or again of the sacred objects which Apuleius (*Apol.* 55) kept in his house. Thereafter he is admitted--to the *Epoptia*, in the usual language of the mysteries,[77] or to the ἐμβατεύειν, as it is called here. That is the second act of the procedure, which as a whole is called ἐπετέλεσε καὶ μυστήρια.[78] And therefore I do not believe that this "entering" refers to the oracle grotto. The use of the oracle is perhaps alluded to in the ἐχρήσαντο of the first of our six inscriptions. Such an allusion would be altogether unnecessary, since the envoys are every-where introduced as θεοπρόποι. Rather, ἐμβατεύειν is to be connected with the "entering" of the inner shrine (in the temple).[79] Thus ἐμβατεύειν would be a technical designation of the mystery proper, legitimate partici-pation in which was rendered possible by the *muēsis* (or the παραλαμβάνειν τὰ μυστήρια). No further proof is needed that a mystery can be designated by ἐμβατεύειν, since also the content of the ceremony in Apuleius has turned out to be essentially such an "entering" under divine protection.[80] It remains open to question whether also in the case of Claros there is a sanctuary which is the image of a cosmic space; perhaps the archaeologists will assist us to still further knowledge. But this much can be affirmed: that the inscriptions from Claros attest a technical, cultic use of ἐμβατεύειν in the second century A. D. (see above, notes 69, 70) and, moreover, in relation to a mystery celebrated there. Not every θεοπρόπος seems to have become a member of this cultic association; on the other inscriptions the statement is lacking. The question of the prerequisites for admission--whether the status of the delegation or individual choice or perhaps the payment of a contribution--remain provisionally unanswered.

But that which we can know is sufficient to explain the Pauline passage. In the propaganda of a foreign cult which has established itself in Colossae the key word ἐμβατεύειν plays a role. The object of ἐμβατεύειν is probably indicated by the relative clause ἃ ἑώρακεν. From that fact

alone it is possible to conclude that ἐμβατεύειν is used as a technical
term. The inscriptions of Claros confirm that ἐμβατεύειν was used technically in the language of at least one mystery cult of Asia Minor from the
second Christian century on. Thus the religion that made its way into
Colossae in the first Christian century, whose language used ἐμβατεύειν
technically, may also have been a mystery religion. This result is no
surprise, but hitherto evidence has been lacking.

        Therefore ἃ ἑώρακεν ἐμβατεύων belongs to the words which Paul
quotes from the language of that mystery. The allusion is fully comprehensible only to the initiated, since they will not have confided *what*
they saw even to their Christian brothers. The sentence probably cannot
be construed quite so freely as: μηδεὶς ὑμᾶς καταβραβευέτω θέλων ἐν
ταπεινοφροσύνη ... (καὶ ἐν τούτοις) ἃ ἑώρακεν ἐμβατεύων--"who takes
pleasure in that which he saw in the initiation." In any case it is
better, as proposed above, to take ἐμβατεύων as parallel to θέλων and
ἃ ἑώρακεν as its object: "who enters (in the initiation) that which he
saw." Perhaps one should think of sacred symbols which were first exhibited
and then played some role at the ἐμβατεύειν. In that case, ἐμβατεύειν
would stand for "be initiated," having lost its strict connotation. Alter-
natively, one might better retain its proper connotation and refer ἑώρακεν
to the preparatory vision:[81] in a trance the initiate first sees the sacred
rooms which he will later be admitted to. Among the numerous visions
reported by Apuleius, the one experienced in Rome before the second,
Osiris initiation (*Metam.* 11.27) comes closest as a parallel: *nam proxuma
nocte vidi quendam de sacratis linteis iniectum* (that is the future
mystagogue), *qui thyrsos et hederas et tacenda quaedam gerens ad ipsos
meos lares collocaret et occupato sedili meo religionis amplae denuntiaret
epulas* (that is apparently a part of the future initiation) ["For the next
night I saw one of the initiates, wearing linen robes, who brought the
thyrsus and ivy and other things which cannot be mentioned and laid them
before my household gods. Then he sat down in my chair and ordered a
banquet befitting elaborate rites."].

        This reference of the Pauline phrase to a visionary experience
is all the more attractive since we can assume here as well that the rooms
which the initiate "enters" represent cosmic regions. For it is cosmic

deities which are revered in the θρησκεία τῶν ἀγγέλων [worship of angels]:[82]
the στοιχεῖα (2:8). Other words of Paul confirm the impression that the
φιλοσοφία was basically a mystery religion. Perhaps a good many of the
statements about Christ relate antithetically to the salvific content
of the mysteries: Paul speaks of the μυστήριον revealed in Christ (1:26)
and of the treasures of σοφία [wisdom] and γνῶσις [knowledge] hidden in
him (2:3). Perhaps also κατὰ τὴν παράδοσιν τῶν ἀνθρώπων (2:8) is an
allusion to the initiatory procedure which is called παράδοσις = *traditio*.
Possibly it is also no accident that the depiction of Christian salvation
in 2:11 f. uses concepts from the mysteries (συνταφέντες, συνηγέρθητε
[being buried with; you were raised with]), so that one could read the
sentence to mean, "You have already received the greatest mystery." But
certainly we shall connect the ascetic commandments in 2:21, μὴ ἅφῃ μηδὲ
γεύσῃ μηδὲ θίγῃς ["Do not touch, nor taste, nor handle"] with the
continentia prior to the initiation (Apuleius 11.23) and thus be able to
relate them to the ταπεινοφροσύνη ["humility"] in the sentence already
quoted (2:18; cf. 2:23 ταπεινοφροσύνη καὶ ἀφειδία σώματος). Also the
problematic expression ἐθελοθρησκεία ["willing worship"??] (2:23)--
surely a catchword of the opponents--probably finds its explanation in the
character of the mystery religions. Insofar as the mysteries do not cultivate their religion in national or municipal societies but in the voluntary union of a free association, they are really "voluntary cults." And
that is what the Greek word must mean by analogy with related forms, even
though it is unattested. This voluntary character is emphasized especially
in those mysteries which initiate individuals separately and not by the
hundred. We are acquainted with the ethos of the personal religion which
surrounds such an initiation from Apuleius, and we may presuppose it also
for the mysteries at Colossae, because they are called ἐθελοθρησκεία. For
this term, like its two neighbors ταπεινοφροσύνη and ἀφειδία σώματος, is
to be understood as a proud title in the mouth of the initiates.

As in the case of Apuleius, we are confronted here with a cosmic
mystery. It involves a cultic veneration of the elements, and everything
which I said above about motifs and interpretation of such a cult--a propos
of the journey of Lucius *per omnia elementa*--applies here to a heightened
degree, because *only* the elements are mentioned. Their circle lacks the

monarchical zenith. There is lacking the one to whom one could say, *tibi serviunt elementa*[83] or *una quae es omnia* [84]; one worships only *omnia*, the All represented in the elements. Why this is so, one can only surmise (see below, section V), but the fact has its importance in the context of the history of religions. This is the second of the two forms of cultus which--as I showed above--guaranteed man's liberation from the control of εἱμαρμένη [fate]: not worship of a superior deity, as of Isis, is the means here, but a cult of the cosmic tyrants themselves. But Paul's polemic attacked at just this point, and in the opposite sense. He recommends the cult of the superior god; he depicts the cosmic rule of Christ. And he does this, in 2:19, in words which are related to the στοιχεῖα τοῦ κόσμου. He calls Christ the κεφαλή, ἐξ οὗ πᾶν τὸ σῶμα διὰ τῶν ἁφῶν καὶ συνδέσμων ἐπιχορηγούμενον καὶ συμβιβαζόμενον αὔξει τὴν αὔξησιν τοῦ θεοῦ.

As we saw, the letter of Paul did not address directly those who had introduced this cultus into Colossae. Rather, he turned to the Christians who had given an audience to those people. These Christians were the instigators of the hybrid structure that joined the Christ-cult and στοιχεῖα-worship. From the whole tenor of the second chapter, especially 2:20 (εἰ ἀπεθάνετε σὺν Χριστῷ ἀπὸ τῶν στοιχείων τοῦ κόσμου, τί ὡς Ζῶντες ἐν κόσμῳ δογματίζεσθε), it is possible to conclude that this connection was already established. Members of the Christian congregation have joined the mysteries of the "elements." But they remain Christians; neither have they been expelled from the congregation nor have they withdrawn. This combination of cults, particularly in the mysteries, is nothing unheard-of.[85] It represents a kind of double insurance and in our case is perhaps made easier by the want of a monarchical god in the one cultus. It is certainly facilitated by the different sorts of salvation expected in the two cults. Christianity grants security in the future judgment; the cult of the elements, protection from the εἱμαρμένη, the *Fortuna caeca* as Apuleius calls it. By opposing this combination, Paul stands both for the *superiority* and for the *exclusiveness* of his religion. It is superior because Christ gives protection not only from the coming wrath (1 Thess. 1:10) but also from the rulers of this cosmos (Col. 2:15). It excludes every other mystery because in Christ is revealed everything which mysteries could offer (Col. 1:26; 2:3).

V

One might ask why the notion of exclusiveness did not matter to
the other side, the proclaimers of the mystery. The question is to be
answered first of all by calling attention to the syncretistic tendencies
of the period, which favored the thought of combination while opposing
that of rejection. The most striking evidence, again in Apuleius (*Metam.*
11.2 and 5) and in the Attis hymn of Hippolytus (5.9) are familiar. Thus
the priests and initiates of the Colossian mystery would have seen in
Christianity one of the other cults of equal rank. They could therefore
admit its adherents to their communion without scruple. Thus syncretism
possessed these Christians, and we recognize in the events at Colossae
the first stage of a process which has decisively influenced Christianity's
union with Hellenism as well as the argument between them. In our conclusion we shall take another look at the driving forces behind this process.
It is the process of the *syncretization* of Christianity,[86] the infiltration
of gnosis into the Christian congregations.

The fact that around the year A.D. 56[87] members of the Christian
church in Colossae were initiated into the mystery cult of the "elements"
cultivated there constitutes probably the earliest certainly datable and
historically recognizable case of an early and germinal Christian-gnostic
formation. What is lacking of the full development of gnosticism can be
stated forthwith: a fleshed-out dualism,[88] the gnostic redeemer-figure,
and consequently also the Christian-gnostic docetism. It was by no means
asserted by the Christians who turned to the cult of the elements that
Christ was a redeemer from the cult of the cosmic powers--otherwise Paul
would not have taken the field against them with just this thought. Thus
we see that here on both sides there are starting points for the later
development. Paul teaches a cosmic meaning of Christ--starting point for
the Christ-myth of later gnosis, which must occupy our attention later.
First, we look to the other side. Christians became cult-associates of
mysteries which are evidently "pagan." With all due caution we may also
believe that this "paganism" was already influenced by gnosis. The worship of the στοιχεῖα suggests, probably with certainty, that this cult was
ultimately of oriental origins. Bousset has gathered the evidence which
argues for such a provenance.[89] Yet the framework of the pagan pantheon

is evidently lacking in these στοιχεῖα. Therefore Paul's attack upon them
lacks any specific anti-pagen polemic. Instead, the positive trains of
thought of Colossians evince the effort to replace the cosmic speculations
of the opponents by comparable Christian notions. Consequently it seems
that the mysteries into which members of the Christian congregation had
been initiated were not hellenistic mysteries like those of Isis and Attis,
modified forms of Oriental religions propagated in the form of mysteries
fitted out with mystical initiations. Rather, they were still further
removed from the circle of "pagan" religions than those familiar cults.
They were, so to speak, detheologized [*entgöttert*], in that their mythical
basis was transformed into cosmic speculation. They were not "hellenistic"
but *gnostic* mysteries. Thus pre-Christian gnosis--an entity whose existence has hitherto been a matter of controversy--appears before our eyes
in an individual case, and a datable one at that.

      We observe here a most significant process in the history of
religions. To sum it up in a formula, it is the *origin of a Christian-
gnostic formation by double initiation*, by Christian baptism and by
initiation into mysteries already transformed in a gnostic direction.
Presumably this process did not take place only in Colossae. From a later
time we have evidence for a similar occurrence, although its significance
is diminished by the circumstance that the Christians in the latter case
were already Christian gnostics, so that the process in question did not
create the Christian-gnostic formation, but only carried it further. The
case is that of the Naasenes, who, according to the unambiguous testimony
of Hippolytus,[90] were initiated into the mysteries of Attis. Numerous
clues suggest that these Attis mysteries were already influenced by
gnosticism. In the first place, Reitzenstein[91] has at least demonstrated
the probability that the expositions which Hippolytus opposes originally
contained nothing Christian, but were a "pagan" commentary on the Attis
hymn quoted at their conclusion. But these expositions identify Attis
with the primal Man, and this blending of the god of the mysteries with
cosmic speculation must be attributed to the beliefs of those particular
Attis initiates who were joined by the Naasenes. This is all the more
likely since the Attis hymn itself shows traces of the equation of Attis
and the primal Man--in the name Adamas for the Samothracian image of

Attis.[92] Besides this, Bousset has proved[93] that in Julian and Sallust
(*De diis et mundo*) the Attis beliefs are transformed in a similar fashion.
Hence the cultic merger which the Christian Naasenes entered into with the
gnostically-influenced Attis mysteries is comparable to the development
we have observed in Colossae.

Hippolytus' report of the preachings of the Christian Naasenes
provides yet another indirect proof for the appearance of such cultic
mergers on this soil. These pneumatics describe themselves as those who
celebrate the mystery in the third gate, or who have entered through the
third gate.[94] That has to be understood not only symbolically, but in
the first instance realistically: of rooms in the sanctuary, in which the
mysteries are celebrated, and which are the image of cosmic zones. But
that is the same situation which I have undertaken to demonstrate for the
mysteries, and εἰσέρχεσθαι [to enter] in Hippolytus corresponds to *pervadere*
in Apuleius and ἐμβατεύειν in Paul. Thus we have evidence here, in the
Christian-gnostic cultus, for a mystery that is analogous to those cosmic
initiations. And therewith we have a testimony also to the fact that the
parents of this gnosis were Christian and Mystery initiations: cultic
merger by double initiaton!

Furthermore, in many Christian-gnostic sects the figure of the
redeemer is still lacking, their mysteries transmit the names of the archons,
they teach or presuppose how to accomplish the passage of the soul through
the world of these archons.[95] All these characteristics point to the per-
sistence of cults similar to that which we can presuppose in Colossae, and
show that the hypothesized process there was a typical case of the emergence
of Christian gnosis by cultic merger.

A typical case, but not the only type! The investigation of
Colossians itself leads to recognition of a second type. I have tried to
show that the mysteries to be postulated from Col. 2 were already influenced
by gnosticism. We found traces of such influence also in the Attis initiates of the Naasene preaching. The same text presents yet a further
example, to which Dieterich has called attention.[96] In Hippolytus 5.8
(p. 164) the cry of the hierophant in Eleusis is mentioned, which refers
to the birth of Iacchos: ἱερὸν ἔτεκε πότνια κοῦρον Βριμὼ Βριμόν ["Her
Majesty has given birth to a sacred boy, the strong one to a strong one"].

This cry now receives a thoroughly mystical interpretation: πότνια δέ
ἐστι, φησίν, ἡ γένεσις ἡ πνευματικη, ἡ ἐπουράνιος, ἡ ἄνω· ἰσχυρὸς δέ
ἐστιν ὁ οὕτω γεννώμενος ["'majesty,' they say, is the spiritual, heavenly
origin above; 'the strong one' (masc.) is he who is thus born"]. But this
interpretation, to which similar explanations of 'Ελευσίν and ἀνακτόρειον[97]
are added, is, we are told, not a new invention of the Naasenes, but stems
from the circle of the initiates themselves: τοῦτο, φησίν, ἐστίν, ὃ
λέγουσιν οἱ κατωργιασμένοι τῶν 'Ελευσινίων τὰ μυστήρια ["This, they say,
is what those who have undergone the rites of the Eleusinian mysteries
report"]. From that it appears that even the Eleusinian mysteries, at
least in certain circles, were modified by gnostic teaching. Thus we see
that gnosis as mythical-mystical speculation gains entry into various cults
without endangering the existence of these cults or breaching their cultic
fellowship. Christianity has also been affected by this process, and therewith we encounter a second kind of Christian-gnostic formation alongside
of the double-initiation variety: *the gradual gnostic influence of an
existing cultus*. This can be demonstrated in a set of notions long since
described and investigated, but whose relationship with the phenomena
treated here requires further emphasis.[98]

I have sought to demonstrate in an earlier work[99] that Paul conceived of Christ's incarnation after the manner of a descent-to-Hades
myth, and thus constructed an actual Christ-myth. Evidence is found above
all in 1 Cor 2:6 ff., Phil 2:5 ff., but also 2 Cor 8:9 and especially the
expositions in Colossians: Christ descended unrecognized through the
spheres of the archons, in order then, ascending in glory, to triumph
over the deluded archons.[100] The earth has here the place of the underworld in the Hades myths. There the unrecognized Son of God suffers death,
the work of the ἄρχοντες--to be sure, εἰ γὰρ ἔγνωσαν, οὐκ ἂν τὸν κύριον τῆς
δόξης ἐσταύρωσαν (1 Cor 2:8). The expanded form of the myth we can read
in the Ascension of Isaiah. One can argue whether Paul developed his conception in similar fashion, but Colossians proves that he did develop it
beyond the allusions in particular passages. For our problem another
observation seems to me more important than this question: if such a
mythical schema was available and invested with Paul's authority, then it
could attract related extra-Christian myths and assimilate them. Thus a

beachhead was established within the Christian world of symbols for a host
of Oriental, Hellenistic speculations. The history of the Christian-
gnostic movement shows that the beachhead quickly became a colony.

We can no longer say with certainty by what means these conceptions came to the apostle Paul,[101] but we can discern which phenomena of
the religious life they undergirded for him. It is a matter of the
security of the Christian's mystical union with God in spite of all
oppression by the cosmic powers. That security is guaranteed by the victory
of the Son of God over the ἀρχαὶ καὶ ἐξουσίαι [princes and powers]. Also
in this area one needs to pay more attention than has hitherto been the
case to the question whether this goal was achieved by cultic actions or
by inner experience. In the Letter to Romans (6:3, 4) and in a brief
allusion in Colossians (2:12), Paul names baptism as the means by which
the Christian re-experiences the Christ myth: the dying and rising of the
Son of God are imitated in the sacrament. Thus baptism ought really to
be a dying, but the form of the action contradicted that, unless one
interpreted it--as Luther later did--as a veritable "being drowned." So
in the passages mentioned it is understood as an imitation of Christ's
burial--a forced interpretation, for the burial is not a salvific act of
Christ. That fact proves, so far as I can see, that this evaluation of
baptism was not original and that the baptismal ritual was not formed
according to these concepts, but arose from another world of symbols.
The Christian congregation probably borrowed baptism, as an eschatological
sacrament, from the circle of John the Baptist. But the Christians of the
hellenistic world felt the need to understand it as a hellenistic mystery.
Here the analogy of the mysteries explains everything; there is no trace
of any gnostic modification.

Now this evaluation of baptism is by no means idiosyncratic to
Paul; he presupposes it in the Roman congregation, where he is a stranger.
When he mentions it he is only the mouthpiece of the hellenistic Chris-
tianity which he joined after his conversion.[102] His own view of the
mystical union of the Christian with the mythically-conceived fate of the
Son of God, while related, is in one essential point of a different sort.
His view has no connection with the sacrament; it transfers the conception
of the mystery cult to the mystery of life ἐν Χριστῷ, which needs no cultic

apparatus. It is comparable to that mystery initiation which, according
to a familiar passage in Dio of Prusa,[103] was bestowed on mankind by the
gods, as the true mystagogues, by means of a contemplation of the cosmos.
Such a cultless mystery is depicted by Paul directly after the words about
baptism which were cited above. From the breadth and emphasis of this
passage, we may discern that *here* Paul follows the dictates of his heart,
while in the previous passage he was striving to clarify an initiatory
experience for the community. Now there is nothing more said about baptism,
and therefore also nothing else about the mystical burial with Christ.
Rather, Rom 6:6 ff. says: our old man is crucified with Christ; we have
died with Christ that we may live with him. Thus, by the testimony of
other passages, the whole life of the Christian is a mystery[104]--his suffering and his scars,[105] but also his longing, loving, and hoping,[106] his
humility and his power,[107] are no longer human but divine. Or, as Paul
says, they are attributes and effects "of Christ."

     This Christ-mysticism of Paul did not arise from his taking over
the thoughts and moods of cultic mysticism, starting from the concepts of
the mysteries, and translating them, without the cultic aparatus, into
Christian language. The investigation of Romans 6 showed us that the
cultic-sacramental connection was not primary for Paul--in contrast to the
hellenistic churches. The separation of this mysticism from cultus, if it
had ever been connected, took place before Paul, on extra-Christian soil.
He follows a mystical theology that is not attached to cultus, as a similar
theology affected Philo. This theology can enter into new relationships
with cults of different provenience--as Philo and Paul themselves show--
but it can also produce new rites and new systems within these cults.
Thus we recognize also in this theology a root of gnosticism or, if one
wants to use the expression, a kind of pre-Christian gnosis.

     The emergence of Christian-gnostic formations from this mysticism
can be plausibly conjectured, after all, but it can also be demonstrated
by examples. Without any reference to a cultic action, Paul spoke of the
Christian being crucified with Christ. Then this thought was joined *de
novo* with a cultic action, evidence for which we have in two Odes of Solomon. The twenty-seventh Ode,[108] following Staerk's translation, reads:

     I stretched out my hands and sanctified them to my Lord,

for the extension of my hands is his sign,

and my extension is the upright tree. Hallelujah.

The beginning of the forty-second Ode has almost the same word-
ing with the exception of the third verse, whose text cannot be reconstructed with certainty.[109]   In both Odes an action is depicted in which
the believer--probably while using the gesture of prayer--assumes the
position of the Crucified. And this action is a sacrament. The *orans* is
deified by it and now speaks, in 42:4 ff., as Christ (cf. n. 100 above).
Perhaps the allusion here, as Bousset has conjectured,[110] is not to the
earthly cross of Christ, but to its cosmic countertype, the heavenly light-
cross of gnosis. Speculations about the latter may possibly be older than
Christianity and be connected with Plato's description of the world-soul
οἷον Χεῖ ["a sort of X"] (Timaeus 36BC). In any case, the cross-mysticism
that Paul presented without any cultic action is here turned into something
cultic and sacramental, perhaps assimilated at the same time with a pre-
Christian speculation--a typical example of gnostic development.

The small prayer collection of the Berlin papyrus 9794 (*Berliner
Klassikertexte* VI, 110 ff.)[111] offers the most obvious, though late, witness for the way the mysticism attested in Paul and the Odes--with its
restraint or even complete suppression of the human ego--perceived non-
Christian material as spiritually related and assimilated it. The papyrus,
as is well known, contains alongside of Christian texts also the concluding prayer of the Poimandres (*Corp. Herm.* 1. 31 f.) with slight modifications. The Christian who borrowed it, from whatever source, perceived
the prayer's mysticism as kin to his own. Evidently he did not perceive
that at the prayer's conclusion the mystic's self-consciousness--more
correctly, his mystical God-consciousness--is intensified in a way that
seems intolerable within Christianity: ὁ σὸς ἄνθρωπος συναγιάζειν σοι
Βούλεται, καθὼς παρέδωκας τὴν πᾶσαν ἐξουσίαν αὐτῷ ["Your man wants to join
you in the act of sanctifying, as you have granted him all authority"].
The last words refer to the complete initiation, the knowledge of deification that is "delivered" to the mystic. *Corp. Herm.* 1.26 offers the
parallel: τοῦτό ἐστι τὸ ἀγαθὸν τέλος τοῖς γνῶσιν ἐσχηκόσι, θεωθῆναι.
λοιπὸν, τί μέλλεις; οὐχ ὡς πάντα παραλαβὼν καθοδηγὸς γίνῃ τοῖς ἀξίοις κτλ.

["This is the excellent goal of those who have obtained knowledge: to
see God. Now, why do you delay? Should you not, as one who has received
everything, become a guide for those worthy ...?"] The conclusion of the
prayer sounds so little Christian, in fact, that the editors of the papyrus
Schubart and Schmidt, not recognizing the text's agreement with the Poimandres, postulated a lacuna. They were forced to assume that αὐτῷ referred to Christ. Regardless whether the prayer collection was catholic or
gnostic, the fact remains that Christian mysticism accepted a prayer of
non-Christian origin.

Already in Paul's time, however, mysticism could occasionally
exercise an influence on the myth which would reach its full development
only in the gnostic realm of ideas. That is shown by Romans 14:9. After
the union of the faithful with Christ has been depicted in the famous
words of 14:7 f., the incarnation of Christ is itself explained in the
sense of this mysticism. Christ had to become man in order that Christians
could become like him: εἰς τοῦτο γὰρ Χριστὸς ἀπέθανεν καὶ ἔζησεν, ἵνα καὶ
νεκρῶν καὶ ζώντων κυριεύσῃ ["For this purpose Christ died and came to life,
that he might rule the dead and the living"]. The motto of Angelus
Silesius, "I am as great as God, he as small as I," would fit here.[112]
But this is an ad hoc formulation by Paul, with at most one other parallel,
2 Cor 8:9. Rom 8:3 presents the incarnation under a different viewpoint,
and even in 14:9 the Christian's likeness to God is essentially limited by
the word κυριεύσῃ [rule]. In the piety of the Odes of Solomon, however,
where mysticism and mythical speculation stand in the center, this notion
which is only alluded to by Paul also takes central place. Read Ode 7:4 ff.:
"He revealed his nature to me richly and undisguised, for by his kindness
he caused his greatness to become small for me. He became like me, that
I might receive him; he appeared in likeness to myself, that I might put
him on."[113] Think how many starting points for mythical exposition this
form of the thought not only might offer but in the Odes actually does
offer! Thus here again it is apparent to what an extent Paul's mysticism
carries within it the germ of gnostic developments.

I have attempted to demonstrate by examples two types of the
syncretization of Christianity. We have seen how already in Paul's time

mystical Christianity attached itself to gnostic mysteries in what one
might call a personal union. We have seen further how hellenistic mysticism
and speculation--without any cultic connections and in part already of
gnostic coloration--crept into earliest Christianity and thus prepared
the way for the invasion of gnostic myths and speculations. There is yet
a third type of connection, which is however less readily recognizable, and
which I therefore shall only mention in conclusion. This is the case of
syncretistic religions adapting themselves to Christian beliefs and assim-
ilating them. To the mystery priests in Colossae--as stated above--
Christianity seemed so tolerable that they initiated Christians without
separating them from the Christian congregations. The same sensibility
may have moved other proclaimers of syncretistic religions to approach
Christianity from their side, without giving up their own piety.

    In all probability Simon Magus should be included in this con-
text. To be sure the historical figure behind this name can scarcely be
recognized through legendary transformation. But the picture drawn in
Acts 8:9 f. can at least claim credence in depicting a *type*:[114] one of the
syncretistic prophets who wandered the lands of the Near East in those days
becomes acquainted with Christianity. He is attracted by the results obtained by its proclaimers, documented in word and deed, for his own public
image as the new great revealer of God rests upon such results. Thus he
seeks to join the competing movement, in order to get possession of its
technique by participation in its cultus--that is, the ceremonies, verbal
formulas, and rites which, in his opinion, produce such powers.

    The more strongly Christianity emphasized its exclusivity, the
more quickly the loose ties would be broken. The less the Christians perceived the distinguishing factor, the more readily they could tolerate
such an outsider. A few allusions in the gospels and in the Acts testify
that such cases were repeated and were judged by the Christian congregations
sometimes in a friendly manner, sometimes in a hostile way. I have on
another occasion collected the passages and investigated them under the
catchword "Half-Christianity."[115] According to circumstances, the development led either to lasting fusion or to repulsion. In the latter case the
representative of the syncretism might retain some Christian reminiscences
in the form of names, formulas, or rites. Thus Christian influences in

syncretistic religions should not surprise us,[116] especially since this
process was not limited to Christianity. For the syncretist religiosity
is also attracted to Judaism and bears certain traces of this approach.
Jewish reminiscences in the magic papyri can serve as evidence.[117] A still
better proof is provided by the conjecture, if it should prove true, that
the Old Testament citations in the Naasene preaching in Hippolytus were
already contained in the original "pagan" gnostic text.[118]

      Thus movement and countermovement are revealed: gnostic invasion
of Christianity and adaptation of Christian material by syncretism. And
to these relationships must be added the phenomenon investigated at the
beginning of this essay, the merger of cults. Yet all three factors are
working toward the same goal for which the Isis mysteries in Apuleius and
the cosmic mysteries in Colossae strove: by means of a revelatory religion
to set man free from cosmic compulsion and to make him master of his fate.
Christianity resists with the same resources that Paul already used: it
emphasizes its exclusivity and its superiority and constantly reinforces
these bastions.

      Christianity shows its exclusive character not only in the fact
that it repells the syncretistic developments and thus overcomes the
crisis of the anti-gnostic struggle,[119] but especially by establishing
the uniqueness of its divine revelation in the unique greatness of God.
That is, it overcomes Hellenistic syncretism by means of the concepts of
Hellenistic philosophy. The Gospel of John is an important witness to this
process, which is far from having been adequately evaluated. It not only
bans the strange shepherds as thieves and robbers from the kingdom of the
good shepherd (10:8), already in the prologue it also links the mode of
the salvific revelation with the concept of God. Because God cannot be
seen by any mortal eye, only the μονογενής can reveal him. It was the con-
viction of the syncretistic sons of God and God proclaimers that man,
superior to the gods, could ascend to heaven in the spirit and thus see
and learn heavenly things. The belief receives typical expression in the
Κλεύς of the Hermetic Corpus (10.25): οὐδεὶς μὲν γὰρ τῶν οὐρανίων θεῶν ἐπὶ
γῆς κατελεύσεται, οὐρανοῦ τὸν ὅρον καταλιπών, ὁ δὲ ἄνθρωπος εἰς τὸν οὐρανὸν
ἀναβαίνει καὶ μετρεῖ αὐτόν ... ["For while none of the heavenly gods will
descend upon earth, abandoning the bounds of heaven, yet man ascends to

heaven and measures it ..."]. John 3:13 sounds like the Christian answer
to such claims: οὐδεὶς ἀναβέβηκεν εἰς τὸν οὐρανὸν εἰ μὴ ὁ ἐκ τοῦ οὐρανοῦ
καταβάς, ὁ υἰὸς τοῦ ἀνθρώπου.

From *our* perspective, the superiority of Christianity is documented above all in the fact that it offered more and different things than
mysteries, gnosis, and syncretistic prophets. But its *success* vis a vis
these forces depended in the first instance on the fact that believers
found in Christ the *same* value as in Isis: liberation from the cosmic
tyrants of existence, from the *fortuna caeca*. For although Christianity
resembled its rivals in this particular, yet it was also superior to them
by force of its original content and its tendency to exclusivity, by which
it secured this content. However, in order to equal the competitors and
to show to the Christians their mastery of fate, the Christian proclamation
had to become involved in the cosmic problems of existence. This new orien-
tation could not be carried through without borrowing from Hellenism, but
while Christian gnosticism fell into syncretism in the process of transformation, the greater part of the congregations were saved from this fate
by that exclusive tendency.

Thus this process, which begins with Paul and reaches its high
point in the ecclesiastical gnosis of Alexandria, proceeds by absorption
and exclusion. Its significance becomes visible precisely when one looks
at the initiation rites of the mysteries which have been investigated in
this essay. That which the reoriented Christianity bestowed on its
believers was formulated as follows by a contemporary of Apuleius, the
Christian Tatian, himself a product of Hellenism: ἡμεῖς δὲ καὶ εἱμαρμένης
ἐσμὲν ἀνώτεροι ["We are superior even to fate"] (*Oratio ad Graecos* 9; ed.
Schwartz, p. 10). The priest of Isis points the transformed Lucius to the
same goal: delivered from all oppression, rejoicing in the divine providence, to triumph over the power of fate--*en ecce pristinis aerumnis
absolutus Isidis magnae providentia gaudens Lucius de sua Fortuna triumphat*
["Behold Lucian triumphs, saved from his former troubles by the providence
of the great Isis, rejoicing in his Fortune"].

* * *

NOTES

[1]Especially the following works: Richard Reitzenstein, "Zum
Asclepius des Pseudo-Apuleius," *Archiv für Religionswissenschaft* 7 (1904)
393-411; *Die hellenistischen Mysterienreligionen* (Leipzig and Berlin, 1910;
[3d ed. reprinted Darmstadt, 1956]) especially 8 ff., 84 f., 204 ff.

[2]K. H. E. de Jong, *De Apuleio Isiacorum mysteriorum teste* (Diss.
Leiden, 1900); *Das antike Mysterienwesen in religionsgeschichtlicher,
ethnologischer und psychologischer Beleuchtung* (Leiden, 1909). I cite
the latter as "De Jong," the former as "De Jong, *Dissertation*."

[3]The attestations of παράδοσις, παραδιδόναι, and *tradere* in the
mysteries are to be found in [Christian A.] Lobeck, *Aglaophamus* [Königsberg,
1829] 1. 39, n., and in [Gustav] Anrich, *Das antike Mysterienwesen in seinem
Einfluss auf das Christentum* [Göttingen, 1894] 54, n. 4.

[4]Reitzenstein (*ARW* 7. 406, n. 1) rightly criticizes De Jong,
Dissertation, for failing to take this viewpoint into account. But Reitzenstein himself applies it to the purifying bath (11.23), although in the
text itself the depiction of voluntary death can be found only in *accessi
confinium mortis*. Apuleius leaves us in the dark about the meaning of
that "baptism," whether it was indeed a parallel ἀναγέννησις. Hence we
cannot take as our starting point an attempted interpretation of this
ceremony.

[5]Cf. [Paul] Vallette, *L'Apologie d'Apulée* (Paris, 1908) 281:
"The initiate completed a journey to the land of the departed. That was
the central fact, and the culminating point of the ceremony was the return
from death to life."

[6][Antoine Isaac] Silvestre de Sacy in the second edition of
[Guillaume E. J., Baron de] Sainte Croix, *Recherches historiques et
critiques sur les mystères du paganisme* (Paris, 1817) 2. 163, translates:
"J'ai été en présence des Dieux supérieurs et inférieurs." The same in-
version occurs in the translation by [Adolf] Jacoby, *Die antiken Mysterien-*

Religionen und das Christentum, 40. The mistake is characteristic. On the work by Silv. de Sacy just cited, see De Jong, *Dissertation,* 6.

[7]To build a proof on this stylistic argument alone appears open to question. One could well imagine that the eclectic stylist Apuleius, who modifies his style according to subject matter, might produce ornate language with the most sensuous effect possible for the Fotis scenes, but could here speak in hieratic simplicity in the mode of older mystery symbols. Cf. [Eduard] Norden, *Antike Kunstprosa* [2d. ed., Leipzig, 1909; 5th, unchanged, Darmstadt, 1958] 2. 600-605.

[8][Albrecht] Dieterich (*Eine Mithrasliturgie* [Leipzig, 2d. ed., 1910; 3d. ed. reprinted Darmstadt, 1966] 126-27) provided the evidence for this meaning of παστός and set it within a broad context in the history of religions. Thereafter it would seem that no further consideration need be given the remaining possible interpretation, which recalls the *pastophori* of Isis and finds evidence in the σύνθημα for a corresponding procession with temple models. Cf. [Hugo] Hepding, *Attis* [Giessen, 1903] 193 f.

[9]Thus explained by Hepding, *Attis* 188. But he is led to this interpretation by the introductory words of Firmicus Maternus, and these statements of the Christian author seem to me open to suspicion (see further below).

[10]The valuable investigation of *moriturus* by [Ernst] Maass, *Orpheus* [Munich, 1895] 176, n. 3 (cf. De Jong 203) thus remains entirely valid. Its conclusion can also be supported further by the observation that Firmicus, 18.2 (Ziegler 43 f.), probably plays on the designation *moriturus,* in the same sense that elsewhere (20.1; 21.2) as well he emphasizes the relative truth of the pagan terminology: *Male miser homo de admisso facinore confiteris. Pestiferum veneni virus hausisti, et nefarii furoris instinctu letale poculum lambis. Cibum istum mors sequitur semper et poena.* He is in very truth a *moriturus.* Cf. Friedrich, *In Julii Firmici Materni de errore profanarum religionum libellum Quaestiones* (Giessen Dissertation, Bonn, 1905) 42 f. We shall have to disregard all conjectured emendations.

([Christian August] Lobeck, *Aglaophamus*, [Königsberg, 1829] 1. 24:
oraturus; Bursian in his edition: *introiturus*; Halm the same in the
Vienna *Corpus*.

[11]Ziegler, in the apparatus of his edition (p. 43), also advocates the possibility that Firmicus constructed Form C himself, pointing
to two passages with similar terminology in the astrological work of
Firmicus, *Math.*, 1. 4. 11 (Kroll 13): *divinae dispositionis secreta perdi-
dicit* and 5.1.26 (p. 14) *absconsarum religionum secreta perdiscens*.
Ziegler adds: *unde cognoscimus Latinam eam interpretationem ab ipso Firmico
conceptam neque in Attidis sacris usitatam fuisse*. In contrast to others,
Ziegler also assumes a large lacuna at the end of chap. 18 (p. 47): *nos
plura (fortasse folium exempli librarii Palatini) excidisse rati*, etc.

[12]Considering the probability that the saying circulated in
several recensions, we should probably do better to refrain from reducing
Forms A and B to a single text (so [Hermann Karl] Usener, *Altgriechischer
Versbau* [Bonn, 1887] 89). Cf. Dieterich, *Mithrasliturgie* 217; Friedrich 42.

[13][Georg] Wobbermin, *Religionsgeschichtliche Studien [zur Frage
der Beeinflussung des Urchristentums durch das antike Mysterienwesen*
(Berlin, 1896)] 177: "One cannot with certainty derive anything more from
him than that he found out that the formulae which he recounts were used
in mysteries." I believe that I have shown above that this mistrust is
well founded, so Friedrich's defense of Firmicus (pp. 36 ff.) seems to me
not to have succeeded in this point.

[14]Wobbermin 177. Clement, *Protrepticus* 2.15 (Stählin, p. 13),
uses σύμβολον of the sacred formula of the Attis cult; that of the Eleusinian
mysteries is called σύνθημα (2.21, p. 16). He calls ἀστράγαλος, σφαῖρα,
στρόβιλος, etc. τὰ ἀχρεῖα σύμβολα (2.18, p. 14), just as ὀρίγανον, λύχνος,
ξίφος, κτεὶς γυναικεῖος are called ἀπόρρητα σύμβολα (2.22, p. 17). In 2.16
(p. 13), Σαβαζίων γοῦν μυστηρίων σύμβολον τοῖς μυουμένοις ὁ διὰ κόλπου θεός,
σύμβολον probably refers to the object, but perhaps also to a formula. In
any case we have no occasion for reading out of the word σύμβολον the use
of the sacred saying.

[15]As is well known, the beginning of the symbol is not preserved, nor can it be reconstructed with certainty. Friedrich, 47, supposes on the basis of his conjecture (ι)δέ that the initiate is admonished to gaze at the image of the god. Since the restoration is questionable (cf. the proposals of Dieterich, *Mithrasliturgie*[2] 214, 236), it seems simpler to me to assume that the words represent the greeting by the initiate of the god at his epiphany.

[16]Cf. the conjecture made above about the forms of the Attis symbol. Perhaps too the meaning would be possible which Arnobius attributes to the Eleusinian symbol (*Adversus nationes* 5.26): *quae rogati sacrorum in acceptionibus respondetis*--if this remark is to be believed at all.

[17]On the whole question of maintaining secrecy, see further below.

[18]This meaning here is confirmed besides in the fact that in the following scene, 11.24, the initiate is shown to the people as a god. In addition, see Reitzenstein, *Hellenist. Mysterienreligionen* 112 ff.

[19]Dieterich 14: κύριε, πάλιν γενόμενος ἀπογίγνομαι αὐξόμενος καὶ αὐξηθεὶς τελευτῶ ἀπὸ γενέσεως ζωογόνου γενόμενος εἰς ἀπογενεσίαν ἀναλυθεὶς πορεύομαι ὡς σὺ ἔκτισας, ὡς σὺ ἐνομοθέτησας καὶ ἐποίησας μυστήριον.

[20]The cultic language of these Isis mysteries was naturally Greek. I refrain from the attempt to re-translate the Isis text, since the terminology of these mysteries is not known to us; it would perhaps become better known if for once a systematic re-translation of all technical expressions in the eleventh book of the *Metamorphoses* were to be undertaken.

[21][Albrecht] Dieterich, *Die Grabschrift des Aberkios* (Leipzig, 1896).

[22]For the interpretation, cf. Dieterich, *Mithrasliturgie*, 170 ff.

[23]Thus in Tertullian, *Apologeticus* 8. See also Lobeck,
Aglaophamus 64 ff., Anrich, *Antikes Mysterienwesen* 31 f.

[24]Rohde has expressed this insight, in part based on Lobeck's
exposition (*Aglaophamus* 1. 48 ff.), as follows: "It was not easy to
divulge the 'mystery,' for strictly speaking there was nothing to divulge"
(*Psyche* [Freiburg i.B., 1st. ed., 1894] 1[4]. 289 [ET, 1. 222]) Cf. also
the brief presentation in Anrich, 31 f.

[25]It is probably these formulae which are referred to in the
passage in Pseudo-Lysias, *Adversus Andocides* 51: οὖτος γὰρ ἐνδὺς στολήν,
μιμούμενος τὰ ἱερὰ ἐπεδείκνυ τοῖς ἀμυήτοις καὶ εἶπε τῇ φωνῇ τὰ ἀπόρρητα,
on which see Rohde, 1. 289, n. 2. [ET, 1. 233, n. 20].

[26]Cf. Abt, *Die Apologie des Apuleius von Madaura und die antike
Zauberei* (Religionsgeschichtliche Versuche und Vorarbeiten, IV/2) 214.
The speaker means presumably the Eleusinian cult and the mystic κίστη with
the phallus. Also the *signa* and *monumenta* in the cloth, from Apuleius'
allusions, must be objects. So *signum*, too, is ambiguous in relation to
the mysteries, like σύμβολον (see n. 14 above) denoting both objects and
formulae (*signum* = "formula" in the passage cited immediately below,
Apologia 56, and in Firmicus Maternus 18, cited above).

[27]Neither Abt nor Vallette offers an explanation of the passage.

[28]*Apol.* 55 (ed. Helm, p. 63), referring to Apuleius' speech in
Oea, says: *dicite aliquis, si qui forte meminit, huius loci principium.--
audisne, Maxime, multos suggerentis? immo, ecce etiam liber offertur.
recitari ipsa haec iubebo, quoniam ostendis humanissimo vultu auditionem
te istam non gravari.*

[29]Abt deals with the probability of reworking, pp. 6 ff., and
with the misreading of the passage from the Asclepius speech, p. 4.
Naturally not the whole section about the mysteries, but only the appeal
to the cult brother would be attributable to the redactor. In favor of

this assumption is the consideration that in case of trouble Apuleius
would have taken care that the third party was really present; in the same
way he had planted an acquaintance in the audience with a copy of the
Asclepius speech.

[30]Hildebrand (Leipzig, 1842) connects *audiat* with the following
clause, which would otherwise be meaningless. Both Van der Vliet and
Helm print *audias*; see Helm's note in the apparatus, p. 64.

[31]Thus the translation by Fritz Weiss (Leipzig, 1894).

[32]Since Isaac Casaubonus, Eleusinian and Attis symbols from
Clement have been cited at this passage, beside ἀστράγαλος, σφαῖρα,
στρόβιλος, κτλ., although σύμβολον in this case refers to objects (see
above, n. 14). In addition, it is customary to refer to Plautus, *Miles
gloriosus* 4.2.1016: *cedo signum, si harunc Baccharum es.*

[33]Dieterich, *Mithrasliturgie* 125, sought to show that Lobeck's
emendation ἐγγευσάμενος was unnecessary, and took the passage to denote a
sexual object, in my judgment correctly. For that reason alone a veiled
expression seems appropriate, yet it is remarkable nevertheless that the
other formulas as well are kept intentionally vague.

[34]De Jong did not give an unequivocally affirmative answer to
this question, but by and large he associated himself with [Karl Ludwig]
Du Prel (*Die Mystik der alten Griechen* [Leiden, 1888], 68-120), who sees
spiritualist phenomena in the depicted events.

[35]Cf. Vallette, *L'Apologie d'Apulée* 280.

[36]In a letter several years ago, Eduard Norden called my attention to this observation. It is evident to every reader of the book that
Apuleius used numerous technical expressions of the cult in his presentation. It is something else again when [Richard] Perdelwitz adduces the
words *fani quidem advena* (11.26) and the inscription *adven(tor) huius templi*

(mithraeum in Dorstadt) in order to prove that προσερχόμενοι in 1 Pet 2:4
originated in the mysteries (*Die Mysterienreligionen und das Problem des
I. Petrusbriefes* [Giessen, 1911] 70). For *advena* at least designates, in
the passage named, just the one who has not yet been initiated into the
cult--antonym: *indigena*.

[37]Cf. Franz Cumont, *The Oriental Religions in Roman Paganism*
[ET, Dover edition, 1956, 238, n. 84]: "De Jong, the latest commentator
on this passage, seems inclined to take it as a mere ecstatic vision, but
the vision was certainly caused by a dramatic scene in the course of which
hell and heaven were shown in the dark." The expression "dramatic" seems
to me subject to misunderstanding in this case, since the person to be
initiated was a participant in the "drama."

[38]Evidence is provided by Maass, *Orpheus* 132, n. 10; 176, n. 3.

[39]In this context the ancient testimonies to the suffering of
the initiate receive their justification, also in the Isis initiation.
This is particularly true of the famous fragment that stands under the
name of Themistios in Stobaeus (*Anth.* 5, ed. Hense, p. 1087) and is rightly
or wrongly (cf. Maass, *Orpheus* 303 ff.) traced back to Plutarch. It compares dying (τελευτᾶν) with the mystery initiation in these frequently
quoted words: πλάναι τὰ πρῶτα καὶ περιδρομαὶ κοπώδεις καὶ διὰ σκότους τινὲς
ὕποπτοι πορεῖαι καὶ ἀτέλεστοι, εἶτα πρὸ τοῦ τέλους αὐτοῦ τὰ δεινὰ πάντα,
φρίκη καὶ τρόμος καὶ ἱδρὼς καὶ θάμβος. It is unlikely that this passage
refers directly to the Isis mysteries. Anrich, *Das antike Mysterienwesen*,
33, n. 2, gives further evidence; cf. also Dieterich, *Mithrasliturgie*, 163.

[40]Hence no guess about the Egyptian basis of the initiatory
celebration should be expressed; cf. [Richard] Reitzenstein, *Hellenistische
Wundererzählungen* (Stuttgart, 1906; reprinted, 1963) 114-17. I am not concerned here with the origins of the idea, but with its appropriate place
within the meaning of the Hellenistic world view.

[41]Perhaps this offers an answer to the question posed by Reitzenstein (*Archiv für Religionswissenschaft*, 7, 408): "It strikes us as odd

that an initiation of this sort can be expanded into two further initiations."

[42]De Jong, 309, in agreement with [Edouard] Schuré, *Les grands Initiés* [Paris, 1889] 437 ff. Cf. also De Jong 271 ff.

[43]Cf. Diels, *Elementum* (Leipzig, 1899); [Adolf] Deissmann, art. "Elements," *Encyclopaedia Biblica*; Pfister, *Philologus* 69, 410 ff., and my expositions in *Die Geisterwelt im Glauben des Paulus* (Göttingen, 1909) and *Kommentar zu den Kleinen Paulusbriefen*, 78 f. [cf. the third edition, *An die Kolosser, Epheser, an Philemon*, ed. Heinrich Greeven (Tübingen, 1953) 27-29].

[44]Cf. Reitzenstein, *Hellenistische Mysterienreligionen*, 85: "Apuleius, too, beheld the *dei superi et inferi* and felt himself in all the elements." But this formulation suggests an interpretation as purely subjective experience, corresponding more or less to the passage cited by Reitzenstein, 121, from *Corpus Hermeticum* 11.20: πάσας δὲ τὰς αἰσθήσεις τῶν ποιητῶν σύλλαβε ἐν σεαυτῷ, πυρός, ὕδατος, ξηροῦ καὶ ὑγροῦ, καὶ ὁμοῦ πανταχῇ εἶναι, ἐν γῇ, ἐν θαλάττῃ, ἐν οὐρανῷ ... However, there is a difference between this text and ours: there a contemplative, ecstatic experience, here a cultic action with accompanying ecstatic phenomena.

[45]*Geisterwelt*, 78 ff.; 125 ff.; 227 ff.; *Kommentar* 71, 78 f., 85 f. [see n. 43 above].

[46]["Contingency and law--and all will is only a wishing, because we must."]

[47]Probably the κλῆσις of the so-called Mithras Liturgy, in which the person praying addresses the "firstlings" of the elements which are united in him, one after another. In Gal 4:3 Paul regards all ancient religions from this perspective. The mysteries of Colossae will be treated below.

[48] Cf. Reitzenstein, *ARW* 7. 408.

[49] On the various enumerations of στοιχεῖα, see Wilhelm Bousset, *Hauptprobleme der Gnosis* (Göttingen, 1907) 223 ff.

[50] Dio Chrysostom, *Oratio* 12, 33 (ed. Arnim, 1. 163): σκότους τε καὶ φωτὸς ἐναλλὰξ αὐτῷ φαινομένων, specifically in a mystery sanctuary of the Athenians. The fragment preserved by Stobaeus (*Anth.* 5, ed. Hense, p. 1087) under the name of Themistius: ἐκ δὲ τούτου φῶς τι θαυμάσιον ἀπήντησε καὶ τόποι καθαροὶ καὶ λειμῶνες ἐδέξαντο (continuation of the passage cited above, n. 39).

[51] *De errore prof. rel.* 2. 4 (ed. Ziegler, p. 5) in the polemic against the Isis cult: *nec ostensi tibi luminis splendore corrigeris*. Cf. also Aelius Aristides, *Sacr. serm.* 3. 46 (ed. Keil, II, 424): ἐγένετο δὲ καὶ φῶς παρὰ τῆς Ἰσιδος καὶ ἕτερα ἀμύθητα φέροντα εἰς σωτηρίαν (but in this passage there is no mention of an initiation).

[52] Cf. in Apuleius 11. 17 the mention of *simulacra spirantia*: icons of gods with especially "lifelike" appearance are meant. Cf. the evidence in Hildebrand's edition.

[53] Thus the opinion of De Jong (313 ff., 353 ff.), who here again, however, suppresses the question of the cultic apparatus so far as possible (cf. p. 332).

[54] The question may be left open, to what extent *sol* is understood personally in the sentence *vidi solem candido coruscantem lumine*. If perhaps Sol is thought of here as an incarnation of the highest deity, then one could speculate whether there is an allusion to this in the depiction of the Osiris epiphany (11.30) *non < in > alienam quampiam personam reformatus*. However, the passage could also be understood as the negative counterpart to *coram*.

[56] The sacred meals on the second and third days (11.24) naturally

do not have this meaning, since already before that the initiate has been
shown to the populace as a sun god.

[57]Cf. Paul Wendland, *Die hellenistisch-römische Kultur* (2d ed.,
Tübingen, 1912) 105, 156, 157.

[58]For details of interpretation see my commentary in Lietzmann's
"Handbuch zum Neuen Testament" [3d ed., revised by Heinrich Greeven,
appeared in 1953 (Tübingen)].

[59]In mentioning the beginnings in 1:7, 8, Paul has only happy
things to report. But more important: in this case, too, Paul would not
have neglected to point out the reactionary elements in the cult of the
elements. We can see how easy that would have been for him from Gal 4:1
ff., where he depicts paganism and Judaism alike as service of the
στοιχεῖα τοῦ κόσμου.

[60]This reading occurs in the so-called Koine tradition, but also
gets accepted in branches of other recensions. The introduction of the
negative is understandable, but its omission would not be. Naturally that
still says nothing about the correct interpretation of the passage.

[61]*Geisterwelt* 141. Cf. also Hermann von Soden in his commentary.

[62]In the fall of 1913, Macridy and Picard, under the auspices
of the Ottoman Museum and the Ecole française d'Athènes, carried out new
excavations at the same site, which they reported in the *BCH* 39 (1915)
33-52. Because of difficulties of communication during the war, I first
learned of this after the present essay was in press and, despite every
effort, have still not seen this volume of the *Bulletin*. A kind communication from Hermann Winnefeld tells me that the publication contains no new
inscriptions and that the excavation was limited to the uncovering--still
uncomplete--of a *propylon* and an adjacent *excedra*

[63]The most important geographical note is in Strabo, 14. 1. 27
(p. 642) εἶτα τὸ Γαλλήσιον ὅρος καὶ ἡ Κολοφών, πόλις Ἰωνική, καὶ τὸ πρὸ

αὐτῆς ἄλσος τοῦ Κλαρίου 'Απόλλωνος, ἐν ᾧ καὶ μαντεῖον ἦν ποτε παλαιόν.
Cf. also Pausanias 7.3.2; 5.3, 10. Tacitus, *Annal*. 2.54, says of the
oracle: *non femina illic, ut apud Delphos, sed certis e familiis et ferme
Mileto accitus sacerdos numerum modo consultantium et nomina audit; tum in
specum degressus, hausta fontis arcani aqua, ignarus plerumque litterarum
et carminum edit responsa versibus compositis super rebus, quas quis mente
concepit*. This description, however, as the inscriptions show, applies
to prophets. Cf. also pseudo-Iamblichus, *De mysteriis* 3.11: τὸ δὴ ἐν
Κολοφῶνι μαντεῖον ὁμολογεῖται παρὰ πᾶσι δι' ὕδατος χρηματίζειν. εἶναι
γὰρ πηγὴν ἐν οἴκῳ καταγείῳ καὶ ἀπ' αὐτῆς πίνειν τὸν προφήτην· ἔν τισι δὲ
τακταῖς νυξὶν ἱερουργιῶν πολλῶν γενομένων πρότερον, πιόντα δὲ χρησμῳδεῖν
οὐκέθ' ὁρώμενον τοῖς παροῦσι θεωροῖς. In addition, cf. [Karl Friedrich]
Hermann, *Lehrbuch der gottesdienstlichen Altertümer der Griechen* [= Lehrbuch der griechischen Antiquitäten, 2. Teil] (2d ed., Heidelberg, 1858)
§40, nn. 24, 26; [Georg Friedrich] Schoemann, *Griechische Alterthümer*
(4th ed., Berlin, 1897-1902) II, 330 f.

[64]The imprecise statements of the ancients have led to frequent
confusion of Notion, Claros, and Colophon. Beside the discussion by
Macridy (following note), see especially Fontrier, Περὶ Κλάρου, Κολοφῶνος,
Νοτίου, in Μουσεῖον καὶ Βιβλιοθήκη τῆς Εὐαγγελικῆς Σχολῆς [Smyrna], 3
(1880) 187 ff., especially 193 ff.; C. Schuchhardt, "Kolophon, Notion und
Klaros," *Athenische Mitteilungen* 11 (1886) 398-434; B. Haussoullier,
Revue de philologie, n.s. 22 (1898) 257 ff.

[65]In the following, I cite the inscriptions according to the two
publications of Th. Macridy, "Altertümer von Notion," *Jahreshefte des
österreichischen archäologischen Instituts* 8 (1905) 155-73 and "Antiquités
de Notion II," *ibid.*, 15 (1912) 36-67, designating the former "1905" plus
the Roman and Arabic numbers of the inscriptions, the second "1912" plus
the Arabic numbers.

[66]For the following, cf. Macridy 1912, 42 ff.

[67]A visit to the *Seven Churches in Asia* (London, 1828) 306.

[68]The designation θεωροί (Pausanias 7.5.3: ἀποστέλλουσιν οὖν ἐς Κλάρον θεωροὺς οἱ Σμυρναῖοι) occurs also occasionally in the inscriptions; see 1905 III 1, 12.

[69]The stone was discovered inside the early Byzantine church mentioned above; the inscription dates from A.D. 132.

[70]This stone as well seems to come from the church, but it was removed at an earlier time. The text was published by Chamonard and Legrand, *BCH* 18 (1894) 216, No. 3; Haussoullier, *Révue de Philologie*, n.s. 22 (1898) 259; Dittenberger, *Orientis Graeci inscriptiones selectae* (Leipzig, 1903-05) 2, No. 530. An observation by R. Heberdey, *JÖAI* 8 (1905) 169, n. 9, shows that the stone belongs together with 1905, V; both are parts of the same plinth. The text is dated in the 163rd year of the freedom of Amisos, i.e. A.D. 132; cf. Haussoullier 260; Dittenberger, n. 12.

[71]On the lower drum of the first column of the Apollo temple to be discovered.

[72]On the inner side of the western wall of the Apollo temple.

[73]Below the previous inscription.

[74]On the stone next to that bearing 1912, 15, 16; cf. 1912, Fig. 25. The statement of the editor on p. 52 contradicts this drawing.

[75]This is the opinion of Haussoullier, *Rev Ph.* 1898, 268, and Dittenberger, *OGIS* 2. 194, n. 11.

[76]This is also Ramsay's explanation, *Athenaeum* 1 (1913) 107.

[77]Cf. Lobeck, *Aglaophamus* 1. 31 ff.

[78]μυστήρια in ἐπιτελεῖν τὰ μ. is therefore something different from the same word in παραλαμβάνειν τὰ μ. Similarly in the Eleusinian

mysteries μύησις is the act before the Epoptia (Lobeck, I, 35) but in Theo Smyrnaeus, *Expos. rer. math.* 1 (ed. Hiller, p. 14) μύησις is the entire action, including the Epoptia. Also, in this passage παράδοσις is the action between καθαρμός and ἐποπτεία, while *traditio* in Apuleius, *Met.* 11.21, is the whole initiation.

[79]Ramsay (*Athenaeum* 1 (1913), 107) offers an explanation which I do not understand: "Perhaps, then, ἐμβατεύειν implies 'to put foot on the threshold,' i.e. enter of [sic] the new life of the initiated."

[80]Here again I call attention to the summarizing expression in Apuleius, *Met.* 11.21, *ad arcana purissimae religionis secreta p e r v a d e r e.*

[81]Obviously the author of the variant ἃ μὴ ἑώρακεν was of the opinion that a vision was involved.

[82]The use of ἄγγελοι rather than στοιχεία here certainly does not have to be understood as accommodation by the mystery priests or by Paul to Jewish-Christian usage. For ἄγγελος is employed outside this circle as well, as by the Sabazius priest who dedicated to his wife Vibia the famous grave painting in the Praetextat catacomb. On that and other examples, see my book, *Die Geisterwelt im Glauben des Paulus* 209 ff. In fact there is no statement at all in Paul's letter that compels us to assume Jewish influence in Colossae. For 2:11 περιετμήθητε περιτομῇ ἀχειροποιήτῳ--said to the Christians--may not be an antithetical allusion to the mystery religion at all, but simply a reproduction of Christian baptismal doctrine. Even if it should have reference to the foreign cult, in the sense, "you need not have yourselves externally 'circumcised,'" it could recall the self-mutilation of mystery priests. And if the new cult that had penetrated Colossae celebrated festivals by astral reckoning-- which would be probable in any case--then Paul could write (2:16) μὴ οὖν τις ὑμᾶς κρινέτω ... εν μέρει ἑορτῆς ἢ νεομηνίας ἢ σαββάτων, without any- one having on that account to think of the introduction of the Jewish festival calendar. And it is probably not accidental that the passage

about the law, 2:14, is kept so general: Through the cross of Christ God
freed us from the δόγματα and--2:15--at the same time triumphed over the
ἀρχαὶ καὶ ἐξουσίαι. Both seem to belong together--a reference to the
δόγματα of the στοιχεῖα-religion!

[83]Apuleius, *Met.* 11.25. Which cosmic powers belong to the
elementa is as uncertain in Paul as in Apuleius.

[84]*CIL* 10.1, 3800, of Isis.

[85]Cf. Anrich, *Das antike Mysterienwesen*, 55.

[86]On this definition of gnosis, cf. the discussion by Karl
Müller, *Kirchengeschichte* (Freiburg i.B., 1892-1919) Vol. 1, §19, 20.

[87]Because of Philemon 22, I am inclined to put the composition
of the Letter to Philemon and the contemporary Letter to Colossians in
Paul's imprisonment in Caesarea. According to Acts 24:27, the duration
of this imprisonment seems to me--despite the doubts of [Eduard] Schwartz,
["Zur Chronologie des Paulus"] *Göttinger Nachrichten* (1907) 294 f.--to
amount to two years. According to the studies of Adolf Deissmann, *Paulus*
159 ff. [ET: Appendix I, pp. 235-60] and Hans Lietzmann, *Zeitschrift für
wissenschaftliche Theologie* 52 (1911) 345 ff., these years are to be reckoned as approximately A.D. 55-57.

[88]Otherwise Paul would polemicize against them. Compare the
attack on food asceticism in Col. 2:20 with the opposition to the same
phenomenon in 1 Tim 4:3, 4. In the second case dualistic thoughts seem
to be a contributing factor among the opponents, in the former they are
not.

[89]*Hauptprobleme der Gnosis* 223 ff.; cf. also *Göttingische
gelehrte Anzeigen,* 176 (1914) 697-755.

[90]Hippolytus 5. 9 (ed. Schneidewin, p. 170): διὰ τούτους καὶ τοὺς

τοιούτους λόγους παρεδρεύουσιν οὗτοι τοῖς λεγομένοις Μητρὸς μεγάλης
μυστηρίοις, μάλιστα καθορᾶν νομίζοντες διὰ τῶν δρωμένων ἐκεῖ τὸ ὅλον
μυστήριον.

[91]*Zwei religionsgeschichtliche Fragen* (Strassburg, 1901) 96;
Poimandres (Leipzig, 1904; reprinted 1966) 81 ff.

[92]Hippolytus 5. 9 (Schneidewin, p. 168): Σαμοθρᾷκες ᾿Αδαμνα
σεβάσμιον.

[93]*Hauptprobleme der Gnosis*, 184 f.

[94]Hippolytus 5. 9 (Schneidewin, p. 174): ἡμεῖς δ᾿ ἐσμέν, φησίν,
οἱ πνευματικοί, οἱ ἐκλεγόμενοι ἀπὸ τοῦ ζῶντος ὕδατος τοῦ ῥέοντος Εὐφράτου
διὰ τῆς Βαβυλῶνος μέσης τὸ οἰκεῖον, διὰ τῆς πύλης ὁδεύοντες ἀληθινῆς,
ἥτις ἐστὶν ᾿Ιησοῦς ὁ μακάριος. Καὶ ἐσμὲν ἐξ ἁπάντων ἀνθρώπων ἡμεῖς
Χριστιανοὶ μόνοι ἐν τῇ τρίτῃ πύλῃ ἀπαρτίζοντες τὸ μυστήριον καὶ χριόμενοι
ἐκεῖ ἀλάλῳ χρίσματι κτλ. 5. 8 (p. 160) explaining Matt 3:10; Luke 3:9:
καρποὶ γὰρ οὗτοι, φησίν, εἰσὶ μόνον οἱ λογικοί, οἱ ζῶντες ἄνθρωποι, οἱ
διὰ τῆς πύλης εἰσερχόμενοι τῆς τρίτης. Moreover, 5. 8 (p. 158) speaks of
the ἀνάστασις ἡ διὰ τῆς πύλης γινομένη τῶν οὐρανῶν. On these passages
see Bousset, 318.

[95]Bousset, 321.

[96]*Mithrasliturgie*, 138--one of the numerous places where Dieterich,
on the way to his goal, has stated merely in passing a most important and
productive perception.

[97]ὅτι ἤλθομεν, φησίν, οἱ πνευματικοὶ ἄνωθεν ἀπὸ τοῦ ᾿Αδάμαντος
ῥυέντες κάτω· ἐλεύσεσθαι γάρ, φησίν, ἐστὶν ἐλθεῖν, τὸ δὲ ἀνακτόρειον
τὸ ἀνελθεῖν ἄνω.

[98]Our understanding of the entire process has been advanced most
of all, probably, by Paul Wendland's book, *Die hellenistische-römische*

Kultur, especially his eighth (in the first edition the tenth) chapter,
"Synkretismus und Gnostizismus." Over against his presentation, I should
like to emphasize two things: 1. The difference between "hellenistic"
mysteries and "gnostic" mysteries. This involves the matters I believe I
have proved for Colossae, and which I stressed above as differences between the Isis mysteries and the στοιχεῖα-mysteries: dispossession of the
old deities, which become cosmic powers, and joining the mystery of redemption with cosmological speculation. 2. I emphasize more than Wendland's
presentation envisions the beginning of the influence on Christianity
already in the first century. 3. I should like to illustrate the different
kinds of exchange, a question Wendland did not go into.

[99]*Die Geisterwelt im Glauben des Paulus* passim; summary 203 ff.
Cf. also the concurring discussion in Wilhelm Bousset, *Kyrios Christos*
(Göttingen, 1913) 161, n. 3 [Compare, in 3d and subsequent edd., pp. 32 f.
and 205 f., n. 2; ET, pp. 67 f. and 270, n. 84].

[100]I still find an allusion to this myth in Phil 2:5 ff., even
though W. W. Jaeger's article (["Eine stilgeschichtliche Studie zum
Philipperbrief"] *Hermes* 50 [1915] 537-53) has convinced me that οὐχ
ἁρπαγμὸν ἡγήσατο contains no reference to the "robbery" of the angelic
powers (cf. *Theologische Literaturzeitung* 40 [1915] 557 f.). But the
triumph over the spirits is attested clearly enough in Phil 2:11 to let
us recognize the mythical outline.

[101]The foremost question is whether the transmission took place
within Judaism. Much seems to speak in favor of that assumption. Recently
it has been pointed out how in the Gospel of John Moses is represented as
nothing other than the "savior" (in the Hellenistic sense) of the Jews,
especially John 9:28 f. (G. P. Wetter, *Der Sohn Gottes* [Göttingen, 1916]
167 ff.). Evidence from Philo would yield still more, at the very least
the suggestion of a very strong hellenization of the relationship between
Moses and Israel. How little we know of the inner life of the Jewish congregations on Hellenistic soil is shown by the newly discovered, so-called
Damascus Document (Solomon Schechter, *Fragments of a Zadokite Work*

[Cambridge, 1910]). [This work, two partial manuscripts of which had been
found in the storeroom of the old Cairo synagogue, is now known to have
been linked with the Essene group that occupied Khirbet Qumran near the
Dead Sea. The Qumran discoveries have underscored the truth of this
statement by Dibelius, but also the ambiguity of his phrase "Hellenistic
soil" -Ed.]

[102]Cf. the essay by Wilhelm Heitmüller, *ZNW* 13 (1912) 320-37
[abridged ET in *The Writings of St. Paul*, ed. W. A. Meeks (New York, 1972)
308-19].

[103]Dio Chrysostomus, *Or.* 12.34 (ed. Arnim, p. 164): ξύμπαν τὸ
τῶν ἀνθρώπων γένος τὴν ὁλόκληρον καὶ τῷ ὄντι τελείαν τελετὴν μυούμενον....

[104]It suffices to recall the most famous passage, Gal 2:20.

[105]Cf. Col 1:24 and the excursus thereon in my commentary;
2 Cor 1:5; 4:10 (νέκρωσις τοῦ Ἰησοῦ); Gal 6:17 (στίγματα τοῦ Ἰησοῦ);
Phil 3:10; see also Steubing, *Der paulinische Begriff "Christusleiden"*
(Diss. Heidelberg; Darmstadt, 1905).

[106]Phil 1:8 (ἐπιποθῶ πάντας ὑμᾶς ἐν σπλάγχνοις Χριστοῦ Ἰησοῦ
1 Thess 1:3, where τοῦ κυρίου ἡμῶν Ἰησοῦ Χριστοῦ belongs to πίστις ἀγάπη
ἐλπίς.

[107]Humility, Phil 2:5; power, Phil 4:13; 2 Cor 12:9; 13:3.

[108]I assume that in Ode 27 and in Ode 42:1-3, an almost identical
text, the praying subject (Christian gnostic) speaks. That is disputed by
pointing out that 42:4 ff. is a triumph song of Christ. But the two are
not mutually exclusive. First, it must be kept in mind that the cited
text ("his sign") and probably also 42:3 (a verse somehow out of place,
where Christ is spoken of as the "upright" or "up-raised"; see next note)
speak of the Redeemer in the third person. Further, the allusion to the
gesture of prayer is more likely attributable to the Christian than to

Christ. Then 42:1-3 contains the depiction of the consecration: the
praying person is deified by the sacrament depicted here and thus becomes
like Christ. In 42:4-12 he now speaks as Christ of his communion with the
faithful (42:6, "I speak through your mouth"--that is just what is happening in this Ode); in 42:13-26 this Christ portrays his descent to Hades.
In the same way Ode 17:1-7 describes how the mystic received "countenance
and form of a new person," how God's grace caused him "to become great."
Then, 17:8-14, there follows the portrayal of Christ's descent to Hades,
and in the hymn at the end, 17:15, the praying person, now human again
(or the congregation) greets the "Anointed." Also in Ode 10:4 ff. and
36:3 ff. the poet speaks as Christ, and also there one can at least conjecture that the first verses are intended to depict the way he was deified,
how he became Christ: He caused "his immortal life to dwell in me" (10:1);
the Spirit of the Lord "raised me to the height" (36:1). Accordingly,
since the transition from human to divine "I" occurs in several Odes, I
cannot agree with the interpretation that seeks to avoid this phenomenon
in Ode 42 by excising the first three verses or by applying the first
verses to Christ. Cf. also [Gerhard] Kittel, *Die Oden Salomos* [Leipzig,
1913], 136 ff.

[109]Deviations in Ode 42: in v. 1, "approached me" instead of
"consecrated them"--but the variants only confirm the sacramental character
of the action; in vs. 2, "the sign therefor" (Codex H) rather than "his
sign," but Ungnad already corrected it according to Ode 27, and the second
Codex N (see Kittel, *ZNW* 14 [1913] 91) confirms that "his sign" should be
read also in Ode 42. Vs. 3 in 42 reads, "My extension (is) the extended
wood, that was hung up at the way of the Upright." Frankenberg (*Das
Verständnis der Oden Salomos*, 44) corrects according to 27; Gressmann (*ZNW*
11 [1910] 302) conjectures: "and the extension of the extended wood, on
which the up-raised hung on the way."

[110]*ZNW* 14 [1913] 273 ff.

[111]Cf. Richard Reitzenstein [and Paul Wendland, "Zwei angeblich
christliche liturgische Gebete"], *Göttinger Nachrichten* (1910) 324-29;

Carl Schmidt, *Theologische Literaturzeitung* 35 (1910) 829; Reitzenstein, *Göttingische Gelehrte Anzeigen* (1911) 537 ff.; Reitzenstein, *Historia monachorum* [Göttingen, 1916] 213.   The papyrus is from the third century.

[112]On the thought and the text, as well as on the understanding of the Ode of Solomon quoted in the following, cf. my essay, "ἐπίγνωσις ἀληθείας," in *Neutestamentliche Studien für Heinrici* [Leipzig, 1914] 176 ff.

[113]A more developed parallel is offered by the view expounded by Irenaeus (2.22.4), that Christ experienced all the ages of life: *omnes enim venit per semetipsum salvare; omnes, inquam, qui per eum renascuntur in Deum, infantes et parvulos et pueros et iuvenes et seniores.   Ideo per omnem venit aetatem.*   According to Corpus Hermeticum 11.20, on the contrary, it is the prerequisite of knowledge of God that man, like God, incorporate all elements, places, and times in himself, and thus also the stages of life: μηδέπω γεγενῆσθαι, ἐν τῇ γαστρὶ εἶναι, νέος, γέρων, τεθνηκέναι, τὰ μετὰ τὸν θάνατον.

[114]Since I am concerned only with the type, I leave aside the question, to what extent the author of the Acts edited the traditional report and, especially with 8:14 ff., worked it into his presentation in the context.

[115]Cf. my essay, *Die urchristliche Überlieferung von Johannes dem Täufer* [Göttingen, 1911] 90 ff.

[116]Wendland, *Hellenistische-römische Kultur* (2d ed.) 167 and n. 3.

[117]Wetter has recently investigated examples in the book *Der Sohn Gottes* 33 f.

[118]Reitzenstein, *Poimandres* 82.

[119]The process of forcefully establishing the ecclesiastical organization--no less important than the phenomena reflected on here, but

by their nature properly part of these reflections--has its place in this context.

THE HERESY OF COLOSSIANS

Günther Bornkamm*

The Letter to Colossians gets its peculiar stamp from Paul's opposition to erroneous teaching. While the apostle explicitly contends against it only in the limited section 2:4-23, his positive unfolding of the gospel in 1:15-20 is already determined, in terminology and in thought, by antithesis to the heresy, and the structure of the letter as a whole becomes transparent and its peculiarity comprehensible in view of this confrontation.[1] To be sure, the letter does not give a complete picture of the opponents' teaching, nor one that is certain in all details. Scholarship rather unanimously recognizes that Paul alludes to it verbally in several passages, takes up its termini and characteristic slogans polemically in some, and makes positive use of its concepts for his own exposition in others. Still, the extent and manner of his reference to the opposing doctrine cannot be determined with certainty.[2] Thus the attempt to reconstruct the Colossian heresy remains encumbered by guesses and possibilities. Nevertheless, a series of characteristic features can be extracted from the statements of the letter and fitted together into a whole. If we succeed in assigning the details and the whole to a place in the history of religions, then we shall have attained the desired degree of certainty and avoided the suspicion of vague combinations and hypotheses.

I

What information about the false teaching can be drawn from the Letter to Colossians itself? The first and most important characteristic of the Colossian heresy is, according to 2:8, 20, its teaching about the cosmic elements. In 2:8 Paul sets them over against Christ; in 2:10 and 2:15 he calls them ἀρχαί and ἐξουσίαι and characterizes the false teaching

*First published in *Theologische Literaturzeitung* 73 (1948) 11-20; reprinted in *Das Ende des Gesetzes*, © 1952 Chr. Kaiser Verlag, Munich, 139-56; translated by permission of Chr. Kaiser Verlag. Günther Bornkamm (b. 1905) was Professor of New Testament in Heidelberg until his retirement in 1972.

summarily in 2:18 as θρησκεία τῶν ἀγγέλων [worship of angels]. It follows
that the στοιχεῖα τοῦ κόσμου [elements of the world] are personal, angelic
powers. The polemic against the στοιχεῖα-worship in Galatians confirms
the picture. Paul could hardly have compared them in Gal 4:2 with the
ἐπίτροποι and οἰκονόμοι [guardians and trustees] to whom minor children
are subject, and designated them as φύσει μὴ ὄντες θεοί [beings not gods
by nature], whom the Galatians served, unless the latter had regarded
the στοιχεῖα τοῦ κόσμου as personal, divine beings. Since worshipping
them, according to Gal 4:10 as well as Col 2:16, included the observation
of certain festival days and periods, one must also think at least of the
worship of astral powers.[3] Evidently the heretical doctrine declares
that in the στοιχεῖα τοῦ κόσμου the πλήρωμα [fulness] of deity dwells, as
becomes apparent from the clearly polemical and antithetical formulation
of Col 2:9 ὅτι ἐν αὐτῷ κατοικεῖ πᾶν τὸ πλήρωμα τῆς θεότητος σωματικῶς [For
in him the whole fulness of deity dwells bodily] (cf. 1:19).[4] The στοιχεῖα
τοῦ κόσμου, according to 2:20, place men under certain δόγματα; they are
the authorities and guardians of the νόμος [law], to whom the believer
must subject himself in "humility" (2:18, 23). Whoever obeys these
"regulations," keeps the established festivals and seasons, and satisfies
certain ascetic prescriptions, has the promise that he will receive a share
of the divine power that holds sway in the elements. That is the heretical
doctrine which one may infer from the formulation, probably also antithetical, καὶ ἐστὲ ἐν αὐτῷ πεπληρωμένοι [and in him you have been fulfilled]
(2:10).[5] Again confirmation is supplied by statements in Galatians, which
like Colossians identifies the στοιχεῖα τοῦ κόσμου with the angels that
give the law (3:19) and describes existence under the slavery of the
στοιχεῖα as being under the Law (4:5, 3:13, 23).

But one can say more. On the basis of the unambiguous fact that
the Colossian heresy is a Christian error and not just any kind of pagan
or Jewish religion, one may reasonably conclude that the false teachers
did not merely juxtapose their στοιχεῖα-doctrine with the doctrine of Christ
without any connection, much less develop it in conscious opposition to
christology. Rather they held the worship of the world-elements to be an
integral constituent of the faith in Christ. Over against just this heretical amalgamation of the στοιχεῖα-doctrine with the faith in Christ, Paul

places the incompatibility of the two at the beginning of his polemic,
with radical sharpness (2:8). He undergirds this blunt antithesis with
that sentence, ὅτι ἐν αὐτῷ κατοικεῖ πᾶν τὸ πλήρωμα τῆς θεότητος σωματικῶς
(2:9). Certainly the false teachers did not want to represent the opinion
that the fulness of God did not dwell in Christ. A Christian doctrine of
redemption which accorded divinity to the angelic powers but not to Christ
is unthinkable in the history of early Christianity. On the contrary, the
heresy for its part will also have accepted the sentence 2:9, only with the
difference that it did not put the ἐν αὐτῷ [in him] in *opposition* to the
indwelling of the divine πλήρωμα in the στοιχεῖα, but regarded the divine
fulness in Christ as given *in his relationship* to the elements. The mythological and christological expression of this doctrine may have taken the
form that the opponents understood the στοιχεῖα τοῦ κόσμου themselves as
the σῶμα [body] of Christ, or as his limbs, and Christ as the totality of
the world-elements.[6]

II

All of these individual traits, extracted and inferred from the
statements of Colossians, are confirmed when one searches through the
broader and more immediate comparative religious background against which
they emerge. Only from that perspective will a series of further traits
and motifs become understandable, which we have so far passed over among
the statements of the letter.

We have been spared the necessity of having to enter into a precise investigation here of the prehistory of the concept στοιχεῖα τοῦ
κόσμου and its meaning in the syncretistic milieu of early Christianity.
This work has been performed repeatedly and with converging results.[7]
The term means the elementary powers and forces of the cosmos, which hold
sway mysteriously and peremptorily in the phenomena of nature and the
destinies of the human world, threatening and bestowing life. In view of
the extensive attestation of the term's astral, theological, and demonol-
ogical use in Persian-Chaldean astrology, Oriental-Hellenistic mysteries,
and gnostic speculations, it ought not to have been questioned recently
that the term was idiomatic and contained a slogan of the heresy.[8] To be
sure, the speculative and mythological pictures in which the concept of

the elements occurs are so manifold, and the formulas of Colossians and
Galatians so meagre, that a number of questions about the heresy in question must remain unanswered. What pictures were connected in detail with
the concept of the elements, in what order and number they were connected
with one another, how constellations or the zodiak were connected in their
doctrine with the material elements of the cosmos--on these questions no
clarity can be obtained. No doubt seems possible to me, however, on one
point: The Colossian doctrine of the elements belongs to the ancient
mythology and speculation of the Oriental Aeon-theology, which was widespread and active in Hellenistic syncretism. Its origins reach back to
the Indo-Iranian cosmogony and its conception of a world-deity, whose
gigantic body was composed of the elements of the universe.[9] The cosmogonic
myth of the body of the world-god and of the elements as his limbs occurs
again in gnosis in the form of the myth of the primeval man, in which it
receives a cosmic-soteriological meaning. In consequence of the dualistic
world view of gnosis, the στοιχεῖα become elements of the light world, as
opposed to the world of darkness, which is also composed of a certain
number of elements. This is most consistent in the Manichean system. The
salvation of the gnostic means now his transformation into the form of the
primeval man as his heavenly image, and at the same time his rebirth from
the elements of the upper world, to which his authentic self belongs by
origin. Redemption means apotheosis of the gnostic to the Aeon.[10] The
process of redemption is served by the mystery procedures, revelatory dis-
courses, and magical prayers, which transmit to the gnostic and initiate
the vision of the heavenly elements and thus accomplish his deification.[11]

From a series of peculiar expressions in the Letter to Colossians
can be inferred that the Colossian heresy promised to its adepts redemption
and deification in this sense. The gnostic character of the false teaching
can be perceived already from its designation as φιλοσοφία (2:8). Without
doubt Paul takes up with this term a self-designation of the opposing
doctrine. For syncretistic thought it has long since ceased to designate
rational learning, but has become equivalent to revealed doctrine and
magic.[12] Its representatives appear as mystagogues, appeal, as can be inferred from 2:8, to special παράδοσις [tradition], and affirm that they
have based the content of their teaching on a mysterious vision (2:18).[13]

Also from the polemic phrase εἰκῇ φυσιούμενος ὑπὸ τοῦ νοὸς τῆς σαρκός
[vainly puffed up by the mind of flesh] (2:18) can be gathered that Paul
satirizes the self-consciousness of the gnostic mystagogues.[14] Finally
the expression ἐθελοθρησκία [a word of disputed meaning, otherwise unattested, from the root meaning "will" plus "religion"] (2:23) probably
intends to say that the initiate who has joined the heresy underwent a
voluntary initiation into its mysteries.[15] Through recognition of the
world-elements, initiation into their secrets, and submission to their
regulations, he wants to receive a share in the divine πλήρωμα that fills
the στοιχεῖα. This promise of the heresy echoes clearly from its antithesis in 2:10, "And in him you have been fulfilled." In these words the
Apostle emphatically holds up to the congregation not the goal which they
must achieve by subjecting themselves to the δόγματα of the powers, but
that which has long since been won as the origin of their faithful
existence in Christ.

The conceptual world that emerges from Colossians has far-reaching
parallels in the mystery texts assembled by Reitzenstein, above all in the
deification mystery that A. Dieterich called a "Mithras liturgy." It is
obviously no accident, and betrays the kinship of the Colossian heresy
with the view of the mysteries, that in the principal prayer of the so-
called Mithras liturgy the παράδοσις [tradition] character of the mysteries
is underscored right at the beginning: the initiate wants to receive them
from the ἀρχάγγελος of the deity and wishes to achieve the vision of the
All on his heavenly journey.[16] The rebirth (ἀθάνατος γένεσις) takes place
amid invocation of the elements (πνεῦμα, πῦρ, ὕδωρ, οὐσία γεώδης [wind/
spirit, fire, water, earth-substance]). Together they comprise the σῶμα
τέλειον [perfect body] of the initiate, who is here still trapped in the
transitory φύσις [nature], presently still oppressed by necessity (χρεία,
ἀνάγκη), but now, by the divine will (ἐὰν δὴ ὑμῖν δόξῃ--κατὰ δόγμα (!) θεοῦ
ἀμετάθετον) is to be led to the vision of the elements, i.e. of the
ἀθάνατος Αἰῶν [immortal Aeon] and therewith to rebirth and deification.[17]

So here are the same ideas that we conjectured for the Colossian
heresy: an Aeon that comprises the world-elements within itself; a vision
of it that effects deification; the initiate's bondage to the world of
darkness and death (notice the antithesis ἐν ἀφωτίστῳ καὶ διαυγεῖ κόσμῳ ἐν

τε ἀψύχῳ καὶ ἐψυχωμένῳ [in a world unilluminated yet bright, with no living soul, yet with a living soul][17a] who must leave behind the φθαρτὴ
βροτῶν ψύσις [perishable human nature] and undergo sacred rites (ἁγίοις
ἁγιαθεὶς ἁγιάσμασι), in order to ascend to the light-world. From here the
expressions in Colossians, θρησκεία τῶν ἀγγέλων, which characterizes the
cult of the στοιχεῖα; ἃ ἑόρακεν ἐμβατεύων [which he saw when he entered]
2:18; and the sentence in 2:20, εἰ ἀπεθάνετε σὺν Χριστῷ ἀπὸ τῶν στοιχείων
τοῦ κόσμου, τί ὡς ζῶντες ἐν κόσμῳ δογματίζεσθε; ["If you died with Christ
from the elements of the world, why do you submit to regulations as if
still living in the world?"] make clear and adequate sense. The Colossians
also seem to have celebrated a mystery of rebirth. Evidently they called
it, in dependence on Judaism, "circumcision," an expression that Paul takes
up in 2:11 f. as a designation of baptism. He interprets it by means of
the completely un-Jewish expression, which is however understandable from
gnosticism, ἀπέκδυσις τοῦ σώματος τῆς σαρκός [stripping off the body of
flesh].

          Paul's disagreement with the heresy and its conception of baptism
consists in the fact that it does not hold to Christ the head (2:19) and
to the rebirth which had already happened to the faithful in his death and
resurrection, but rather to the στοιχεῖα. It is from the στοιχεῖα that
it expects to be filled with the powers of the πλήρωμα and seeks to achieve
for the individual that which, according to Paul, had long since been fulfilled in the σῶμα of the church. The term σωματικῶς [bodily] (2:9) must
already refer to the σῶμα of the church, as does σῶμα in 2:19.[18] Paul
attributes to the church that growth which, according to the doctrine of
the mysteries, belongs to the rebirth of the initiate.[19] In the church as
the body of Christ the πλήρωμα of the deity is accessible to the believers,
and they already participate in it; therefore they need no new mysteries
and no regulations "as if they were still living in the world" (2:20).

          If this interpretation is correct, then the question is decided,
whether the heretics understood the στοιχεῖα τοῦ κόσμου as divine or as
evil powers, the latter in the sense that gnosticism understood the plane-
tary spheres as the region of demonic forces who hostilely barred the way
of the redeemer and of the souls ascending to the light-world. Obviously
the Colossian heresy understood them as divine elements, as did the Mithras

Liturgy, the Isis mystery in Apuleius, and Corpus Hermeticum 13.11, where
the initiate becomes one with the All by means of rebirth and deification
("I am in heaven, in the earth, in water, in air; I am in animals, in
plants; I am in the womb, before the womb, after the womb, everywhere."
Cf. §13: "I see the All and myself in the mind"). This conception of the
divinity of the elements does not exclude, but rather includes the dualism
between the visible world, dominated by hostile spiritual powers, and the
higher world, from which the soul originates and to which it must be
liberated. Mysteries and gnosticism show that unequivocally. The purification which the initiate undergoes in the mystery of rebirth means, according to *Corp. Herm.* 13.7 ff., the expulsion, by means of God's powers, of
the punitive spirits that hold sway in matter, and who have captured the
inner man (ἐνδιάθετος ἄνθρωπος), until the initiate's σῶμα is composed of
these divine powers (ibid., §14) and deification is complete ("mental
birth has been accomplished ... and we have been deified by this birth"
13.10).

Paul's statements about the powers and authorities and thus about
the στοιχεῖα τοῦ κόσμου (1:15 ff. and 2:9 ff.) seem at first to be self-
contradictory. On the one hand, he coordinates them with Christ as the
totality of creation (1:16 ff.), designates him κεφαλὴ πάσης ἀρχῆς καὶ
ἐξουσίας [head of all rule and authority] (2:10), and includes the powers
in the reconciling work of Christ (1:20); on the other hand, he says that
they are disarmed and publicly exhibited, that is, they are conquered
enemies over whom Christ triumphs (2:15). With that he breaks through the
gnostic dualism, even though he makes use of the language of gnosis, and
accords to the powers their place in the creation. But precisely for that
reason he cannot let them count any longer as bearers of the divine πλήρωμα
and as the σῶμα of Christ. Even if they retain their place in creation,
they still remain representatives of the old, transitory aeon over against
Christ as bringer, ruler, and content of the coming aeon (1:13). With the
exaltation of Christ their claim to dominion expires. It only seems that
Paul renews and radicalizes the gnostic dualism with this secularization
of the στοιχεῖα and their coordination with the cosmos. Actually he is no
longer concerned with the gnostic opposition between visible and invisible,
matter and spirit, but with the opposition between Christ and world in the

history of salvation. The death and resurrection of Christ mean the
shattering of the sphere of the σάρξ [flesh] because they bring to the
believers forgiveness of sins (2:13) and thereby annul the authority which
the powers exercise over the unredeemed--n.b.: destroy their *authority*,
which accrues to them from the guilt of men. The unredeemed men's bondage
to them is therefore not understood as a tragic destiny or fate suffered
by the heaven-born Man because the powers unjustly exercised superior force.

III

So far we have not adequately taken into account certain features
of the Colossian heresy which more narrowly limit and more clearly delineate
its religious-historical background. The Letter to Colossians leaves no
doubt that the heresy was a variety of Jewish gnosticism. This Jewish
character of the heresy is shown by the very fact that Paul sets στοιχεῖα
and law over against Christ in the sense of the antithesis between σκιά
[shadow] and σῶμα [body] (2:17). For the concept σκιά means not only a
depreciation, but also the recognition of the salvific function of the
στοιχεῖα and their laws.[20] This evaluation of the law[21] obviously has
meaning only if the heresy is of Jewish and not pagan origin. Possibly
circumcision also belonged to the religious practices of the false teachers,
perhaps with the altered meaning of a mystery-like initiation rite.[22] The
emphasis that circumcision took place for the believers once and for all
in Christ's death and resurrection (2:11 ff.) could also, of course, be
understood as opposed to the repeated washings and baptismal ceremonies
of the heretics. In any case the designation of baptism as "circumcision"
presupposes that it could be so understood by the heretics. Also the
characterization of the στοιχεῖα-cult as θρησκεία τῶν ἀγγέλων ["worship
of angels"] (2:18) points most likely to a Jewish origin of the heresy.
The coordination of the angels with world-elements and constellations is
widely attested in the documents of apocryphal Judaism.[23] Not only
Colossians, but also Galatians and the Pastoral Epistles give evidence that
the Judaizing movement grew up on the soil of a gnosticizing Judaism.[24]
Paul himself (Gal 3:19 f.) borrows from this gnosis the thought that the
law was not the revelation and gift of the gracious God, but from the hands
of the angels and transmitted by a μεσίτης ["mediator"].[25] Only in this

way is it understandable that he calls the Judaizing return to the law
ironically a "conversion" back to the poor and weak στοιχεῖα (Gal 4:9).
The στοιχεῖα for him as for the Galatian Judaizers are the angels of the
law, except that for Paul their power is broken, while for the Judaizers
their claim to dominion is still valid. Also the Pastoral Epistles show
the characteristic blending of gnostic aeon-speculation with a strict
legalism. Col 2:14 f., 20 belongs in this same context. The δόγματα of
the powers for the heretics are rules for life, still valid, which must
be respected by the believers. Paul does not contest the reality of the
ἀρχαί and ἐξουσίαι and their claim to dominion manifested in the δόγματα,
but he does contest the idea that they still have power over the believers
who have died and risen with Christ and that their δόγματα are still ob-
ligatory for them. The death and resurrection of Christ expose them as
laws not of life, but of death. They do not point the way to life, but
hold before us "the bond against us" (2:14), which condemns us to death,
until we receive forgiveness in Christ's death and resurrection and are
liberated from the dominion of the powers, to seek life in Christ, the
exalted and coming one.

Also the festivals which are kept by the heretics point towards
a syncretistic-gnostic origin of the Colossian Judaizing movement. Paul
mentions New Moon and Sabbath (Col 2:16), days, months, seasons, and years
(Gal 4:10), i.e. in each case days and seasons that do not stand under the
sign of the history of salvation, but under the sign of the periodic cycles
of nature, i.e. corresponding to the movement of the stars. Thus the
στοιχεῖα τοῦ κόσμου provide their content and meaning.

Finally, also the taboos and the ascetic requirements of the
heretics (Col 2:21 ff.) expose the erroneous doctrine as a variety of syncretistic Judaism. These are requirements which cannot be derived from
the Jewish law--indeed, in strict Judaism they are expressly rejected--but
most likely belong to the practice of pagan philosophical schools and
gnostic mystery circles. These prescriptions have nothing to do with
Jewish fasts. On the contrary, they correspond entirely to the attitude
and intent of gnosticism, which wants to lead its adepts along this path of
voluntarily adopted pious practices and asceticism to "fulfillment" with
the divine powers of the elements of a higher world.[27]

The meagre data of the Letter to Colossians thus yield a picture
of the heresy which, while certainly not complete, is nevertheless sufficiently clear. It is confirmed by documents of Jewish gnosticism, in
which the most important motifs and characteristics which we have uncovered
almost all reappear. These are the fragments of the Book of Elchasai,
which Hippolytus, *Refutatio* 9.13 ff., has preserved, and the Pseudo-
Clementines, which are very closely related. Here we encounter not only
the requirement of circumcision and the worship of the elements, but also
the images of the Iranian Aeon-myth. Elchasai received the book of his
teachings, according to Hippolytus *Ref*. 9.13 (Epiphanius, *Haer*. 30.17;
19.4; 53.1), from the Son of God, who appeared to him as an angel in
gigantic form, i.e. as the world-spanning Aeon.[28] The Aeon-primeval-man
speculation is also evidently the origin of the Ebionite christology of
the Pseudo-Clementines, according to which Jesus appears, after his incarnation in the seven righteous, the "seven pillars" of the Old Testament, as the eighth and thus as revealer and redeemer. The schema of the
Aeon-mythology, originally intended cosmogonically, here is made the basis
of a speculation about salvation history, while cosmology recedes altogether.
Bousset already conjectured "hidden connections" here.[29] If one sees how
in Christian gnosticism the redeemer figure is understood as ὁ ἐν πᾶσιν
ὢν καὶ διερχόμενος διὰ πάντων ["he who is in all and passes through all"]
(Acts of Thomas 10),[30] and how his role is taken over by the apostles, and
how, on the other hand, biblical events and figures are frequently interpreted mythologically,[31] then the transposition of the myth onto the whole
history of salvation is no longer astonishing.[32] The connection of the
teachings of the Pseudo-Clementines with the Persian Aeon-theology was so
carefully worked out by Bousset that a reference to his work is sufficient
here.[33] The author of the Pseudo-Clementines is thoroughly familiar with
the conceptual world of the Iranian religion, just as the preface to the
Book of Elchasai, in the note that the mysterious book of the prophet was
of Parthian provenance, shows unmistakably the influence of Iranian thought
on the doctrine of the Elchasaites that, in other respects, arose on Jewish
soil.

This christology derived from the Iranian Aeon-myth is connected
in Jewish-Christian gnosticism with a strict legalism. The Preachings of

Peter at the very beginning polemicizes against the abolition and invali-
dation of the Law, with a sharp rejection of Paul. The same is true,
according to Hippolytus (*Ref*. 9.14), also for the teaching of Elchasai,
although the latter to be sure rejected the Old Testament sacrificial cult.
In its place come repeated baptisms for forgiveness of sins; moral directives, which the baptizand accepts with a vow, while invoking the elements;
the observation of certain times, which are threatened by the influence of
evil stars; and the keeping of the Sabbath. We know from Ps.-Clem. Hom.
8.15; 12.6; Epiphanius, *Haer*. 30.15, 3, that vegetarian prescriptions also
belonged to the δόγματα of the Ebionites.

It goes without saying that these agreements between the Ebionite
or Elchasaite doctrine and the Colossian heresy do not suffice to identify
the latter with the former. Every particular feature, if we but had more
precise knowledge of the history of early Christian and late Jewish sects,
could certainly be attested, to an even greater measure than is now the
case, from a number of other systems. But one can hardly doubt the fact
that behind the Colossian heresy stands a Jewish or Judaizing gnosticism
that is deeply infected by Iranian views.

That can be corroborated finally by a particular feature of the
heretical ethics which can be extracted from the data of the Colossian
letter. There was without doubt an inner connection between the στοιχεῖα-
doctrine and the regulations which were declared to be binding in Colossae.
Lohmeyer has shown quite correctly, as we saw, that the goal of the heretical
prescriptions and directives was the "filling" of the faithful with the
divine powers that hold sway in the στοιχεῖα. The correctness of this
thesis is confirmed by the observation that the letter shows its dependence
in several passages upon the Pentad-scheme known from Iranian-Gnostic
speculations about the elements. Paul himself takes up the schema in the
vice and virtue lists, with which he opposes the essence of the old man to
that of the new. The "members" of the old man are, according to 3:5,
"fornication, impurity, passion, evil desire, and covetousness," according
to 3:8, "anger, wrath, malice, slander, and foul talk"; the members of the
new man, according to 3:12, are "compassion, kindness, lowliness, meekness,
and patience," summed up by ἀγάπη, the "bond of perfection" (3:14). In
this scheme of moral concepts the physical lists of elements belonging to

the cosmic speculation are sublimated and transposed, as often happens
in gnosticism. The Iranian Pentad-scheme lies at the basis also of the
Elcasaites' lists of elements, as Bousset has shown.[34] Perhaps from that
perspective it is no accident that also in Col 2:23 five key words of the
Colossian heresy occur, although they are unrecognizable on first glance,
since the sentence can hardly be translated with certainty and since Paul's
irony has undoubtedly perverted the last concept into its opposite. Of
the first three, however, we can surely assume that they reflect heretical
formulae: ἐθελοθρησκία, ταπεινοφροσύνη, ἀφειδία σώματος. The first must
contain an allusion to the voluntarily accepted initiation into the
mysteries of the στοιχεῖα; the next two obviously speak of obligations
which the adept takes on with this initiation. The fourth, on the contrary,
seems to reject the opinion of the heretics that from the cult of the
στοιχεῖα and the keeping of the δόγματα an "honor" accrued to the faithful.
The concept τιμή (dignatio, honor) is frequent in the terminology of the
mysteries and means the election and deification which is granted to the
initiate from the deity.[36] The final word is certainly not a slogan of
the opponents, but an angry slap by which the supposed object hoped for by
the gnostic is perverted into its gross opposite. But Paul's formulation
still permits us to see that in the scale of the gnostic watchwords, the
πληροῦσθαι [to be filled] with the divine powers of the στοιχεῖα must have
been spoken of at this point, the deification of the initiate. Paul, of
course, sees in that nothing but a πλησμονὴ τῆς σαρκός [gratification of
the flesh].[37]

         While Paul rejects the ascetic requirements as mere human com-
mandments, he emphatically called for the renunciation of sexual immorality
and covetousness and for brotherly love, whose essence is only unfolded in
the five concepts of 3:12, just as fornication in 3:5 is paraphrased by
several concepts. If one puts together the heretical commandment of con-
tinence, rejected in the polemical section, with the warning against fornication and avarice in the parenesis that follows it, then one obtains
the moral canon that recurs in stereotyped form in later Christian gnosticism.
It corresponds exactly to the tria signacula of the Manichees, by which the
elect and perfect distinguished themselves from the remaining members of
the community. In the Acts of Thomas 28 the basic vices are πορνεία,

πλεονεξία, ἐργασία τῆς γαστρός [fornication, avarice, service of the belly]. They are the chief elements of ἀνομία [lawlessness]; over against them stand holiness (= sexual abstinence), moderation, and kindness towards the poor. The aforementioned vices correspond to the rules of conduct for the elect in Manicheism: purity from gluttony, from avarice, and from sexual intercourse.[38] One may ask whether this canon of gnostic morality is not already to be assumed in a similar form for the Colossian heresy. Then the intention of the letter would aim at erasing from this canon the ascetic commandments because of their contradiction of creation, while bringing to the other two a new validity. Πορνεία and πλεονεξία remain the basic marks of idolatry (3:5); they comprise the limbs of the old man who is bound to the earth, while the new man has his essence in love. Of course, what is new about the Pauline directives is not merely the fact that here the ethical canon of a Jewish gnosis is reduced and varied, but that the commandments as such are torn out of the hedge of those δόγματα and founded solely in the redemption by Christ's death and resurrection from the ἐξουσία τοῦ σκότους [authority of darkness] and in the trans-position into the kingdom of Christ (1:13).

That may suffice for a clarification of the religious-historical background of the Colossian heresy. It originates in a gnosticized Judaism, in which Jewish and Iranian-Persian elements, and surely also influence of Chaldean astrology, have peculiarly alloyed themselves and have united with Christianity.

IV

The syncretistic Diaspora-Judaism that presented the matrix for the Colossian heresy still preserved an independent existence apart from Christianity, open further to the influence of the Persian religion. The history of sects in the later centuries shows that, particularly for Asia Minor. In fourth century Cappadocia we meet such a mixed sect from Judaism and Parseeism in the form of the Hypsistarians,[39] about whom Gregory of Nazianzus, whose father and forefathers had belonged to them, gives note-worthy information in the funeral oration for his father.[40] He calls it a sect put together from disparate elements, pagan error and legal fraud, in which pagan idols and sacrifices were rejected, but fire and lights were

worshipped, in which Jewish circumcision was declined, but Sabbath and the
proscription of certain foods were kept. They called themselves Hypsistarians and worshipped only the Pantocrator.

        Gregory of Nyssa similarly depicts them as confessors of the
ὕψιστος [Most High] or παντοκράτωρ [Omnipotent].[42] There are numerous
attestations of cultic associations of Hypsistos from the early imperial
period on. In almost every instance they point to influences of Jewish
monotheism and are the fruit of its propaganda.[43] Hypsistos is a common
designation for the God of Israel. His congregations were probably
recruited originally from the circles of σεβόμενοι [devotees, i.e., "God-
fearers," gentiles attracted to Judaism who had not actually converted],
who worshipped the God of Israel without submitting completely to the
Mosaic law, and developed into independent cultic associations. On the
basis of this worship of Hypsistos a very intensive amalgamation of different religions took place. The Jewish Yahweh merged with the deities
of Syrian, Egyptian, and Asia Minor local cults; ὕψιστος became an attri-
bute of Attis, the Phrygian Zeus-Dionysus, as of the Syrian Ba'alim.[44]
But the emergence of this Hypsistos cult indicates not only the mixture of
such Jewish and pagan elements, but also stands clearly under the influence
of Chaldean astrology and Persian beliefs. The "Most High" has his seat in
heaven, "in the immense orb that contained the spheres of all the stars
and embraced the entire universe which was subject to his domination."[45]
He is the creator and preserver of cosmic harmony and the director of
fate.[46] In the course of the stars, above all in the sun's rule, his
power is experienced and worshipped. It is indubitable that this Hypsistos
cult is the root of the sect of the Hypsistarians that is attested later.
It is not surprising that in this latter sect the Jewish and Persian elements mixed even more strongly than is recognizably the case in the older
cult of Hypsistos, especially on the soil of Asia Minor. For there, under
the rule of the Sassanians, the old Persian religion experienced a revival,
but even earlier it had persisted tenaciously.[47] The paucity of extant
witnesses prevents our ascertaining whether specific speculations about
stars and elements were already connected with the faith in Hypsistos in
earlier times. For the Hypsistarian sect the association of their devotion
to Hypsistos with their worshipping fire and light seems unconditionally

to point in that direction, just as their observance of the Sabbath and
of certain dietary prohibitions, which brings them into immediate connection with the Colossian heresy and to the Jewish gnosis which lay behind
the latter. The probability of this connection is also reinforced by the
fact that the designation ὕψιστος occurs also among the Elchasaites and in
the Pseudo-Clementines.[48] That all points toward the assumption that in
the Asia Minor sect of the Hypsistarians, however it may have changed in
details, the same Jewish gnosis lived on as that out of which the Colossian
heresy sprang.

In the history of thought these connections are of some interest,
because no less a person than the aging Goethe became acquainted in a
strange way with the sect of the Hypsistarians, showed a lively interest in
them, and believed that he could find in their confession of faith a reflection of his own.[49] In fact as a "Hypsistarian" he took up with zest
the cult of the elements in the "legacy of ancient Persian faith,"[50] and in
the famous religious dialogue with Eckermann a few days before his death
(March 11, 1832) he repeated a classical formulation of the doctrine of
the Colossian heresy, even though in new language. After the much-cited
words, "There is at work in the gospels the effulgence of a majesty that
radiated from the person of Christ, and of such divine fashion as only
once the divine has appeared in upon the earth," follow these words: "If
someone asks me whether it is in my nature to accord him worshipful reverence, I say: Absolutely! I bow before him as the divine revelation of the
highest principle of morality. If someone asks me whether it is in my
nature to worship the sun, I say again: Absolutely! For it is likewise a
revelation of the highest, and indeed the mightiest that is granted to us
children of earth to perceive. I worship in it the light and the genera-
tive power of God, through which alone we live, move, and have our being."
So at the conclusion the astonishing fact emerges that in a thoroughly
historical sense Goethe was the last, in any case probably the greatest,
representative of the Colossian heresy.[51]

* * *

NOTES

[1]The question of the literary genuineness of Colossians will not be raised here. Since the appearance of this essay in *TLZ*, the weight of the arguments against composition by the apostle himself and for its origin in the school of Paul (language, style, peculiarities of christology, ecclesiology, sacramental doctrine, relationship to Ephesians) has become so much greater for me that I count it among the deutero-Pauline letters. Even the major monograph by E. Percy, *Die Probleme der Kolosser- und Epheserbriefe* (Lund: C. W. K. Gleerup, 1946) has not convinced me to the contrary. Nevertheless, I have no objection to speaking of "Paul" in the sense of the letter.

[2]Cf. above all M. Dibelius, *An die Kolosser, Epheser, An Philemon* (Handbuch zum Neuen Testament, 12, 3d ed.; Tübingen: Mohr, 1953), excursus to 2:8 and 2:23, and Ernst Lohmeyer, *Der Brief an die Kolosser* (Göttingen: Vandenhoeck & Ruprecht, 1930) 3 ff. Percy (*Probleme*, 137 ff.) goes a very different way.

[3]Cf. H. Schlier, *Der Brief an die Galater* (Göttingen: Vandenhoeck & Ruprecht, 1949) 134. Patristic exegesis already thought of the worship of the heavenly bodies (Chrysostom, Theodoret; see Albert Klöpper, *Der Brief an die Kolosser* (Berlin: Reimer, 1882) on Col 2:8.

[4]Cf. Dibelius, *Kolosser*, 29; Lohmeyer, *Kolosser*, 4, 105-06.

[5]Lohmeyer, *Kolosser*, 4 ff., 106 ff., 129.

[6]Ibid. 125, n. 3; Ernst Käsemann, *Leib und Leib Christi* (Beiträge zur historischen Theologie; Tübingen: Mohr, 1933) 140.

[7]See the references in Schlier, *Galaterbrief*, 133; already A Dieterich, *Abraxas* (Leipzig: Teubner, 1891) 56 ff.; Percy, *Probleme* 156 ff.

[8]Against Percy, *Probleme* 166-67.

[9]Richard Reitzenstein and Hans Heinrich Schaeder, *Studien zum antiken Synkretismus aus Iran und Griechenland* (1926, 2d ed., Darmstadt: Wissenschaftliche Buchgesellschaft, 1965) 72 ff. The Iranian-Babylonian provenance of the element and angel speculation and of the Aeon myth is especially clearly proved by the passage from Nicomachos of Gerasa (cited by Richard Reitzenstein, *Die hellenistische Mysterienreligionen* [henceforth: *H.M.R.*; 3d ed., 1927 = 4th, Darmstadt: Wissenschaftliche Buchgesellschaft, 1956] 171, and *Die Vorgeschichte der christlichen Taufe* [1929, 2d ed., Darmstadt: Wissenschaftliche Buchgesellschaft, 1967] 127 ff., and by Lohmeyer, *Kolosser* 7, n. 2, who recognized its peculiar parallelism to expressions in Col), where Athena is designated as the Seven (i.e., as Aeon) and the stellar spheres, as angels and archangels. The prototype of the three-fold function of the στοιχεῖα, in which the πλήρωμα of divinity presents itself, the cosmos subsists, and the life of the pious finds its divine norms, is the Iranian doctrine of the Amesha Spentas. Consequently, as Schaeder has shown, the Christian-Sogdian translation of στοιχεῖα in Gal 4:3 is consistently *amahraspands*, which later in Manichaeism is used to denote the elements (Reitzenstein-Schaeder, *Studien* 2. 279; Lohmeyer, *Kolosser* 6-7).

[10]Käsemann, *Leib* 59 ff.

[11]Cf. Reitzenstein, *H.M.R.* 222 ff.

[12]Cf. Theon of Smyrna, *Expositio rerum mathematic.* (ed. E. Hiller, 1873) 14: τὴν φιλοσοφίαν μύησιν φαίη τις ἂν ἀληθοῦς τελετῆς καὶ τῶν ὄντων ὡς ἀληθῶς μυστηρίων παράδοσιν; see further my article μυστήριον, *TWNT* 4 (1942) 814 ff. [=*TDNT* 4 (1967) 808-13]. To my knowledge there is no monograph on the history of the concept φιλοσοφία; even Pauly-Wissowa fails us. According to Stobaeus, *Anth.* 1. 407 (*Corpus Hermeticum*, ed. Nock-Festugière, 4, frag. 23, 68), philosophy and magic exist for the nurture of the soul. In magic papyri the magician is called σοφιστής (=philosopher) (Reitzenstein, *H.M.R.* 236-37). Cf. also the fragment of an alchemical text published by Reitzenstein (*Nachrichten der Gesellschaft der Wissenschaften*, Göttingen, 1919, 24; cf. *H.M.R.* 129). This text

presents itself as βύβλος περιέχουσα τῶν φώτων καὶ οὐσιῶν τὰς ἀποδείξεις
διδασκάλου Κομαρίου τοῦ φιλοσόφου ἀρχιερέως (a gloss on the name, which
means "high priest") πρὸς Κλεοπάτραν τὴν σοφήν and its philosophy as
mystagogia. According to Col 2:23, readiness to accept the heretical
doctrines also counts as "wisdom." To the Colossian στοιχεῖα philosophy
cf. also the phrase διὰ τεσσάρων στοιχείων γυμνάσας [exercising through
four elements] in the continuation of the alchemical text. In view of the
Judaic character of the Colossian heresy, to be discussed further below,
it is not unimportant to note that Hellenistic Judaism frequently presented
itself as a philosophy. Cf. Philo, *Leg.* 156; *Mut.* 223; Josephus, *Ant.*
18.1, 2; *JW* 2.8, 2. The Jewish martyrs in 4 Macc 7:7, 9 appear as representatives of the true philosophy and are mocked by Antiochus for their
"philosophy" 5:10, 22; cf. the introduction to the book, 1:1). Also the
mystagogic style of the Wisdom of Solomon (Wisd 6:22; 8:4) shows the influence of mystery perspectives. Cf. *TWNT* 4 (1942) 820, lines 14 ff.
[*TDNT* 4 (1967) 814, top]; T. Arvedson, *Das Mysterium Christi* (Leipzig: A.
Lorentz; Uppsala: Lundquist 1937) 80 ff., 162 ff.

[13]The reading ἃ ἑόρακεν ἐμβατεύων P46 H D* *et al.* becomes in-
telligible by Dibelius' proof that ἐμβατεύειν is a term from the mysteries,
so it requires no emendation, such as Percy (*Probleme* 170 ff.) advocates
anew. One cannot say for certain whether ἐμβατεύειν suggests the cultic
act of "entering" the sanctuary, or whether, more likely, the word has the
more general meaning, "investigate."

[14]Φυσιοῦσθαι [to be puffed up] is a frequent expression characterizing the gnostic self-consciousness: 1 Cor 4:6, 18 ff.; 5:2; 8:1; 13:4;
2 Cor 12:20. Is this term chosen perhaps as a parody of the opponents'
declaration that they are "filled" by gnosis?

[15]Dibelius, *Kolosser* 39. Ἐθελοθρησκία (slogan of the opponents,
or formed by Paul as a parody of one?) could stand in connection with the
emphasis on the voluntary decision to which the candidate for initiation
was called. Cf. *voluntaria mors* (Apuleius, *Metam.* 9.21); θέλησον καὶ
γίνεται (*Corp. Herm.* 13.7).

[16]Text in Reitzenstein, *H.M.R.* 174 ff. [An abridged ET in C. K. Barrett, *The New Testament Background* (New York: Harper, 1956) 102-04].

[17]It is well known that Reitzenstein (*H.M.R.* 46 ff., 169 ff., and often) has argued for the same view from a multitude of related texts, especially Apuleius, tractates 1 (Poimandres) and 13 of *Corpus Hermeticum*, Philo, and magical papyri. Hence I can dispense with further parallels.

[17a][Trans. Barrett, *NT Background* 103].

[18]Cf. 1:18, 24.

[19]Thus in the concluding prayer of the Mithras liturgy (Dieterich, *Eine Mithrasliturgie* [1923, 4th ed., Darmstadt: Wissenschaftliche Buchgesellschaft, 1966] 14: γινόμενος ἀπογίγνομαι αὐξόμενος καὶ αὐξηθεὶς τελευτῶ ["having been born again I depart; increasing and having increased I die"--Barrett].

[20]Thus Percy, *Probleme* 140, correctly.

[21]It corresponds to what Paul says about the law in Gal 3:24.

[22]Lohmeyer, *Kolosser* 6, 108; Dibelius, *Kolosser* on 2:11 and his excursus on 2:23.

[23]Evidence in Schlier, *Galaterbrief* on Gal 4:3.

[24]Cf. O. Cullmann, *Le problème littéraire et historique du roman Pseudo-Clémentin* (Etudes d'histoire et de philosophie religieuses, 23; Strassburg, Paris: Jouve, 1930) 170 ff.

[25]Schlier, *Galaterbrief* 111-12. Percy's argument against the pre-Christian origin of this gnosis and for its derivation from Pauline theology (*Probleme* 165) I regard as completely wrong-headed.

[26]1 Tim 1:3-4, 7; 4:7; 2 Tim 4:3-4; Tit 1:10 ff.; 3:9. Cf. also
Ignatius, Magn. 8.9; Philad. 6.

[27]See my article λάχανον in *TWNT* 4 (1942) 67 [=*TDNT* 4 (1967) 67];
Johannes Haussleiter, *Der Vegetarismus in der Antike* (Berlin: Töpelmann,
1935); Percy, *Probleme* 141-42.

[28]Edgar Hennecke, *Neutestamentliche Apokryphen* (2d ed., Tübingen:
Mohr, 1924) 424 [ET: New Testament Apocrypha, ed. R. McL. Wilson (Philadelphia: Westminster, 1965) 2. 747].

[29]Wilhelm Bousset, *Hauptprobleme der Gnosis* (FRLANT, 10;
Göttingen: Vandenhoeck & Ruprecht, 1907) 175.

[30]G. Bornkamm, *Mythos und Legende in den apokryphen Thomasakten*
(FRLANT, n.s. 31; Göttingen: Vandenhoeck & Ruprecht, 1933) 108.

[31]Ibid. 117 ff.

[32]One analogy is surely the peculiar prophetology in Manichaeism
(Reitzenstein-Schaeder, *Studien* 287), according to which prophecy divides
itself into the four prophets Buddha, Zarathustra, Jesus, and Mani. Another
is the incorporation of various divine figures of the Zoroastrian, Mithraist,
and Christian religions in the Manichaean pantheon.

[33]*Hauptprobleme* 136 ff.

[34]Ibid. 229.

[35]See n. 15 above.

[36]Reitzenstein, *H.M.R.* 252 ff.

[37]The absence of any adversative particle remains surprising.
However, the opposition has already been expressed in the οὐκ ἐν τιμῇ τινι

[not of any honor]. I therefore paraphrase 2:23: "While that has the
appearance of wisdom (namely, following the δόγματα)--one calls that
'voluntary service,' 'humility,' 'curbing the body'--yet it has nothing
whatever to do with 'honor' and serves (only) to glut the flesh."
Πλησμονή [satiety, gratification] is thus probably chosen in allusion to
the πληροῦσθαι [to be filled] striven after by the Colossians; τῆς σαρκός
[of the flesh] as in 2:18 perhaps an insulting antithesis to the divine
νοῦς [mind] to which the opponents appeal. Lohmeyer, although he takes
the latter expression as an antithesis to ἀφειδία σώματος ["curbing the
body"], speaks correctly of "irony and sarcasm, which rejects the propagated slogans all the more sharply the more precisely it seems to agree
with them" (*Kolosser* 131).

[38]Bornkamm, *Mythos und Legende* 109-10.

[39]Cf. E. Schürer, "Die Juden im bosporanischen Reiche und die
Genossenschaften der σεβόμενοι θεὸν ὕψιστον," in *Sitzungsberichte der
Akademie der Wissenschaften zu Berlin*, 1897, 200 ff., especially 221 ff.,
and F. Cumont, ὕψιστος, in Pauly-Wissowa, *Realencyclopädie der classischen
Altertumswissenschaft* 9. 444.

[40]*Orat.* 18, 5 (Migne, *PG*, 35. 990 f.).

[41]ἐκ δυοῖν τοῖν ἐναντιοτάτοιν συγκεκραμένης, Ἑλληνικῆς τε πλάνης καὶ
νομικῆς τερατείας. ὧν ἀμφοτέρων τὰ μέρη φυγὼν ἐκ μέρων συνετέθη. Τῆς
μὲν γὰρ τὰ εἴδωλα καὶ τὰς θυσίας ἀποπεμπόμενοι τιμῶσι τὸ πῦρ καὶ τὰ
λύχνα· τῆς δὲ τὸ σάββατον αἰδούμενοι καὶ τὴν περὶ τὰ βρώματα ἔστιν ἃ
μικρολογίαν τὴν περιτομὴν ἀτιμάζουσιν. Ὑψιστάριοι τοῖς ταπεινοῖς ὄνομα,
καὶ ὁ Παντοκράτωρ δὴ μόνος αὐτοῖς σεβάσμιος.

[42]*Contra Eunom.* 2 (Migne, *PG* 45. 482 ff.).

[43]Schürer (see n. 39 above) 200 ff.; F. Cumont, *Die orientalische
Religionen im römischen Heidentum* (3d ed., 1931) 58 ff., 117 ff., 273
[cf. ET of 2d ed., *Oriental Religions in Roman Paganism* (New York: Dover,
1956) 62-66; 127-34; 257], and *Hypsistos* (Revue de l'instruction publique

en Belgique, Supplément, 1897).

[44]Cumont, *Die orient. Rel.*, passim. See also especially Reitzenstein, *H.M.R.* 145 ff. On the Phrygian Sabazius cult, see Cumont, *Die
orient. Rel.* 58 ff. [ET 64-66] and "Les mystères des Sabazius et le
judaïsme," *Comptes rendus des séances, Académie des inscriptiones et
belles-lettres,* 9 Feb. 1906, 63 ff.

[45]Cumont, *Die orient. Rel.* 117 [ET 128].

[46]On Yahweh as Aion, see Reitzenstein, *H.M.R.* 148 ff.

[47]Reitzenstein, *Vorgeschichte* (see n. 9 above) 218 ff.

[48]Hippolytus, *Ref.* 9. 15; Ps.-Clementine Homily 18.4; Bousset,
Hauptprobleme 90.

[49]Letter to Boisserée, March 22, 1831 (begun on March 20): "I am
now compelled to conclude the last page, in jest and in earnest, with something wonderful. No man can escape religious emotion, but it is also impossible for him to assimilate such a thing in himself alone; hence he
seeks or makes proselytes. The latter is not my style; the former I have
faithfully carried out and, from the creation of the world on, I have not
found a confession which I could have fully affirmed. Yet now, in my old
age, I discover a sect of the Hypsistarians which, hemmed in between pagans,
Jews, and Christians, professed as far as it knew how to treasure, to marvel
at, and to revere the best, the most perfect, and, insofar as it thus had
to come into close relationship with the deity, to worship it. At once
there came to me from a dark age a joyful light, for I felt that I had
been striving my life long to qualify myself to be a Hypsistarian. But
that is no small effort, for in the limitation of one's individuality,
how can one become aware of the sublime? At least in friendship we do not
want to outdo ourselves" (Vol. 48, 155, 26). On the prehistory of the
letter, the further correspondence between Goethe and Boisserée on the
Hypsistarian question, and the development of his credo in his whole

literary work, see the fine essay by A. Kippenberg, "Die Hypsistarier. 'Goethe,'" *Viermonatschrift der Goethe-Gesellschaft* 8 (1943) 3 ff.

[50]Cited by Kippenberg. Cf. E. Beutler, *Eckart* 18 (1942) 225 ff.

[51]Cf. also in *Dichtung und Wahrheit* (part 2, end of 8th book) Goethe's statement about Gottfr. Arnold's history of the church and of heresy: "His sentiments agree closely with my own, and what especially intrigued me about his book was the fact that I received a more favorable conception of many heretics who had been represented to me previously as stupid or godless." The question how Goethe came to know about the Hypsistarians has recently been investigated and convincingly answered by Bernhard Wyss, "Zu Gregor von Nazianz," in *Phyllobolia für P. von der Mühll* (Basel: B. Schwabe, 1945) 172 ff. In all probability it was through the biography by the Heidelberg theologian, pupil of Creuzer, C. Ullmann, who had connections to Weimar through his wife, a daughter of the poet Sophie Mereau, a protégée of Goethe who had married C. Brentano. Ullmann revered Goethe. His book (*Gregorius von Nazianz, der Theologe* ... [Darmstadt: C. W. Leske, 1825], Appendix V, 388-94, "Über die Secte der Hypsistarier") appeared in 1825, its preface dated August 28 (Goethe's birthday), and was perhaps sent to Goethe by the author. [Ullmann had published a 34-page pamphlet on the subject two years earlier: *De Hypsistariis, seculi post christum natum quarti secta, commentario* (Heidelberg 1823)--Trans.]. Goethe's first remarks about the Hypsistarians are from 1826 (letter to Riemer of October 7, *Weimarer Ausgabe* 4. 41, 190, 3). His later statements correspond entirely to Ullman's conception of the sect. (For this added note I am grateful to H. von Campenhausen.)

PAUL'S ADVERSARIES IN COLOSSAE

Stanislas Lyonnet, S. J.*

The "gnostic" vocabulary of the letters to Colossians and
Ephesians is no less revealing [than that of First Corinthians][1] about the
adversaries who are the Apostle's target, directly in the first letter,
indirectly in the second--that is, insofar as the latter reflects the former.[2] Less "revolutionary" perhaps than in the case of First Corinthians,
the results to which Father Dupont comes are none the less of great interest.

No doubt many interpreters had already freely acknowledged that
the gnosis of Colossae probably entailed elements of Jewish origin. Dupont
cites, for example, the categorical judgment of G. A. Jülicher in the
Encyclopedia Biblica (2, col. 1742) defining the heresy of Colossae as a
"gnosticizing Judaism." E. Percy surely holds no different opinion.[3]
Nevertheless, the majority of commentators, without denying every element
of Jewish origin, continue to interpret the gnosis of Colossae essentially
as a hellenistic syncretism. Thus again recently G. Bornkamm, describing
"the heresy of Colossians," considers it to be "beyond any possible doubt"
that, for example, "the doctrine of the στοιχεῖα ["elements"] belongs to
the oriental theology of the Ἀιών," whose "origin goes back to the Indo-
Iranian cosmogony and its conception of the primordial man."[4]

One of the great merits of Father Dupont is his having been able
to distinguish here in the terminology of the letters two elements which
are usually confused but are in reality very different: one group of terms
deriving from "popular Stoicism" (p. 430) and another deriving uncontestably
from Judaism. Then he has demonstrated that the former, characterized by
words like πλήρωμα [fullness] and σῶμα [body],[5] "do not refer to the

---

*Father Lyonnet is Professor of New Testament Exegesis at the Pontifical
Biblical Institute in Rome. This essay first appeared as part of a series
of reviews of contemporary New Testament research, "L'Étude du milieu
littéraire et l'exégèse du Nouveau Testament," *Biblica* 37 (1956) 27-38,
and is translated by permission of the editors of *Biblica*. The trans-
lator has added notes (below, notes 12, 30) indicating points at which
Lyonnet has extended or modified his position in his more detailed and
technical article, "L'Épître aux Colossiens (Col 2:18) et les mystères
d'Apollon Clarien," *Biblica* 43 (1962) 417-35.

adversaries' mode of speech," but that the vocabulary in question was
"familiar to St. Paul," who "used it when he wished to insist on the idea
of unity" (p. 493), as was precisely the case in our letters. On this
point as well he finds himself in complete agreement with E. Percy, who
was the first, we believe, who ventured to defy the commonly held opinion,[6]
maintaining that the term πλήρωμα itself was not borrowed by the Apostle
from the heretics whom he combatted. If the term is introduced by Paul,
it belongs to the Stoic literary milieu from which Paul had already borrowed σῶμα, and in Colossians-Ephesians the two terms are in fact closely
associated (e.g. Col 2:9; Eph 1:13). On the other hand, the notion itself
does not seem at all new, and Father Dupont effectively connects the
supreme goal proposed to the Ephesians, "to be filled by becoming part of
the *pleroma* of God" (Eph 3:19) with the end assigned to the world in 1
Corinthians 15:28: "God will be all in all," where Paul is dependent on
exactly "the same cosmological conceptions of popular Stoicism" (pp. 475 f.;
cf. p. 492).

The other set of terms, on the contrary, obviously comes from
the gnostics themselves, indeed is explicitly attributed to them, for
example in chapter 2 of Colossians. And everything here calls to mind
Judaism. Not only do the names ἀρχαί and ἐξουσίαι given to the "Powers"
reveal "a literary milieu typically Jewish," as G. Delling and W. Foerster
have shown (*TDNT* 1, 483-84; 2, 571-73; cited by Dupont pp. 285 and 490),
but the expression τὰ στοιχεῖα τοῦ κόσμου [the elements of the world] (Col
2:8, 20), which Paul sets in opposition to Christ, is connected in the
Letter to Galatians, where it first appears, to a context which is universally recognized as purely Jewish (Gal 4:3, 9). Following Father Huby,
Father Dupont sees here "the cosmic forces and more particularly the stars,
whose course regulated the religious life of the Jews."[7] Moreover, in
Galatians as in Colossians, it is precisely a question of "observing certain times," designated in general terms in Galatians 4:10, "days, months,
seasons, years," but with all the precision one could wish in the parallel
passage Colossians 2:16: "festivals, new moons, and sabbaths." There is
another detail which will not deceive us: the Judaizers of Galatia sought
to impose circumcision on the believers (6:12 *et passim*). The fact that
in Colossians 2:13 Paul assimilates baptism to a circumcision "not made by
human hands" suggests at least that the same was true at Colossae.[8]

The Colossians add, it is true, restrictions in drinking and eating (Col 2:16, 21) and a "veneration of the angels" (2:18) which are unknown in the Letter to Galatians.

But one certainly does not have to have recourse to Pythagoreanism in order to explain the former. The importance held by dietary prescriptions in Judaism is well known, and more than once Paul recalls, referring to "Jewish terminology" (p. 308), that for a Christian "nothing is impure (κοινόν)," that "all things are pure (καθαρά)" (Rom 14:14, 20, as already Acts 10:14 f. and 11:8 f.). In this connection Father Dupont appropriately notes that in the Pastoral Epistles it is against the Judaizers again, explicitly mentioned as such (cf. Titus 1:14: "adhering to Jewish fables and human commandments"), that Paul reaffirms the same principle (Titus 1:15; 1 Tim 4:3-5).

As for the alleged "cult of angels" of Colossians 2:18, it seems at first sight scarcely possible to harmonize it with rigid Jewish monotheism, and one has rather supposed a pagan origin. In fact, though, some church writers did accuse the Jews of such a cult. St. Jerome even speaks of "victims offered not to God but to the angels and to the impure spirits" (*Epist.* 121, 10). Origen associates it with magic (*c.Cels.* 1, 26), and Aristides sets this cult over against that of the true God (*Apol.* 14, 4).[9] But for the last-named, who seems to draw all his information from the exegesis of Colossians, it is a matter of a "cult" of a very special kind: it consisted, he says, in "observing the Sabbaths, the new moons, the festivals of Passover and the great Day of Atonement, as well as circumcision and dietary prescriptions." It is probably some such, in fact, that suggested the term used by Paul: θρησκεία, which the Vulgate translates exactly *religio*, in the classic sense of the word designating a group of practices regulating the moral life (cf. Acts 26:5; James 1:26 f., the only [other] two passages where the word is found in the NT). In reality, that with which Paul seems to reproach the gnostics at Colossae is not at all that they worship the angels or offer them sacrifices, but that, instead of honoring God as he wanted to be, they multiply observances "which are inspired by a tradition altogether human" (Col 2:8; cf. vs. 22 and the expression used in Titus 1:14 a propos of Jewish observances),[10] and intended rather to render honor to the angels who assisted in the promulgation of the Mosaic law and are supposed to preside over its observance (Gal 3:19; cf. Acts 7:38, 53; Heb 2:2; Josephus, *Ant.* 15, 5, 3).[11]

One may say that the gnostics of Colossae appear to connect this "cult of angels" with certain "visions" (Col 2:18: ἃ ἑώρακεν) bestowed upon the initiate "when he crossed the threshold of the temple" (ἐμβατεύων, precisely as in the inscription of the temple of Apollo at Ephesus [sic]: οἵτινες μυηθέντες ἐνεβάτευσαν [who, having been initiated, entered], 2d century A.D.). But the sense of the passage is one of the most controversial, the text itself is scarcely certain,[12] and it would be imprudent at least to erect a whole theory on this single term. All the more since the Judaizers of 2 Corinthians in all probability made a point also of "visions and revelations" (cf. 2 Cor 12:1), as Father Dupont properly notes, pointing out the similarity to Colossians 2:18 (p. 259). Even better, is it not the case that the manuscript from Qumran entitled "The War of the Sons of Light," translated for the first time by M. Delcor,[13] speaks of the "people of the saints of the Covenant, who receive the law in teaching, ...hear the voice of the Venerable (=God), *see the holy angels*, have their ears opened and hear unfathomable things" (10, 10-11)? Besides, "visions of angels" are a familiar theme in Jewish apocalyptic literature. Thus the Greek Testament of Levi (2:6 ff.), an Aramaic fragment of which has just been found at Qumran, describes at length the celestial vision of Levi: "And I saw the heavens opened and I saw above me a high mountain that reached the heavens, and I was on it. And the gates of heaven were opened to me, and *an angel said to me* ...."[14]

* * *

At the time of the publication of *Gnosis* (1949), Father Dupont could not take account of the manuscripts discovered at Qumran. He also does not mention the Essenes. We have seen, however, how the doctrine of both illustrated certain tendencies of the Corinthian gnostics.[15] With the gnosis of Colossae, as we have already seen, the comparison is even more striking.

It bears not only on certain details, however suggestive, nor only on such expressions as "the body of flesh," which in fact one finds in Colossians 2:11 as well as in the Habakkuk Commentary 9:2, nor on the

unparalleled place assumed in both by "religious knowledge," knowledge
which "God loves" (CD 2:3), which he "reveals to the elect" (1QpHab 11:1),
knowledge to which "God opens the heart of his servants" (1QS 11:15-16).[16]
It is a matter in both cases of a "revealed knowledge" very similar in
nature if not identical. To the sectaries of the New Covenant the Zadokite
Document declares that "God has confirmed the Covenant which he concluded
with Israel for ever, *revealing to them the hidden things* (the mysteries,
the secrets), concerning which all Israel had erred: his holy sabbaths,
his glorious festivals, his righteous testimonies, and his true paths,
and the desires of his good pleasure by which man shall live, if he fulfills
them" (CD 3:13-16; cf. 6:18-19). Now the "philosophy" of the Colossian
teachers (2:8) involved a teaching on the same subject and perhaps amounted
to just that.

In this way, moreover, an explanation appears for the importance
given in the sect to the question of the "calendar," which in effect controlled the whole religious life of its members. We know now that they
followed a calendar different from that of official Judaism: a solar rather
than a lunar calendar, dividing the year into four equal seasons of ninety-
one days, the same as that presupposed by the book of Jubilees (e.g. 6:23-
38) and the book of the Similitudes of Enoch (1 Enoch chap. 72 and 80:2-6).
The Rule makes at least two allusions to it (1:14-15 and 10:1-9), mentioning, exactly as Gal 4:10 does, "days, months, seasons, and years."[17]

In addition to the multiple prescriptions regulating the observance of the sabbath (e.g. CD 10:14-11:18),[18] which correspond rather well
to the information we obtain from Josephus about Essene customs on this
point (*JW* 2. 8, 9 §147), the distinction between pure and impure foods was
equally severe (CD 6:18, where the prescription is joined with that concerning sabbaths and festivals, again exactly as in Col 2:16; cf. CD 11:11-
15). Josephus reports how heroically the Essenes were faithful to these
(*JW* 2. 8, 10 §152. Moreover, it was probably in order to assure the observance of these rules that, according to Josephus, "they choose priests for
the preparation of food and drink" (*Ant.* 18. 1, 5 §22). Elsewhere he calls
attention to their sobriety: "Purified and clothed in a white robe, the
members enter their refectory as into a sacred shrine. They take their
places without disturbance; then the baker serves to each guest a loaf,

the cook places before each one a plate containing a single course. The
priest pronounces a prayer before the meal, and none may taste anything
before the prayer is said" (*JW* 2. 8, 5 §129-31). It was with reference
to this text that St. Jerome extolled "these men who always abstained from
wine and meat and acquired the custom of daily fasting" (*Adv. Iovinianum*
2. 14). Perhaps Jerome was thinking of the "Therapeutae," brothers or
cousins of the Essenes. In any case, the latter, according to Philo, took
their only frugal meal at evening, composed of water, bread, salt, and
hyssop, to the exclusion of wine.[19] Besides, in order to be convinced
that practices of dietary abstinence were honored in these Jewish milieux,
it is doubtless sufficient to recall John the Baptist and his disciples
(Luke 1:15; Mark 1:6; Matt 11:18; 9:14) or what Hegesippus relates about
James of Jerusalem: οἶνον καὶ σίκερα οὐκ ἔπιεν (like John the Baptist)
οὐδ᾽ ἔμψυχον ἔφαγεν,[20] without having the least reason to resort to who
knows what Pythagorean or Hellenistic influence in order to explain such
practices.[21]

Finally, Josephus again informs us that the angels enjoyed a
special veneration among the Essenes, as in general elsewhere among the
Jews,[22] noting that the novice undertook by very formidable oaths "to
guard the books of the sect and *the names of the angels*" (*JW* 2. 8, 7 §142).
In the Book of Jubilees, which formed part of the library of Qumran,[23] we
see not only that God on the first day of creation created along with
heaven and earth every kind of angel, but also that when it came time to
reveal the calendar, it was the angel of God who descended from heaven
and through Enoch taught men righteousness and the signs of the Zodiac in
order to observe the days, months, and sabbaths (Jub 4:15 ff.).[24]

As for the documents from Qumran, angelology holds a rather large
place in the Rule (cf. 3:13-4:16; 11:8, etc.), and the "Rule of the Congregation," attached to the Rule, excludes from the communal assembly the
crippled, the lame, and the blind (cf. n. 19 above) because "the holy
angels are present in their congregation."[25] Moreover, Fr. Barthélemy
remarks with good reason that this "mystical communion between the earthly
congregation of Israel and the celestial, angelic court" is presupposed
by 1QS 11:8 and many passages of the "Benedictions."[26] In another fragment
found in the first cave of Qumran and which the editors have called the

"Book of Noah," the angels appear as the intercessors appointed for men: "Well, now, it is to you, the holy ones of heaven, that the souls of men set forth their cause, saying: 'Present our cause to the Most High.'" The remainder of the passage shows that the "holy ones" are Michael, Uriel, Raphael, and Gabriel.[27] Finally, in the War of the Sons of Light, not only do the heavenly spirits appear in visions to the people of the saints of the Covenant (10:10-11; see above, p. 147.) and participate in the combat (7:6; 12:4, 8 ff.) as did the celestial cavalry of 2 Maccabees (e.g., 3:25 ff.; 5:2-3; 10:29-30; etc.), but in 9:13-15 mention is made of "three hundred shields" that "surround the tower of the three spirits of the face,"[28] and "on all the shields of the tower they shall write: on the first, Michael; on the second, ...; on the third, Sariel; on the fourth, Raphael, Michael, and Gabriel [?] ..." In truth, at Qumran no less than among the Essenes, the *names of the angels* were singularly venerated.

There is no need to remind the reader of the testimony of the Testaments of the Twelve Patriarchs,[29] evoking the μεσίτης θεοῦ καὶ ἀνθρώπων [mediator between God and men] (T Dan 6:2), or the statement of Carpocrates who, according to Epiphanius (*Haer.* 28. 1), "adhered to Judaism and claimed that the world was created by the angels." One understands without much difficulty how these tendencies could have engendered the errors which St. Paul combatted in his letter to the Colossians,[30] and why he insisted so energetically in it on the primacy of Christ over "all that has been created, the world visible and invisible, Thrones, Dominions, Principalities, Rulers" (Col 1:16; cf. Eph 1:21 ff.) and is careful to mention explicitly Christ's role in the creation (Col 1:15-20).

* * *

NOTES

[1] [In the preceding section, Lyonnet has argued, drawing on material from the Qumran texts, in favor of Dom Jacques Dupont's interpretation of the Corinthian situation.]

[2] See especially Jacques Dupont, *Gnosis: La Connaissance religieuse dans les épîtres de S. Paul* (Bruges-Paris: Desclée de Brouwer, 1949) 17,

256, 489-93.

[3]See particularly chap. 3 [of E. Percy, *Die Probleme der
Kolosser- und Epheserbriefe* (Acta reg. societatis Humaniorum Litterarum
Lundensis, 39; Lund: C. W. K. Gleerup, 1946)]: "Der Kolosserbrief und die
Irrlehre in Kolossä," 137-78.

[4]G. Bornkamm, "Die Häresie des Kolosserbriefs," *TLZ* 73 (1948)
11-20 [above, pp. 121-43].

[5]"The cosmological theories of popular Stoicism are the only
ones to offer a literary theme which uses the term *pleroma* and which
corresponds to the literary context of this term in the Letters of the
Captivity (471). For σῶμα cf. 15. As for κεφαλή [head], the word comes
from Judaism (440-53).

[6]We hesitated to follow him on this point in *Biblica* 32 (1951)
577.

[7]J. Huby, *Les épîtres de la Captivité* (Verbum salutis), 65,
cited [by Dupont] 490, n. 4. See also the article by Fr. Huby in *Biblica*
15 (1934) 365-68: "Στοιχεῖα dans Bardesane et dans saint Paul."

[8]According to Bornkamm (*art. cit.*, col. 14 [above, p. 126],
Colossians were acquainted with a *mystery of rebirth* which they called, in
dependence on Judaism, "circumcision." Paul took over the expression to
designate baptism, which he interpreted in a sense completely contrary to
Jewish conceptions, but conforming to *gnostic conceptions*, as a "stripping
off of the fleshly body" (ἀπέκδυσις τοῦ σώματος τῆς σαρκός). But the Pauline
expression no more implies a "gnostic" conception than that in Rom 7:24:
τίς με ῥύσεται ἐκ τοῦ σώματος τοῦ θανάτου τούτου; ["Who will deliver me
from this body of death?"--RSV]. The specification τῆς σαρκός [of the
flesh] is the essential thing. That which baptism strips away from the
Christian, initially and *de jure*, is the "fleshly" body. In Rom 6:6 Paul
likewise assigned as an effect of baptism the reduction to a state of

impotence of the σῶμα τῆς ἁμαρτίας [body of sin], that is, the body as an instrument of sin. In other words, baptism transferred the human being from the fleshly state, where he put aside the sin of Adam, ratified as an adult by his personal sins, to the spiritual state, that of the resurrected Christ (Rom 6:4-10; Col 2:12).

[9]The texts have been collected by A. L. Williams, "The Cult of the Angels at Colossae," *JTS* 10 (1908-09) 420-31. To be sure, the Council of Laodicea in 360 condemned an actual cult of angels, "disguised idolatry," but one should note that this was a case of Christians, not Jews, and of a practice three centuries later, which could have developed under the influence of local pagan cults.

[10]Paul denotes them with the word ἐθελοθρησκεία, which he seems to have coined himself, "voluntary service," suggesting simply practices imposed by man, not commanded by God. Bornkamm, on the other hand (*art. cit.*, col. 13 [above, p. 125], following Dibelius (*An die Kolosser*, 2d ed. 29) sees here an allusion to the "initiation" to which the initiate submitted voluntarily, under the pretext that Apuleius speaks of *voluntaria mors* (*Metam.* 11. 21)

[11]On the veneration of angels among the Jews, see J. Bonsirven, *Le Judaïsme palestinien au temps de Jésus-Christ; sa théologie* (Paris: G. Beauchesne, 1934) 1. 213-14: "A very widespread conception assigns angels to the various elements, stars, rain, winds, which they are charged to direct and administer ... While Orthodoxy denied to the angels any participation in the work of creation, it let them intervene in world history ... The tradition is especially abundant about the part played by angels of all kinds in the theophanies of Sinai .... These angels transmit the divine words to the Israelites, *ready to punish them if they should refuse,* kissing them on the mouth and crowning them when they accept. Likewise, they are said to assist God in his *judicial activity,* writing down the actions of men, advocating punishments against them, taking the function of prosecutors at the Judgment." Further on, p. 328, he adds: "The juridical prescriptions forbid any form of *adoration of the angels* in such terms as it

is supposed to have been practiced. It is very likely that the cult of
the angels which threatened among the Colossians to undermine the divinity
of Christ came from Jewish gnostics." On the angels and the Law, see the
article by Bo Reicke, "The Law and this World according to Paul," *JBL* 70
(1951) 259-76.

[12]See for example the excursus which C. Masson devotes to this
passage in *L'Épître de saint Paul aux Colossiens* 135, where he proposes
the translation "riding the clouds." In any case, the use of the verb in
the figurative sense of "scrutinize intellectually" is well attested by
2 Macc 2:30 and by later Greek (cf. F. Zorell, *Lexicon graecum Novi Testa-
menti* [Paris: P. Lethieleus, 1931]). [In Part I of his 1962 article (see
n. on p. 144 above), Fr. Lyonnet surveys the philological evidence for the
meaning of ἐμβατεύειν, concluding that its general sense is "to cross a
threshold, especially of a sacred place," "to tread on (sacred) soil," but
that later it developed the metaphorical use just mentioned, for which he adds
further evidence (Philo, *Plant.* 80, church fathers) (pp. 419-25). Lyonnet
thinks both senses are played on in Col 2:18, but that Paul is using the
word sarcastically (see below, n. 30). Lyonnet also discusses the syntactical difficulties of the verse (425-26), without deciding which of the
possible ways of construing ἐμβατεύων is most likely, and some conjectural
emendations that have been proposed, which he finds unnecessary (426-27)
--Ed.]

[13]M. Delcor, "La Guerre des fils de lumière contre les fils de
ténèbres ou le Manuel de parfait combattant de Qumrân," *NRT* 77 (1955)
372-99 ... [Numerous other translations and studies of 1QM have appeared
since Lyonnet wrote, including the editions by Yigael Yadin, *The Scroll of
the War of the Sons of Light against the Sons of Darkness* (2d ed., Jerusalem: Bialik, 1957); J. van der Ploeg, *La rouleau de la Guerre* (STDJ, 2;
Leiden: Brill, 1959); Jean Carmignac, *La Régle de la guerre* ... (Paris:
Letuzey et Ané, 1958); B. Jongeling, *Le Rouleau de la guerre* ... (Assen:
Van Gorcum, 1962); see further bibliography in Jongeling, 396-97.]

[14]J. T. Milik, "Le Testament de Lévi en araméen. Fragment de la

grotte 4 de Qumrân," *RB* 62 (1955) 398-406. [The translation used by
Lyonnet here, which I have tried to reproduce, does not quite follow the
Greek.] The Aramaic text includes: "Then a vision was shown me ... seeing
the visions, also I saw the heavens ... above me, elevated to reach the
heavens ... to me the gates of heaven and an angel ..." (p. 400).

[15]Thus even concerning the notion of "religious knowledge" (4),
concerning the ascetic tendencies of the Corinthians (22-23) or their
difficulties in accepting the resurrection of the body (25 ff.).

[16]...Whence the extremely elaborate solicitude for the study of
the Law (1QS 6:6-7).

[17]Cf. CD 6:18-19; 16:3-4. G. Vermes remarks also that in
1QpHab 11:8 "the expression 'their Sabbath' and the fact that the high
priest was able to journey on so holy a feast will be more easily understood if, together with M. S. Talmon ("Yom Hakkippurim in the Habakkuk
Scroll," *Biblica* 32 [1951] 549-63) one presumes the existence of two different calendars, the one adopted by the community, the other by official
Judaism" (*Discovery in the Judean Desert* [New York: Desclee, 1956] 99,
n. 68). On the calendar, see the studies of A. Dupont-Sommer, "Contribution à l'exégèse du Manuel de Discipline x, 1-8," *VT* 2 (1952) 229-43,
and A. Jaubert, "Le calendrier des Jubilées et de la secte de Qumrân, see
origines bibliques," *VT* 3 (1953) 250-64. It is known that the author has
tried to resolve by this means the still unsolved enigma of the passion
narrative in the gospels: "La date de la dernière Cène," *RHR* 146 (1954)
140-73. Fr. E. Vogt has given a particularly clear summary of these
diverse studies in *Biblica* 36 (1955) 403-13. Cf. also J. Morgenstern,
"The Calendar of the Book of Jubilees, its Origin and its Character,"
VT 5 (1955) 34-76.

[18]The prohibition against lifting, on the Sabbath, "the beast
which falls into a cistern or into a pit" (CD 11:13-14), or "causing to
climb out, by means of a ladder or a rope or any other instrument, a human
being who falls into a place full of water or a cistern" (11:16-17), shows

that Christ did not evoke a purely imaginary case in Luke 14:5 (cf. Matt
12:11, which only speaks of "a sheep") and perhaps even explains the
doublet, "if his son or his ox falls into a well," which many manuscripts
omit, but which is supported by the Chester Beatty papyrus. In just the
same way, when in Luke 14:21 Christ invites to the Messianic banquet the
"crippled, blind, and lame," it is probably aimed at the Qumran doctrine
which, "faithful to the ancient prohibitions," excludes from the
"assemblies" "whoever is contaminated in his flesh, paralyzed in feet or
hands, lame, blind, deaf, dumb, or contaminated by any bodily defect that
strikes the eye" (1QSa 2:5-6; the passage comes almost immediately before
the description of the eschatological feast).

[19] *Vit. cont.* 73. The text of Philo is quoted by Eusebius, *HE*
2. 17. Eusebius thought that Philo spoke of *Christian* monks; indeed, that
Philo's informer had been no other than St. Peter himself (cf. *VD* 33
[1955] 150-51). On the abstinence of the Essenes, see G. Vermes, *Discovery*
55-56. The Rule also mentions several times (6:4-6; 6:20; 7:20) communal
meals in which the priest "first extends his hand to bless the first fruits
of bread and 'must'" (6:5-6). Yet the use of a word (תירוש) denoting sweet,
unfermented beverage—we would say "fruit juice"—in place of the term
ordinarily denoting wine, does not seem sufficient grounds, in Vermes'
opinion, to permit "a firm conclusion on the subject of the abstinence of
the Essenes," especially since תירוש also signifies "new wine" (Deut 14:13)
(Vermes 56). In the description of the eschatological feast (1QSa 2:11-22),
the word is simply translated "wine," as a "poetic ritual appelation preferred to the more worldly term יין" (*Discoveries in the Judean Desert*, ed
D. Barthelemy and J. T. Milik, vol. 1 [Oxford: at the Clarendon Press,
1955] 118).

[20] ["He did not drink wine and liquor, nor did he eat meat"],
reported by Eusebius, *HE* 2. 23, 5.

[21] Pythagorean influence is often invoked for the Essenes, on the
testimony of Josephus (*Ant.* 15. 10, 4 [§371]). But Fr. F.-M. Braun correctly remarks that "Josephus in no wise claims that the Essenes consciously

imitated the Pythagoreans, nor that their congregation drew upon disciples
of Pythagoras. He merely notes that they lived in a Pythagorean fashion:
γένος δὲ τοῦτ' ἐστιν διαίτῃ χρώμενον τῇ παρ' Ἕλλησιν ὑπὸ Πυθαγόρῳ
καταδεδειγμένῃ ["This is a group which follows a way of life taught to
the Greeks by Pythagoras"--trans. Ralph Marcus (Loeb ed.)]. He dealt in
the same way with the Pharisees, whom he compared with the Stoics, and the
Sadducees, whom he has the good taste not to compare with the Epicureans.
Making allowance for his having colored their doctrines and for the philosopher's mantle with which one should say he has clothed them, what he
writes about them remains typically Jewish" ("Essénisme et Hermétisme,"
Revue Thomiste 54 [1954] 541). On the other hand, Fr. Braun does recognize
the likelihood of hellenistic influence, notably on the anthropology of
the Essenes (*ibid.*). Much has been said about Iranian influence: see especially K. G. Kuhn, "Die Sektenschrift und die iranische Religion," *ZTK*
49 (1952) 296-316; A. Dupont-Sommer, *The Jewish Sect of Qumran and the
Essenes: New Studies on the Dead Sea Scrolls*, (trans. R. D. Barnett (London: Valentine, Mitchell, 1954), 118-30 (on "the doctrine of the two spirits").
The latter chooses to think of the religion of the Essenes as a kind of
syncretism. For a felicitous restatement of the issue, see A. Vincent,
Les manuscrits hébreux du désert de Juda (Paris: A. Fayard, 1955) 261-63.
K. Schubert himself notes correctly that the "dualism" of 1QS 3:13-4:16
is only a "relative" dualism: "The dualism is defined not as absolute, but
only as a relative one." It seems to him in effect more likely, by reason
of 1QS 11:10, that it is the men themselves who, by their good or evil
actions, allign themselves under the domination of the Spirit of Darkness
or of the Spirit of Light (*TLZ* 78 [1953] 506). In any case, the dualism in
question is certainly an "ethical" dualism, not physical, and not without
direct dependence on the OT (cf. Kuhn, 310-16). In particular, one does
not detect any trace here of mythological speculations about the primordial
Man.

[22]See n. 11 above.

[23]A fragment has been found in the first cave at Qumran and published in *RB* 56 (1949) 602-605; another (= Jub 35:8-10) is edited with the

first (= Jub 27:19-21) in *DJD* 1. 82-84. [For fragments in Cave 4, see J.
T. Milik, *RB* 73 (1966) 94-104--Trans.]

[24]Cf. Reicke (above, n. 11), 272-73.

[25]Fragment 28a [= 1QSa] 2:8-9. The parallel with Paul's prescription in 1 Cor 11:10 suggests itself [see further J. A. Fitzmyer, S.J.,
"A Feature of Qumran Angelology and the Angels of 1 Cor 11:10," *NTS* 4
(1957-58) 48-58--Ed.] Note the similar exclusion in 1QM 7:4-6, likewise
motivated by "the presence of the holy angels in their armies."

[26]Fragment 29b [sic: read 28b], in *DJD* 1. 117 [= 1QSb].

[27]Fragment 19 in *DJD* 1. 152. This fragment, like the two others
published under no. 19 (pp. 84-85), belongs to one of the sources of 1
Enoch, whose angelology is well known.

[28][Perhaps an over-literal translation? Virtually all other
translators take *rwḥwt* here in the idiomatic sense of "directions," and
"faces" as the "sides" of the "tower," thus obtaining: "in the three
directions of the front" (Dupont-Sommer), "the three outer sides" (Lohse),
"three frontal directions" (Yadin), "trois cotés de front" (Jongeling),
etc.--Trans.]

[29]A. Dupont-Sommer supposes that this work was also a product of
the sect. Others think, on the contrary, that it is, at least in its present form, a Jewish-Christian writing--thus M. de Jonge, *The Testaments of
the Twelve Patriarchs. A Study of their Text, Composition and Origin*
(Assen: Van Gorcum, 1953); cf. J. T. Milik in *RB* 62 (1955) 297-98. The
arguments have not convinced Fr. Braun (*RB* 62 [1955] 5, n. 4). In any
case, the fragments from Qumran Cave 4 identified by Abbe Milik are a
Testament of Levi in Aramaic reproducing a form preserved in the text of
the Cairo Geniza, "a writing probably distinct from the Testaments of the
Twelve Patriarchs, which it served as a source." And Milik concludes his
article, "Among the materials at Qumran there is no remnant of a Semitic

original of the Testaments of the Twelve Patriarchs. Given the extreme wealth and variety of the discovery, this fact practically excludes a pre-Christian and Palestinian origin of the apocryphon. And everything leads one to believe that the Testaments of the Twelve Patriarchs are a Jewish-Christian composition, making extensive use of the Jewish works properly so-called" (405-6).

[30][In his 1962 article (see first note above) Lyonnet reiterates the solution which he outlines here, though more cautiously emphasizing that he does not necessarily wish to insist on specific "Qumranian infiltrations" in Colossae, but takes the Qumran materials as "particularly clear evidence" for tendencies present in "the whole of Judaism" (432). Somewhat more than in the earlier article, he emphasizes the allusion to "visions" in Col 2:18, affirming that this is more readily explained by Jewish parallels than by recourse to hellenistic mysteries (427-32). And he has a most ingenious explanation for the use of the word ἐμβατεύειν, "to enter," in 2:18. Just as in Gal 5:12 Paul sarcastically equates circumcision with "mutilation," like that practiced in that region by the priests of Cybele, so here Paul uses a term with a double meaning to lampoon the Jewish-Christian "philosophy" of the Colossians. The verb with its metaphorical sense, "scrutinize," can refer to their infatuation with angelic mysteries; but it was a well-known technical term of the mystery at Claros, meaning "to be initiated" (accepting Dibelius' argument to this point). The errorists themselves had not organized any mystery, but Paul satirizes their pretensions with mystery language.--Ed.]

HUMILITY AND ANGELIC WORSHIP IN COL 2:18*

Fred O. Francis

For generations, the exegesis of Col 2:18 has been introduced by statements like that of Ernst Percy: "One could easily characterize this verse as one of the most contested passages in the whole New Testament. It presents extraordinarily great difficulties in language and content"[1].

I

The difficulties encountered in this verse cannot be laid to its textual history. The text reads:

μηδεὶς ὑμᾶς καταβραβευέτω
    θέλων
       ἐν ταπεινοφροσύνῃ
       καὶ θρησκείᾳ τῶν ἀγγέλων
        ἃ ἑόρακεν ἐμβατεύων
    εἰκῇ φυσιούμενος
       ὑπὸ τοῦ νοὸς τῆς σαρκὸς αὐτοῦ

The Greek tradition evidences only two noteworthy variants: 1) the omission of ἐν after θέλων, and 2) the inclusion of a negative after ἃ. The first variant is supported by only the original hand of Sinaiticus. The second has more general support[2] but the quality, and to some extent the breadth, of witnesses favors the text that we read.[3]

While textual problems are minimal, lexical, syntactical, and historical problems abound. The interpretation of nearly every word or phrase has been disputed.[4] The main verb, καταβραβευέτω, is extremely rare. The Greek commentators took it to be synonymous with παραβραβεύειν: to award a prize unfairly (so Meyer). Most modern commentators take it to be the equivalent of κατακρίνειν (Dibelius, Lohmeyer, Abbott, Field, and

*This essay first appeared in *Studia Theologica* 16 (1963) 109-134, and is reprinted by permission.

others).⁵ Some scholars (Lightfoot, Percy, Moule, Scott) assume a moderat-
ing position wherein the term retains the primary sense of the simple verb
βραβεύειν, to act as an umpire or one who gives the prize. Thus the force
of the verb would be to deprive, or disqualify, or encroach upon another's
interest.

θέλων (ἐν) is more vigorously disputed than καταβραβευέτω. Some
commentators have supplied the infinitive ποιεῖν, rendering the phrase,
"wishing to do it in" (Theodoret, Theophylactus, Photius, Calvin, Buttmann,
Eadie, Ellicot, and Robertson [1928]). Other scholars have taken θέλων to
be an adverbial absolute modifying καταβραβευέτω (Beza, Reicke, Tittmann,
Fridrichsen, Dibelius, Scott, Riesenfeld). Still others have taken θέλων
in such an absolute sense but have linked it to ἐμβατεύων (Luther, Tyndale,
Ewald). In both cases the term would be translated "gladly," or "will-
fully," or "arbitrarily." Finally, there are those who understand the construction θέλων ἐν to be a Septuagintism, rendering it "delighting in,"
or "boasting in," or *volens in* (MS d, Chrysostom, Augustine, Theodore
Mops., Bengel, Lightfoot, Haupt, Lohmeyer, Percy, Moule.)

Until recent years, ταπεινοφροσύνη has received little attention
from commentators on this passage. Most exegetes have emphasized that this
is a false humility, and have suggested that its meaning is to be found in
the "worship of angels" (among modern commentators Meyer, Lightfoot, Abbott,
Dibelius 1912, Scott). Some scholars have recognized in the word a technical term for fasting or asceticism (Zahn, Moffatt, Dibelius 1927, Riesenfeld, Percy, Reicke, Lohmeyer, Moule). A few of these have related this
insight to the more general view, suggesting that the rigorism was a means
of worshipping the angels (Percy, Lohmeyer).

All but universally, the θρησκείᾳ τῶν αγγέλων has been taken to
be an objective genitive--the worship directed to the angels. However,
there have been those (Ephraem, Luther, Melanchthon, Wolf, Dalmer, Hofmann,
Zahn, Ewald) who have taken it to be a subjective genitive--the worship
which the angels perform. In addition, it has been suggested that the subjective τῶν αγγέλων also modifies ταπεινοφροσύνη (Hofmann, Zahn, cf.
Strack-Billerbeck).

Ἃ ἑόρακεν has usually been taken to be the object of ἐμβατεύων
(so Dibelius 1912). It could also be a relative clause modifying "humility

and worship of angels," this latter clause being the object of a conjunctive θέλων (so Dibelius 1917). It could have this same relation to what
precedes it when θέλων is understood to be absolute (so Dibelius 1927).
It has also been viewed as the object of φυσιούμενος (Fridrichsen).

ʼΕμβατεύων has variously been rendered "investigating" (Preisker),
"entering at length upon" (Nock), "taking his stand upon" (RV mg, RSV),
"presuming upon" (Syr. ܠܡ), "entering" (Luther), "setting foot upon"
(Lohmeyer), "walking about" (most Latin MSS), "being initiated" (Dibelius,
Fridrichsen, Eitrem, Scott, Reisenfeld). It could also be rendered, "entering into possession," as in the LXX and the papyri. The syntax of
ἐμβατεύων is equally diverse. The participle has been understood as co-
ordinate with the other participles (so Dibelius 1912, MS d), as a distinct
object of θέλων and in an asyndetic relation to ταπεινοφροσύνη ... ἑόρακεν
(so Dibelius 1917), as a temporal modifier of the relative clause ἃ ἑόρακεν
(so Dibelius 1927), and as a temporal modifier of ἃ ἑόρακεν when the clause
is taken to be the object of φυσιούμενος (Fridrichsen). Finally, ἐμβατεύων
could take ταπεινοφροσύνη ... ἀγγέλων as its object or be governed by θέλων
in a purpose clause (both of these possibilities are suggested by Luther's
rendering of the text).

Punctuation too is open to more than one possibility. For example, εἰκῆ is usually taken to modify φυσιούμενος; yet, it could just as
well modify ἐμβατεύων (so MS Dd).

The complexity of interpretation which these manifold possibilities represent has led some to conjecture a complex textual history. In
the words of Hort, "some primitive error" is "probable." Emendation is
suggested for the two phrases that historically have been most difficult
and where there is the slight textual variance noted above: θέλων ἐν ...,
and ἃ ἑόρακεν ἐμβατεύων. None of the emendations is acceptable. Either
they are words unattested elsewhere, or their very plausibility makes it
impossible to explain the present text.[6]

It would seem to be sounder methodology not to make recourse to
conjectural emendation, if at all possible.[7] Rather, one should expect
that the difficulties result from summary historical allusions, a kind of
shorthand between writer and readers.[8] Furthermore, the value of any
approach to the text varies directly with its capacity to illuminate the

concrete historical circumstances referred to in the text. This is to say
that methodological adequacy requires both relative simplicity (that is,
accounting for the data with a minimum of presuppositions or extraneous
additions) and relative comprehensiveness (that is, account for all the
data).

Overagainst a maze of complex, partial solutions, Martin Dibelius
proposed an interpretation which, to an unparalleled degree, answered to
both of these canons. He provided documented historical parallels in the
inscriptions from the sanctuary of Apollo at Claros, and in the Isis initiation of Apuleius. On this basis he gave a developed description of
Colossian practice, suggesting a syncretistic mystery. As a consequence
of the relative adequacy of his proposal he has dominated the interepreta-
tion of the passage for the last half century. Virtually all subsequent
interpreters have been in dialogue with Dibelius. While they have raised
important questions with regard to Dibelius' view, they have provided no
similarly concrete interpretation.[9] In fact the discussion of Col 2:18 has
reached an impasse. More than a generation of intramural criticism has had
a paralyzing effect. This may readily be observed in the presentations of
Percy and Moule. Moule lodges an objection against every possibility of
interpretation he sees, and concludes with the frustrated word that we must
do "the best we can".

It is the purpose of this paper to reopen the discussion of Col
2:18--and the Colossian problem as a whole--by viewing the text against a
background of ascetic and mystic trends of piety. Rigoristicly effected
visionary exaltation obtained generally in the Hellenistic world. At the
same time, Jewish-Christian apocryphal literature is particularly helpful
in illuminating the question.

The text cited above we translate as follows: "Let no one disqualify you, being bent upon humility and the worship of angels--which he
has seen upon entering--being vainly puffed up by his mind of flesh".

We have translated καταβραβευέτω by the word "disqualify" because
it allows for the ambivalence of the main clause. To decide between "judgment" and "deprivation (of a prize)" is to force philology. The particular
nuance of καταβραβευέτω--whether it pertains to judgment in the courtroom
or in the athletic stadium--is not material to the sense of the passage.

This is probably because the writer was communicating the double sense of objective judgment against the readers by those in error, and the subjective judgment (in relation to the prize in Christ) which would result from the readers' adoption of the errorists' ways.

The debate on the syntax and translation of the adverbial θέλων (έν) has become polarized between the absolute and conjunctive uses. It is of material significance that those who argue most strongly for the absolute use of θέλων also provide for a conjunctive sense in their translations of the passage.[10] The sentence simply makes best sense with a conjunctive participle. Of course, this should not become the occasion for grammatical license. At this point it seems reasonable enough to take θέλων έν to be a Septuagintism.[11] In any case, ταπεινοφροσύνη ... αγγέλων is a modal specification of καταβραβευέτω. We have translated θέλων έν "being bent upon" to conform the phrase to the ambivalence of the main clause. "Being bent upon" is either a specification of judgment (as, say, "insisting upon"), or a specification of the community setting in which one might be deprived of the prize of Christ (as, say, "delighting in"). The English idiom, like the Greek, is appropriate to both cases.

Finally, we may note that our translation of ἃ ἑόρακεν ἐμβατεύων is the most natural one. The relative ἃ has its antecedent in what goes before as in vss. 17, 22, 23. The participle ἐμβατεύων is a temporal modifier of ἑόρακεν.

The problem to which we must now direct our attention is the meaning and interrelation of the terms humility, entering, and worship of angels. Insight into these questions should enable us to make some suggestions regarding the Colossian problem as a whole.

II

Humility

We have indicated that most commentators have been content to point our that the ταπεινοφροσύνη referred to in 2:18 (and 2:23) cannot be the same as the ταπεινοφροσύνη referred to in 3:12: it is said to be a false humility.[12] The more important observation has to do with why, when he was to enjoin a life characterized by ταπεινοφροσύνη, the writer used the term at all in this verse. It can only be that this was a technical

term of his opponents. Such a technical use of ταπεινοφρόνησις is clearly
present in Tertullian's discussion of fasting, where he twice interrupts
his Latin text to insert the Greek word.[13] Similarly, Hermas identified
ταπεινοφροσύνη with fasting in Sim. 5, 3, 7.[14] In Col 2:16-23, the reference to food and drink, the prohibition against tasting, and severity to
the body all point to fasting.

But the similarity between these passages in Colossians, Hermas,
and Tertullian is still more striking. Ταπεινοφρόνησις in Tertullian is a
broader term than fasting. It might well be translated "rigor of devotion;"
it encompasses fasting, abstinence, and stations--a discipline not unlike
prison! In Hermas the value of fasting is contingent upon first keeping
oneself from every evil word, every evil desire, and purifying the heart
from the vanities of the world. So in Colossians ταπεινοφροσύνη is bound
up with regulations of much broader effect than fasting. In the LXX the
cognate verb (ταπεινοῦν) and the noun (ταπείνοσις) embrace the use of sack-
cloth and ashes and an abject posture.[15]

Finally, this humility, with its fasting and related rigors, has
the same functional significance among these sources. Hermas Sim. 5, 3
recommends humility to gain the interpretation of the parables. The passage appears to be inspired by Isaiah 58, where humility is thought to aid
in prayer, and the drawing near to God, and the knowledge of his ways.[16]
In Hermas Vis. 3, 10, 6, following a series of visions, Hermas asks for
revelation. This he receives through further visions, but he is first told:
"All inquiries require humility (ταπεινοφροσύνη); fast therefore, and you
will receive what you ask of the Lord".[17] Tertullian employs the Old Testament to support his argument for the value of fasting. By fasting Moses
was able to see God's glory (vi); Elijah went for forty days on one single
(!) meal and met with God (vi); Daniel fasted three days and an angel was
sent to him (vii). Daniel also illustrates that abstinence is efficacious
for revelation (ix).[18]

Tertullian's exegesis of Daniel 10:2 ff. is fully justified.
Many similar examples where rigorist humility is effectual for visions are
to be found in apocryphal literature.[19]

Several of these Jewish-Christian writings specify that the consequence of this ascetic practice is entrance into the heavenly realm.

Needless to say, not all accounts of "visionary" experiences yield to historical analysis. Even the visionary himself may "not know" whether his
experience was "in the body or out of the body".[20] In this regard it is
useful to set the Apocalypse of Ezra[21] along side 4 Ezra. While the latter
makes an ambiguous reference to Ezra's visionary departure (5:16), the former records that Ezra was taken up to heaven (1:7). This follows Ezra's
request for divine secrets (1:2), his being told to fast (1:3), and the
statement that he fasted twice the required period (1:5). Similarly, the
two dominant themes in the Testament of Isaac are the patriarch's fasting
and his entrance into heaven.[22] The Apocalypse of Abraham, in contrast to
Gen. 15, makes the revelation to Abraham contingent upon abstinence from
meat and wine (chap. 9). Then, like Elijah, Abraham is said to go forty
days with no food or drink (chap. 12). Following this he is taken up on a
heavenly journey.[23] In his edition of 3 Enoch, Hugo Odeberg prints a fragment of an ascension of Moses contained in MSS B and L.[24] It relates that
when Moses ascended on high he fasted 121 fasts until the highest heaven
was opened to him. In the Ascension of Isaiah (2:7-11),[25] Isaiah and a
band of prophets withdraw to a desert place where they take up a rigorous
life of fasting and lamentation, being clothed in garments of hair. Five
of the prophets are named; regarding the rest it is said, "and many of the
faithful who believed in the ascension into heaven." Whatever may be the
literary relationship between chapters 2 and 7-11,[26] at some early stage in
the tradition it was recognized that asceticism and belief in ascension
into heaven belong together.

     In several passages Philo treats this conjunction of fasting and
visionary transcendence.[27] Three of these relate to Moses' encounter with
God on Sinai. In *Som.* 1. 33-37 and *Mos.* 2. 67-70 Philo takes up the Deut
9:9, 18 tradition that Moses fasted the forty days he was on the mountain.
In the former passage this is said to necessarily follow from hearing the
heavenly hymns--which Moses did when he had become ἀσώματος. In the latter
passage it is said to be preparation for oracular messages and to be com-
pensated by contemplation when "he ascended an inaccessible and pathless
mountain." The "better food of contemplation" is also treated in *QE* 2. 39.
The reference to eating and drinking on Sinai (Ex. 24:11b) receives this
explanation: "For those who are indeed very hungry and thirsty did not

fail to see God become clearly visible." *Ebr.* 148-52 equates fasting with
a libation, the libation with "pouring out the soul before the Lord," and
pouring out the soul with loosening the chains of mortal life in order to
send the soul to the all for the vision of the uncreated.

Gershom Scholem's brilliant studies indicate that this pattern
of asceticism and mystical ascent continued in Judaism into the middle
ages. He quotes a Babylonian sage of about 1000 A.D.: "... who is desirous
of beholding the merkabah and the palaces of the angels on high, must follow a certain procedure. He must fast a number of days and lay his head
between his knees and whisper many hymns ...".[28]

Scholem is convinced that "Originally, we have here a Jewish
variation on one of the chief preoccupations of the second and third century gnostics and hermetics." Such a comparison is quite instructive, for,
as we have seen, the intimate relation between rigorism and entrance into
the transcendent realm is not characteristic of Jewish apocryphal literature only. It may be said that in many respects Philo bridges the apparent
chasm between the apocrypha and the Hermetic corpus. Asceticism and ascent
are prominent in the Hermetic tractates. It will be useful to quote two
illustrative passages from the many of this type in the tractates. Note
the emphasis on human, moral effort, and the imperative tenor.[29]

> 13. 6-7: ... how can you perceive with the
> senses that which ... can be understood only
> by the effect of its power and activity ...
> Am I incapable of doing so, my Father? ...
> By no means, my child. Draw it to yourself and
> it will come. Desire it and it will be. Abolish
> the senses of the body and the birth of deity
> will take place. Cleanse yourself from the ir-
> rational affections of matter.
> 4. 6-8: If you do not first hate your body,
> my son, you cannot love yourself. ... For
> since there are two kinds of things, the
> corporeal and the incorporeal ... a choice
> of one or the other is left open to the one
> who wishes to choose. It is not possible to
> choose both ... This being the case, O Tat,

the things that come from God are always at
hand [God has done his part], and always will
be; and the part that belongs to us--let it
follow, and not fall short! ... You see, my
son, through how many bodies [i.e., physical
spheres] we must make our way, and through
how many choirs of daemons and series and
courses of stars, in order to press on toward
the One and the Only [God]. ... Let us
lay hold, then, upon this beginning, and let
us go forward with all speed.[30]

In tractates 1 and 13 ethical rigorism is inseparable from the
ascent of the soul. We shall see below that the ascent is not simply
subsequent to the death of the physical body, but is intimately bound
up with the ongoing death to the body.

Entering

The primary meaning of ἐμβατεύειν[31] is "to enter." Beyond this,
the signification of the term derives from the context. In Euripides,
Electra 595, the chorus prays that Orestes may triumphantly *enter* the city.
The same verb is used in Sophocles, *Oedipus Rex* 825, but here it is best
rendered by the English *set foot upon*, for it is not in any abstract sense
that Oedipus wants to enter his homeland. Overagainst this, it is instructive to set the four occurrences of ἐμβατεύειν in 1 Macc (12:25, 13:20,
14:31, 15:40). In each case the verb refers to the incursive action of an
enemy in relation to another's country. Here *invade* is a reasonable translation. 2 Macc 2:30 has the term with no expressed object. However, the
context speaks of the detailed work of an historian. Some have suggested
investigate in this case. While this suits the context, the expression
could simply indicate one's involvement with a task, being translated *enter
in* (this is also idiomatic English). The RSV's figurative rendering of the
verse--*occupy the ground*--is appropriate to the concrete use of ἐμβατεύειν
in Joshua 19:49, 51. In these verses "entering" and "taking possession"
are inseparable. Ἐμβατεύειν in the papyri is quite close to this LXX
usage. One commonly is said to *enter into* possession of something or to

enter into one's inheritance. In the inscriptions at the Apollo sanctuary
at Claros, context again must supply the particular nuance of ἐμβατεύειν.
Some of the many delegates (θεοπρόποι or questioners of the god) to the
oracle were initiated into the mysteries.[32] 'Εμβατεύειν appears in three
records of this practice.[33] Two delegates μυηθέντες καὶ ἐνβατεύσαντες
ἐχρήσαντο κτλ. Two others came οἵτινες μυηθέντες ἐνεβάτευσαν. A fifth
delegate παραλαβὼν τὰ μυστήρια ἐνεβάτευσεν. Besides these inscriptions em-
ploying ἐμβατεύειν, there are three inscriptions which record that a delegate ἐπετέλεσε καὶ μυστήρια. Even in these inscriptions, the primary sense
of the verb is not lost. Rather, the crucial question is what the delegate
entered and when.

        Dibelius' argument from these inscriptions is quite ingenious, and
requires careful consideration. A basic assumption is that the first three
inscriptions are equivalent to the second three. Thus Dibelius takes
ἐμβατεύειν to be the second stage in a whole observance called ἐπιτέλειν
μυστήρια. This is to say, the "when" of "entering" is at the climax of
initiation. The inner sanctuary, or possibly the oracle grotto, is "what"
one enters.[34] Dibelius concludes that ἐμβατεύων stands for initiation in
Col 2:18.

        One must ask whether Dibelius was sufficiently careful in develop-
ing his line of argument. Perhaps the most striking discrepancy between
Dibelius' interpretation and the data lies in his conclusion. There is
absolutely no evidence that ἐμβατεύειν can stand alone for initiation.[35]
And it is begging the question to ascribe the inaccuracy to the writer
of Colossians rather than the modern interpreter.[36] Furthermore, Dibelius'
first assumption--that the first and second groups of inscriptions are
equivalent--is not at all self-evidently correct. It is quite possible
that ἐπετέλεσε καὶ μυστήρια is the equivalent of παραλαβὼν τὰ μυστήρια,
and, hence, of μυηθέντες. 'Εμβατεύειν would not then be simply the climax
of initiation.

        But Dibelius' solution is even more questionable from an historical
point of view. Was there such a high degree of syncretism in the Colossian
church? And more, if this were the case, would not the writer's polemic be
more direct? Dibelius himself considers this question. He states that
the Colossian problem could not involve a "revival of an ancient cult."

In that case the writer would not have failed to brand the teaching
as "paganism".[37] Dibelius concludes that, "These Christians werę
the instigators of the hybrid structure that joined the Christ-
cult to στοιχεῖα-worship."[38] It is curious indeed that syncretistic
revival must be branded as paganism, while syncretistic originality
requires no frontal attack!

Finally, because the merit of Dibelius' solution has been its
comprehensiveness and concreteness, it should be noted that his development of ἐμβατεύων has resulted in a curtailment of ἃ ἑόρακεν. In 1912
it was that into which one was initiated. In 1917 it (and ταπεινοφροσύνη
... αγγέλων to which it was now related) was another interest along side
of initiation. In 1927 ταπεινοφροσύνη ... ἑόρακεν was merely one of the
incidents at initiation. There is some truth in Percy's observation that
this results in a strange initiatory vision.[39] But more important,
Dibelius' results suffer from the same cause as Percy's: concentration on
one aspect of the passage has inhibited the interpretation of the whole.

Some years ago Wilhelm Bousset, in his "Die Himmelreise der
Seele,[40] wrote that 2 Cor 12:2 and 4 represent two stages on the approach
to God. He also suggested that 1 Cor 2:6 ff., 2 Cor 5:1 ff., and Eph 6:11-
17 could be similarly related to the heavenly journey.[41] Some months
later, before the printing of the second half of his study, Bousset felt
that a postscript was necessary. To this discussion of Corinthians and
Ephesians he added, "Also the difficult passage Col 2:17 [sic.]: ἐν ...
(μὴ) ... ἐμβατεύων,: may be explained in this connection." A generation later, A. D. Nock wrote in passing, "...if ἐμβατεύων falls within the relative clause it may indicate some claim to special knowledge obtained on a visionary entry into heaven...".[42]

Materials already used in our discussion of humility are in accord
with such a view. These documents record that, having fasted, Ezra, Isaac,
Abraham, and Moses all journeyed to heaven. An enigmatic judgment drawn
from Gershom Scholem provides a structure for exploring this perspective.[43]
Scholem notes the "idea that the ecstatic sees in his lifetime what other
people see only after death" as a common feature of Paul's (2 Cor 12:2 ff.)
and the rabbis' (bḤagiga 14b) journeys into heaven. He then states, "There
is, however, a significant difference. Whereas Paul is 'caught up' to

Paradise, the rabbis 'enter' it." Scholem does not elaborate on this proposition; we shall have to evaluate it on the basis of our sources. Nevertheless, we shall first look at documents where *entering* is used of the
heavenly journey.[44]

The Greek Apocalypse of Baruch[45] is a clear example of this type
of literature. An angel *leads* Baruch *to* the first heaven. The angel suggests that they *enter* through a door. It is then recorded that they *entered* (2:2). The same sequence is repeated for the second heaven (3:1 f.).
The angel also *leads* Baruch *to* the fifth heaven. Baruch asks if the gate
is not open that they may *enter*. The angel replies that they cannot *enter*
until Michael comes (11:1 f.). It is interesting that, while the text
twice speaks of Michael's *descent* from God (11:4, 15:1), when it would be
appropriate to speak of Michael's *ascent* it is instead simply said that he
departed (14:1).

1 Enoch, 3 Enoch, and the Testament of Levi all speak of ascent
and entrance into heaven, giving greater emphasis to the latter.[46] The
Naasene literature that Hippolytus samples in *Ref*. 5. 8 gives considerable
attention to the theme of entrance into heaven. Explication of the name
Κορύβαντα entails an account of the descent and ascent of the perfect man.
Ascent, unlike descent, is not repeated in the discussion, but is immediately
supplanted by the theme of entrance and the gate. This theme then carries
over into the remainder of the chapter. The Naasenes confirm that "the
apostle Paul knew this gate" by a paraphrase of 2 Cor 12:2-4.[47]

This theme of entrance and gate is basic to Hermas Sim. 9. The
Naasene rule that "the perfect man cannot be saved unless he is regenerated
and enters through this gate" has its counterpart in the elaborate allegory
of Hermas and its summary statement in Sim. 9. 12, "therefore the gate was
made recently, that they who are to be saved may enter through it." In
Sim. 9. 25. 2, apostles and teachers are blessed with πάροδος μετὰ τῶν
αγγέλων, entrance with the angels!

This brief survey is sufficient to indicate that visionary transcendence was often characterized as entrance into heaven. More than this,
our samplings also suggest that "entrance" is not a phenomenon distinct
from "ascent" even when the entrance theme is predominant.[48] This insight
points to that body of literature which treats of the visionary ascent.

We have already referred to the ascent of Ezra, Isaac, Moses,[49]
and Abraham,[50] and to the fact that Isaiah's band believed in ascension.
To these sojourners must be added Sedrach[51] and Elijah.[52] Additionally,
in contrast to 1 Enoch, the movement in 2 Enoch is almost entirely vertical.
Enoch ascends to each of the seven heavens in succession (3:1 ff.), descends
to his house for a thirty-day period of teaching (38:1 ff.), and is finally
taken up to the highest heaven (67:2 ff.). Similarly, in the Ascension of
Isaiah, 7-11, Isaiah is taken up through the seven heavens, and returns to
the body with the promise of heaven when his days are completed. The canonical Revelation to John does not exhibit such schematic clarity with regard
to the standpoint of the visionary. Certain references might be taken to
imply that John did not have the viewpoint of heaven (for example, 18:1,
20:1). However, 4:1-2 clearly involves a visionary entrance into heaven.
Finally, 2 Cor 12:1-4 is an invaluable historical account of the heavenly
journey.

We have now come full circle on the question of entering. And
comparable to Paul's Corinthian note is the Talmudic record (bḤagiga 14b)
that "Four men entered the 'Garden', namely, Ban 'Azzai and Ben Zoma, Aher,
and R. Akiba".[53]

We may conclude this consideration of entering and ascent with
two passages from the Hermetica which illustrate the relation of the ascent
to the continuing death to the body.

> 4. 5. ... as many as partook of the gift sent
> by God, these ... are as immortal gods to
> mortal men, embracing all things in their own
> mind, the things on earth and the things in heav-
> en, and even whatever may be above heaven. Having
> thus raised themselves to such a height, they see
> the Good, and having seen it they look upon their
> sojourn here below as a misfortune. Then, having
> scorned all things corporeal and incorporeal, they
> hasten on to the One and Only.
> 10. 24-25: For man is a being of divine nature ...
> man ascends even to heaven, and measures it; and
> what is more than all beside, he mounts to heaven

without quitting the earth; to so vast a distance
can he put forth his power.

We must now address ourselves to the fact that ἐμβατεύειν is not
used in our primary sources. It is of first importance that, as we observed
at the beginning of this section, the verb never loses its simple meaning,
and derives its particular nuance in each case from its context. Secondly,
specific verbal agreement between vs. 18 and our sources is not required.
It would be gratuitous to presume that for every example of ancient usage
that has survived a second one has also survived. Such a presumption is
unnecessary when that usage is as closely related to its context as is
ἐμβατεύειν (for example, the singular use of the verb in 2 Macc 2:30 is
clear enough). The requirements of historical parallelism are satisfied
when the simple sense of the verb together with its context answers to a
profuse literary tradition.

At the same time, it is possible to develop a reasonable historical hypothesis. The Claros inscriptions record that Laodicea on the Lycus
(Col 2:1, 4:16) sent several delegations to the oracle of Apollo.[54] It is
quite conceivable that the employment of ἐμβατεύειν at Claros spurred
popular use of the verb in the areas to which delegates returned.[55] On
this basis there is greater likelihood that the word would appear in Colossians than in our related sources. A further specification of this solution could involve the errorists' intentional borrowing of the language
of the oracle to characterize their own religious practice.[56] It should
be observed that such a view of the matter does not in itself define Colossian practice.[57] It is reasonable to conjecture that the errorists may
have understood humility followed by visions seen upon entering "the
heavenly temple" to be analogous to initiation followed by reception of
oracles upon entering the Apollo sanctuary.

We turn to consider what was seen upon entering, namely, the
angelic worship.

Angelic Worship

The traditional and scholarly consensus that τῶν ἀγγέλων is an
objective genitive has two principal sources: the Preaching of Peter, and

Theodoret's connection of the phrase with the canons of the Council of
Laodicea.

 The pertinent passage in the Preaching of Peter is quoted by
Clement (*Strom*. 6, 5, 41) and Origen (*Jn*. 13, 17), alluded to by Origen
(*contra Cels*. 1, 26:5, 6), and is adapted in the Apology of Aristides. The
Jews are said to worship angels and observe new moons, etc.

 The thirty-fifth canon of the Council of Laodicea enjoins
Christians not to abandon the worship of the church for assemblies where
angels are venerated. Such a practice is condemned as a secret idolatry.
About seventy to eighty years later (c. 435) Theodoret identified the heresy
with the chapels dedicated to the archangel Michael in his own time, and
with the Colossian error in apostolic times.

 It must be said that the subject itself--angels--resists the
efforts of many modern commentators to set out a definition of the matter
which excludes all others. For example, if the Michael legend, with its
appearances and miracles, were involved in the Colossian error, this would
not in itself preclude the possibility that the angels were at the same
time related to the (physical) elements of the cosmos (so Dibelius) or the
regulations which were observed (so Percy). On the contrary, the most common phenomenon is the proliferation of angelic functions.[58]

 Percy has ably pointed out a fundamental weakness of Dibelius'
solution: it is inconceivable that asceticism would honor the powers behind
the elements and heavenly bodies, and there is no evidence of a choice of
"good" over "evil" elements.[59] But the context does not allow Percy's
solution either. It is for this reason that he emended the text. We shall
return to a consideration of the objective genitive after we have viewed
the evidence for a subjective genitive.

 As we have suggested, the hosts of angels have diverse functions.
The worship which the angels perform is specified in our passage not by
chance. Without exception, the highest office of angels--and of men--is
the adoration of God.[60] The Ascension of Isaiah is quite interesting in
this regard, for, on his ascent, Isaiah sees the hosts of each of the seven
heavens praise and glorify God.

 Many of our sources describe the angelic worship which the
visionary sees. The Ascension of Isaiah 7:13-9:33 is emphatic with its

seven-fold description. The Testament of Levi 3:4-8 details the liturgical
climax of Levi's entry into heaven. The canonical Revelation to John,
chapters four and five, records John's vision of a heavenly liturgy.
1 Enoch 14 presents a comparable tradition of the heavenly halls, praise
and blessing coming at the conclusion of Enoch's heavenly journeys in 36:4.

Participation in the angelic liturgy is detailed in several
sources. Isaiah participates in the worship of the fifth, sixth, and
seventh heavens (Asc. Is. 7:37, 8:17, 9:28, 31, 33). The daughters of Job
hymn and glorify God in an angelic tongue (T. Job 48-50). In 3 Enoch 1:12,
Enoch utters a song before the Holy One. Following his ascent, Abraham
(Apoc. Abr. 17) learns to recite an elaborate celestial song. When Isaac
is taken to heaven (T. Isc. [Arab.] Fo. 16vo., 17), he and all the saints
and the heavenly ones praise God with the trishagion. This description of
visionary participation in the angelic liturgy is anticipated in Isaac's
teaching to his household (Fo. 15).

> And it is required of every man upon the earth ...
> that he keep the testimonies that are appointed.
> Because after a little time they ... shall be
> engaged in holy angelic service, because of their
> purity, and stand in the presence of the Lord and His
> angels because of their pure offerings and angelic
> service, because their earthly service resembles
> their occupation in the heavens, and the angels shall
> be their companions because of their perfect faith
> and purity. And great is their honour in the presence
> of the Lord ... And now be humbling [!] your-
> selves to God ...

Our earlier consideration of fasting touched on Philo's *Som.* 1.
33-37. In this passage, that capacity which distinguishes man from all
other living creatures and the sole purpose for which heaven was tuned as
the archetype of musical instruments is the hymnic worship of God. And
only mind and heaven can render this solemn praise. The man who, like
Moses, hears this perfect harmony abstains from food and drink, and "as a
being awaiting immortality takes his nourishment from the inspired strains."

In his own incisive way, Gershom Scholem has related this mystic participation in the celestial liturgy to Talmudic tradition and to the worship of the synagogue--and even to the earliest Christian liturgy.[61]

Again and again passages appear in the Qumran literature which suggest sharing in the lot of the angels, including participation in the angelic worship. We cite but two.[62]

> 1QSb 4. 25-26 thou shalt be as an Angel of the Face
> in the dwelling-place of holiness for the glory of
> Elohim of hos[ts. ..] [and thou shalt] be in
> the company of God, ministering in the royal palace,
> and decreeing fate in the company of the Angels of
> the Face;
> 1QH 3. 20-22 Thou hast made me rise to everlasting
> heights, and I walked in an infinite plain! ...
> Thou hast cleansed the perverse spirit from great
> sin that he might watch with the army of the Saints
> and enter into communion with the congregation of
> the Sons of Heaven.

A cognate experience finds expression in the Hermetic corpus.

> 1. 26 Then, stripped bare of all that the powers
> in the framework had wrought in it, man enters the
> eighth [ogdoadic] nature, possessing only his own
> proper power, and, together, with the beings which
> are found there, he hymns the Father. Those who
> are present rejoice over his arrival; and being made
> like those with whom he dwells, he also hears a kind
> of sweet sound of certain Powers, who dwell above
> the eighth nature, as they praise God.

The argument that τῶν ἀγγέλων is a subjective genitive referring to angelic worship is further confirmed and not contradicted by the derivative possibility of worship directed to angels. There is evidence in our sources for such misdirected adoration. John twice (Rev 19:10, 22:8-9) fell down to worship an angel, and twice had to be warned against it. Isaiah

(Asc. Is. 7:21) committed the same error in the second heaven. Along these
lines the veneration of Michael in Asia Minor may well have been the reverence that errorists thought due the angelic bearer of revelations. This
would be the natural result of Michael's agency in visionary participation
in the angelic worship.

Two final remarks are necessary with regard to the angelic worship. The first concerns the word θρησκεία itself. The term can stand
for quite divergent meanings: ritual in the most elementary sense (Philo,
Det. 21), and piety in the least ritualistic sense (James 1:27); one's own
religion (1 Clem. 62:1), and pagan cults (Eusebius, *HE* 4, 26, 7); temple
service (Philo, *Legat.* 298), and religious observances (Philo, *Fug.* 41).
It also stands for the act of worship. A noun joined to θρησκεία in a
genitive construction is most commonly the object of the verbal idea (e.g.
1 Clem. 45:7). However, the subjective genitive is attested (e.g. 4 Macc
5:7). Josephus' usage is instructive. In *Ant.* 12, 253 θρησκεία is set in
a genitive relation to Ἰουδαίων; in 12, 271 it is set in a genitive relation to θεοῦ. Both phrases are linked to the law of the country. Together
they refer to the worship that the Jews do when they worship God. Such
proximity (both in terms of space and reference) of the subjective and
objective genitive precludes a purely lexical determination of θρησκείᾳ τῶν
ἀγγέλων in Col 2:17.[63]

Secondly, we should say a few words about the relation of ταπεινοφροσύνη to ἃ ἑόρακεν and τῶν ἀγγέλων. It would appear that ταπεινοφροσύνη
is a referent of ἃ, and thus the subject of visions. Indeed, this is a
common pattern: instruction in humility for the purpose of obtaining visions
is itself the subject of visions.[64] Scholem suggests still another perspective. He indicates that the hymns which are part of the technique of self-
oblivion[65] are also the hymns that "are described as celestial songs of
praise sung by 'the Holy Living Creatures'".[66] This is to say that along
side visionary instruction in humility the visionary ascent itself may not
be rationally distinguishable from the means of access.[67] From the fact
that the preposition ἐν is not repeated before θρησκεία it might be inferred that ταπεινοφροσύνη stands in the same genitive relation to τῶν ἀγγέλων
that θρησκεία does. Such is the most frequently attested syntax of the time.
However, such an arithmetical judgment must be informed by historical-literary

judgments. Infrequently attested syntax is to be preferred to undocumented, purely constructive interpretations of the phrase[68] and merely formal analogies.[69]

III

It has been the purpose of this study to reconsider Col 2:18 and the Colossian problem as a whole from an historical perspective of ascetic-mystic piety, and from a methodological perspective involving a minimum of presuppositions and extraneous additions, and a comprehensive exegesis of the material. It may be useful to make a few additional suggestions relating our findings to the immediate context of the passage and to the epistle as a whole.

In our discussion of ταπεινοφροσύνη we found that humility answers to many of the elements in 2:16-23. Here we shall raise two additional considerations. In the first place, the compound ἐθελοθρησκία in vs. 23 is neither a catch-word of the errorists[70] nor a severe judgment of the writer.[71] Rather it expresses the writer's own ambivalent situation. While he recognizes in the ascetic-mystic bent of the errorists a threat to his readers, he cannot flatly deny the reality of the heavenly ascent as such (cf. 2 Cor 12:1-4). In vs. 23 he simply casts doubt on his opponents' experience of it. The compound is best rendered "would-be worship".[72]

Some recent commentators have found in ἐθελοθρησκία what they think to be a "fatal objection"[72a] to our proposal. Eduard Lohse states, "Francis' interpretation [of Col 2:18] fails because of v. 23 where 'self-chosen worship' (ἐθελοθρησκία) specifically characterizes the concept 'worship' (θρησκεία) as performed by men."[72b] Two brief responses may be appropriate here: 1) The character that εθελο- gives to worship is not all that specific or self-evident. Any standard lexicon of ancient Greek will indicate at least three areas of meaning for compounds formed with εθελο. One is voluntariness, as in "voluntary servitude" (ἐθελοδουλεία). A second is interest (delight/endeavor), as in "aiming at fashion" (ἐθελάστειος). The third is pretence, as in "would-be philosopher" (ἐθελοφιλόσοφος). In all cases the differing nuances overlay the action of the will in

relation to certain circumstances. The grammar of the compound is
the classic subject-object schema in which the self as agent seeks
to effect, desires, or agrees to some conditions. 2) Lohse's rendering of ἐθελοθρησκία as self-chosen worship--or any other possible
translation--presents no obstacle to our construction of the Colossian
problem. The information gained from the term, namely that certain
Colossians chose/aspired to/gave pretence of some worship, does not
in any way specify "a cult performed by men."[72c] We could say, if
we accepted Lohse's translation, that the Colossians chose for themselves the worship performed by the angels. We did indicate above
that in a number of ancient sources a vision of the angels at worship
incorporates participation in the angelic liturgy. Yet even that does
not lead to the conclusion that the Colossian visionaries worshiped
angels. The religiosity of the opponents obviously is behind the
choice of terms here, but our interpretation stands or falls on broader
issues than this particular word. (Spring 1973, F.O.F.)

In the second place there is good reason to understand the σκιὰ τῶν
μελλόντων in 2:17 as a byword of the errorists. The relative ἃ finds
its antecedent in vs. 16 which in turn points beyond itself: judgment in
matters of food and drink cannot be understood apart from the prohibition
against tasting in vs. 21 which is characteristic of the humility of vs. 18;
judgment with regard to festival, new moon, and sabbath cannot be separated
from he regulations of vss. 14 and 20 and the precepts and teachings of men
in vs. 22, and in vs. 23 these are seen to be integral to the question as
issue in vs. 18. Thus the whole of 2:16-23 is a subtle, unified argument.
From this standpoint it is inconceivable that the writer would volunteer
the judgment that these things to which his readers had died with Christ
(2:20-22) bore the very impress of Christ![73] On the contrary, they are not
"according to Christ;" they have the appearance of wisdom but actually
serve the flesh. As in his references to ταπεινοφροσύνη in vss. 18 and 23,
so here the writer employs his opponents' terminology. Philo is quite
helpful in illuminating the Colossian errorists' use of σκιά. He equates
the Platonic conception of knowing the craftsman from his craft with
apprehending God by means of a shadow (*LA* 3. 99). Moses' subordinate
Bezaleel is said to discern God in this way (*LA* 3. 102). However, Moses

(*LA* 3. 100), being more perfect, more thoroughly cleansed, and initiated into the great mysteries does not gain his knowledge of the eternal from created things, but transcending (ὑποκύπτειν) the created, he obtains a clear (ἐναργῆ) vision (ἔμφασις) of the uncreated, so as from Him to apprehend both Himself and His shadow, which is (ἦν) the Word and the world. Thus the lunar and sublunary referents of Col 2:16 were probably held to be the σκιά by which most men apprehend God. That some men apprehend the σκιά in the very vision of God is in accord with our earlier observation that instruction in humility may be the subject of visions. Moreover, the relation of these two--the earthly σκιά and its transcendent disclosure-- derives from the circumstance that although not every Colossian practice would have been an aspect of the visionary technique itself, the errorists probably claimed that everything they enjoined had been gained from visionary access to the throne of God. In two other passages Philo indicates that the vision itself may be said to have the character of a σκιά.[74] The force of τῶν μελλόντων may be grasped from a perspective we previously cited from Scholem: "the ecstatic sees in his life time what other people see only after death".[75] The quest for the higher reality represented by Philo's Platonism and common Jewish-Christian eschatological expectations are not necessarily mutually exclusive. The ascension of Isaiah was at one and the same time a representation of the ascent upon the ladder of reality and an anticipation of what is to come. In his testament Isaac taught his household both that their earthly service resembled their occupation in the heavens, and that after a little time they would be engaged in holy angelic service. Thus in Col 3:3-4 the writer and his opponents have in common a prospective gaze; the issue lies in the specific nature of the prospect--in particular how it relates to past and present.

There is universal agreement that the Colossian error funamentally consists of a limitation of Christology. Interpreters have commonly expressed this in terms of the mediation or rule of powers other than Christ, and the attendant honor paid to them. Our exegesis of vs. 18 indicates that the angelic powers were not thus venerated. Indeed, one who participated in the angelic liturgy would have sung his praise to God and to him who sits at his right hand! The pre-eminence of Christ over all powers was the presupposition held in common by writer, readers, and errorists.

Traditions such as 1:15-19, 2:9, 10b, and 3:1bc were not at issue. The
argument lay in their soteriological and eschatological implications.
The errorists did not have the spiritual wisdom to understand that they
were "now reconciled in his body of flesh by his death," that they had
"come to fullness of life in him," that they "were circumcised ... by
putting off the body of flesh in the circumcision of Christ," that they
were "buried with him," "raised with him," "made alive with him." They
did not give thanks for their share in Christ's "triumph" over the powers,
nor were they established in the faith that they were "being renewed"
after him. The errorists did not question the fact that *Christ* had done
all this--their heavenly songs praised him for it! They simply did not have
the assured understanding that in, with, by, and after Christ *they themselves* had been delivered. Just as Christ put off the body, so they too
had to handle it with severity. Just as he took his place above all rule
and authority, so they too labored to enter the heavenly realms. Christ
was their pattern, the reality or σῶμα after which they fashioned their
σκιά.[76]

    Overagainst this ignorance of the redemption wrought in Christ,
and the consequent struggle to enter into the inheritance of the saints,
the writer prayed that his readers might know the riches that were theirs
and might wait with patience and joy until our life which is hid with
Christ appears with him. Thus it is that the writer's intention and theological method are as active in the Haustafeln and miscellaneous injunctions
as in the rest of the epistle. The ethical commonplace is an affirmation
of both the saving efficacy and the eschatological hiddenness of Christ's
work. The Christian is free to use the world precisely because Christ
has freed him from the world.

    Col 2:18 and the epistle as a whole provide invaluable insights
into early Christian history. A number of the texts most illuminating for
this study have been drawn from apocrypha which are either Jewish works
with Christian interpolations or Christian works based upon Jewish traditions. How far the early church as a whole thrived on such literature is
still an open question, but some circles, of which we have little direct
knowledge, must have done so. Colossians opens up the inner life of such
a community. Moreover, it appears that the use of such literature was

facilitated by the fact that ascetic-mystic piety obtained generally in the Hellenistic world--not specifically gnostic, not entirely Jewish. Finally, Colossians fixes a rather early date for the establishment of ascetic-mystic piety in the church--and for the opposition which it evoked.

* * *

NOTES

[1]E. Percy, *Die Probleme der Kolosser- und Epheserbriefe* (Lund 1946) 143. The present paper has grown out of a seminar conducted by Professor Nils A. Dahl during his year as Visiting Professor of New Testament at Yale University Divinity School. It is due to the kindness of Professor Dahl that the study has been published in *Studia Theologica*. If, as I would like to think, the solution to an old exegetical riddle has now been found, it is due to a close co-operation between teacher and student, and between Scandinavian and American Biblical Scholarship.

[2]Reading μή: C, and most Koine MSS; reading οὐκ: G; reading a negative: most of the Latin tradition, the Syriac, the Armenian, and most fathers.

[3]ℵ* A B P⁴⁶ D* 69 d m Marcion-Tertullian Ambrosiaster. It seems that in this case, the original text of the bilingual edition was preserved by Dd. The reading οὐκ in G was probably a correction from the Latin tradition.

[4]An entire monograph would be required to lay out such an exegetical history. The older commentaries provide a helpful overview. Cf. T. K. Abbott, *A Critical and Exegetical Commentary on the Epistles to the Ephesians and to the Colossians* (Edinburgh 1897) 265 ff.; J. B. Lightfoot, *Saint Paul's Epistles to the Colossians and to Philemon,* (New York 1897 [Rev.]) 195 ff.; H. A. W. Meyer, *Kritich Exegetisches Handbuch über die Briefe Pauli an die Philipper, Kolosser und an Philemon* (4th ed., Göttingen 1874) 341 ff. Cf. also H. Riesenfeld, "Zu ΘΕΛΩ im Neuen Testament," *Arbeiten und Mitteilungen aus dem Neutestamentlichen Seminar zu Uppsala*

(AM), 1 (1935) 1-8.

[5]Note the Syriac ܣܘܚܒܘܐ , condemnation.

[6]Cf. Lightfoot 197; Abbott 267; C. F. D. Moule, *The Epistles of Paul the Apostle to the Colossians and to Philemon* (Cambridge 1957) 105 f.

[7]Cf. Percy (p. 172), who argues similarly, but accepts Lightfoot's emendation. One has the feeling that Percy's conjectural elimination of the words ἃ ἑόρακεν is a work of necessity following upon his failure to treat the passage as a whole in the first place.

[8]Cf. E. F. Scott, *The Epistles of Paul to the Colossians, to Philemon and to the Ephesians* (London 1930) 54 f.

[9]We have indicated that Percy, with all the abundance of his ex- cellent insights, has failed to come to grips with the problem. E. Loh- meyer, *Die Briefe an die Kolosser und an Philemon* (10th ed., Göttingen 1954) imposes a rational construct upon the passage. A. D. Nock, "The Vocabulary of the New Testament," (JBL) 52 (1933) 131 ff., sets forth a philological solution based on "the rhythm of the words" and the usage in 2 Macc 2:30.

[10]Cf. M. Dibelius, *An Die Kolosser Epheser an Philemon* (2nd ed., Tübingen 1927) 24; A. Fridrichsen, "θέλων: Col 2:18," *ZNW* 21 (1922) 137; Riesenfeld, AM 1. 8.

[11]Cf. Percy 146 f.; Moule 104; Lightfoot 195 f.; Lohmeyer 123 f. It need not be presumed that LXX influence is limited to the usage most commonly attested therein.

[12]Such an account is given even by W. Bauer, *Griechisch-Deutsches Wörterbuch zu den Schriften des Neuen Testaments und der übrigen urchrist- lichen Literatur* (5th ed., Berlin 1958) col. 1592.

[13]De ieiunio adversus psychicos xii: sed ad praemuniendam per nosmet ipsos nouissimorum temporum condicionem indicentes omnen ταπεινοφρόνησιν, cum carcer ediscendus et fames ac sitis exercendae et tam inediae quam anxii uictus tolerantia usurpanda sit; xiii: itaque si et ex hominis edicto et in unum omnes ταπεινοφρόνησιν agitatis, quomodo in nobis ipsam quoque unitatem ieiunationum et xerophagiarum et stationum denotatis.

[14]ἐν ἐκείνη τῇ ἡμέρᾳ ᾗ νηστεύεις μηδὲν γεύσῃ εἰ μὴ ἄρτον καὶ ὕδωρ ... καὶ οὕτω ταπεινοφρονήσεις ἵν' ἐκ τῆς ταπεινοφροσύνης σου ὁ εἰληφὼς ... εὔξηται ὑπέρ σοῦ ...

[15]Cf. Isa 58, Ps 34 (35):13-14.

[16]The reflection of Isa 58 in Hermas Sim 5, 3 includes opposition to evil words and desire, and connection between the work of humility and care of the needy.

[17]πᾶσα ἐρώτησις ταπεινοφροσύνης χρῄζει. νήστευσον οὖν, καὶ λήμψῃ ὃ αἰτεῖς παρὰ τοῦ Κυρίου.

[18]ita xerophagiarum miseratio et humiliati metum expellunt et aures dei aduertunt et occultorum compotes faciunt.

[19]Cf. 4 Ezra 5:13, 20; 6:31, 35; 9:23-25; 12:51-13:1; Syr Bar 5:7 ff., 9:2 ff., 12:5 ff., 21:1 ff., 43:3, 47:2 ff. In the apocryphal romance of Joseph and Asenath there is an extended, detailed account (Chap. 10 ff.) of Asenath's ascetic humility and its issue, the appearance of Michael. The Greek text was edited by P. Batiffol in "Le Livre de la priere d'Asenath," *Studia Patristica*, fasc. 1, 2 (Paris: Leroux, 1889-90). It was re-edited by V. M. Istrin, "Apokrif ob Iosife i Asenefe," *Moskovskoe Arkheologicheskoe Obshehestvo: Slavianskaia Kommissiia*, 1898. The latter was not available to me at the time of writing. The noun regularly used for humility in the Greek MSS is ταπείνωσις. E. W. Brooks edited Syriac (Zachariae Rhetori Adscripta I, i, Scriptores Syri XXXVIIII, *CSCO* LXXXIII,

Louvain 1953) and English (*Joseph and Asenath*, London 1918) versions.
The Syriac renders ταπείνοσις with words meaning penitence, suffering,
poverty, and subjection. The most common is the last of these, ‌ܡܟ‌ܝܟܘ .
The Testament of Job, M. R. James, ed., *Apocrypha Anecdota* 2, Vol. 5, No.
1 of *Texts and Studies* (TS), ed. J. A. Robinson, Cambridge 1897, 103-37,
describes Job's provision of girdles of virginity as his three daughters'
inheritance (46:7 ff.). The girdles are said to be of value for life in
heaven (47:3). In chapters 48, 49, and 50 each daughter in turn puts on
her girdle. Thereupon, each begins to speak in an angelic tongue.

[20]Thus it is uncertain as to what is meant when it is said that
Job's daughters were no longer cosmic.

[21]C. Tischendorf, ed., *Apocalypses Apocryphae* (Leipzig 1866) 24-33.

[22]W. E. Barnes extracted and translated an Arabic MS in *The Testaments of Abraham Isaac and Jacob* (TS, 2/2, 1892) 140-51. S. Gaselee
translated a Coptic MS in G. H. Box, ed., *The Testament of Abraham* (London
1927) 57-75. Gaselee (pp. 76-89) also translated the Testament of Jacob
from the same MS. Barnes (pp. 152-54) gave an abstract of the Arabic.
Jacob instructs his family in fasting after his heavenly journey.

[23]Box, *The Apocalypse of Abraham* (London 1918) 44 f., 50.

[24]*3 Enoch or the Hebrew Book of Enoch* (Cambridge 1928) 40 ff.

[25]Cf. R. H. Charles, *The Ascension of Isaiah* (London 1917) 32.

[26]With due regard to the outstanding literary work of the last
generation, this remains an open question.

[27]Cf. notes 49 and 74 and the discussion of σκιά in Sec. III.
Our citations from Philo draw upon the Loeb series, edited by F. H. Colson,
G. H. Whitaker, and R. Marcus (London 1929-1962).

[28]G. Scholem, *Major Trends in Jewish Mysticism* (New York 1954) 49.

[29]The only reliable text is that of A. D. Nock and A. J. Festu-
giere, *Corpus Hermeticum* (Paris 1945-1954). We have made use of the
translation in R. M. Grant, ed., *Gnosticism* (New York 1961) 211 ff. The
translation of 10. 24-5 below is from W. Scott and A. S. Ferguson,
Hermetica (Oxford 1924) 1. 205.

[30]G. Van Moorsel, *The Mysteries of Hermes Trismegistus* (Utrecht
1955) identifies the thrust of passages such as these as effectuating
asceticism. However, he argues that Hermetic piety is so "spiritualized"
that the effectuating asceticism represented in the tractates is only
apparent. Moorsel's refusal to take the passages at face value stems from
what appears to be a basic methodological error. He belittles what he
terms "the statistical method" of adding passage to passage in support of
an ascetic interpretation, calling it "no great feat" (pp. 32, 44 ff.).
"What does carry weight," he says, "is the qualitative point of view."
In response, it first must be observed that Moorsel's own constructive
work is unable to sustain his rejection of an inductive approach to the
texts. For example, on pp. 81 f. he collects a selection of passages
supporting his view on παράδοσις. Secondly, his "qualitative" judgement
that "the ideological element predominates over the moral side of things"
does not in itself "make it difficult for effectuating asceticism to hold
its own." Moorsel does not seem to recognize that ethics is everywhere
conducted in an ideological frame. Moreover, the seeming incompatability
of the two (as in 12. 5 where destiny is said to compel men to do the evil
for which they are punished) is not peculiar to the Hermetic Corpus.
Passages such as 1. 18, 24-26; 4. 5; 7. 2-3, and 1. 22-23 should not be
given over to radical reductionism.

[31]Cf. H. G. Liddell and R. Scott, *A Greek-English Lexicon*, ed.
H. S. Jones (Oxford 1925-1940) 539: J. H. Moulton and G. Milligan, *The
Vocabulary of the Greek New Testament Illustrated from the Papyri and Other
Non-Literary Sources* (London 1914-1919) 205 f.; Bauer, col. 504.

[32]With S. Eitrem, "'Εμβατεύω: Note sur Col 2:18," *Studia Theolog-ica* (*ST*) 2 (1948) 91, it is to be noted that "la myese n'est pas obligatoire à tous les consultants de l'oracle. Les consultants ordinaires n'ont pas été initiés, à ce qu'il semble."

[33]These inscriptions and the related ones which also bear upon the present discussion were brought together by Dibelius in his essay of 1917, "Die Isisweihe bei Apuleius und verwandte Initiations-Riten." This is now available in his collected works, *Botschaft und Geschichte* (Tübingen 1956) 2. 30-79. [See above.]

[34]Compare Dibelius, *Botschaft und Geschichte*, 2. 61, and *An die Kolosser* (2nd ed.), 26. Cf. also W. M. Ramsay, *The Teaching of Paul* (2nd ed., London 1914) 287 ff., who anticipated Dibelius with regard to a two stage ritual and entrance into a sanctuary.

[35]Cf. Eitrem, *Orakel und Mysterien am Ausgang der Antike* (Zürich 1947) 72: "Unzweifelhaft müssen wir nämlich das 'Hineinschreiten' von der Einweihung trennen." Eitrem, in *ST*, 2. 91, explains the term as "*le pas-sage rituel* du myste à *l'oracle*," "le contact direct avec l'adyton," necessitating new purifications and sacrifices. Cf. Percy 172; Lohmeyer 124 n. 2.

[36]According to Eitrem, *Orakel* 73, the Apostle has "... zwei verschiedene Termini der Orakelbefragung, wie wir sie jetzt aus Klaros kennen, ineinander verschlungen ..."

[37]*Botschaft und Geschichte*, 2. 55 f. "Neither does it involve a cult already settled in Colossae, nor the setting up of a στοιχεῖα cult along side a Christ cult." [Above, p. 82.]

[38]*Botschaft und Geschichte*, 2. 65 [Above, p. 90].

[39]Percy 172, actually calls it "eine völlige Sinnlosigkeit."

[40] *Archiv fur Religionswissenschaft* (*ARW*) 4 (1901) 136-69, 229-73.

[41] Ibid. 143 f.

[42] *JBL* 52. 132 f. Here the writer gratefully acknowledges that some of the basic ideas of this study were presented to him orally by Professor Nils A. Dahl. Cf. note 1.

[43] *Jewish Gnosticism, Merkabah Mysticism, and Talmudic Tradition* (New York 1960) 17 f.

[44] The verb regularly used in those sources which have come down to us in Greek is εἰσέρχεσθαι. The significance of this fact for the use of ἐμβατεύειν in Colossians will be treated below.

[45] M. R. James, ed. (TS, 5/1) 83-102.

[46] Cf. 1 Enoch 14:5, 8, 9, 10, 13, and Enoch's journeys from place to place; 3 Enoch 1:1, 5, 6, 2:2, 4:7, 8, 18:19, 31:2; T. Lev. 2:5-7, 10, 5:1, 3.

[47] It is interesting that entrance is bound up with ethical rigor, namely abstinence from sexual intercourse. Sexual intercourse is identified with the work of swines and dogs (*Ref.*5, 8; cf. Mt 7:6). Hippolytus comments, "With all severity and vigilance they enjoin abstention, as if they were emasculated, from intercourse with women" (*Ref.*5, 9).

[48] Even in Hermas Sim. 9, 3-4 the stones that go in through the gate are said to come up from the deep to be builded into the tower.

[49] Cf. the discussion of σκιά in Sec. III and note 74. It should be noted that Philo's treatment of the Sinai vision in *QE* 2, 39 specifies that envisioning God does not take place "in any mortal place at all," but, by "a migration," in "a holy and divine place, which is called by another name, Logos." Cf. also *QE* 2, 27-29, 51.

[50]In addition to the Apocalypse of Abraham, the independent tradition preserved in the Testament of Abraham recounts a heavenly journey
made by the patriarch. Abraham is allowed to see all created things before
his death. Michael conducts him through the heavens in the divine chariot.

[51]M. R. James, ed., *The Apocalypse of Sedrach* (TS 2/3 1893) 130-37.

[52]P. Riessler, ed. "Apokalypse des Elias," *Altjüdisches Schrift-
tum ausserhalb der Bibel* (Augsburg 1928) 114-25.

[53]Cf. Scholem, *Major Trends* 52 ff., *Jewish Gnosticism* 14 ff.
The fact that "entering" and "ascending" refer to the same reality would
seem to derive from the simple fact it is heaven *above* that one enters.

[54]Ramsay 288.

[55]Nock, *JBL* 52. 133, raises the possibility that "there was a
divergent local use of the word." This of course is possible, but nothing
is explained by ascribing a piece of data to an unknown factor. Our suggestion relates general usage to a concrete historical factor.

[56]This is the essence of Dibelius' assumption, for even if the
term were used in mysteries beyond Claros (and Colossae) the *originality*
of the error at Colossae would still make its use there a new application.
The Claros inscriptions are insufficient grounds for postulating extensive
mystery use of ἐμβατεύειν; but more, such generality would be an open door
to the common public usage which we are suggesting.

[57]It did not do so for Dibelius. He never suggested that the
Colossian Christians were initiated at Claros. Beyond an uncertain hint
of mystery initiation, he gets nothing from the Claros inscriptions.

[58]An excellent survey of the subject can be found in J. Michl,
"Engel: 1-9," *Reallexicon für Antike und Christentum*, ed. T. Klauser, 5
(1960) 54-258.

[59]Percy 161. The comprehensive study of W. L. Knox (*St. Paul and the Church of the Gentiles*, Cambridge 1939) follows Dibelius in most respects. However, the great merit of Knox's work is also its chief weakness. He has constructed a mass of syncretistic trends that would have been unrivaled in the ancient world!

[60]Such is the clear implication of most of our documents. Philo sets it out as an explicit principle in *Som* 1. 35.

[61]Cf. Scholem, *Jewish Gnosticism* 20-30. Cf. also *Major Trends* 57-63.

[62]We employ the translation of A. Dupont-Sommer, *The Essene Writings from Qumran*, trans. G. Vermes (New York 1961).

[63]In Num 8:11 and 19 respectively, similar objective and subjective uses of עֲבֹדָה (ἔργον LXX) stand together.

[64]Cf. 4 Ezra, Syr. Bar., Apoc. Ezra, Apoc. Abr., Herm., Tertullian *de ieiun.*, Dan., Philo, *Som.* 1, *Mos.* 2 in the passages cited above. To these may be added Philo, *Sac.* 59-63.

[65]*Major Trends*, p. 49.

[66]*Jewish Gnosticism*, p. 20.

[67]This is certainly the case in the Hermetic corpus. Fasting in Philo, *Som.* 1. 36, is inseparable from the exalted, asomatic state itself.

[68]Hofmann and Zahn.

[69]Chap. 12 of *The Fathers according to Rabbi Nathan* (J. Goldin, ed., New Haven 1955, p. 67) records that angels are more humble than men, "for when they open their mouths and recite the Song ... they defer to one

another, which men do not do." The combination of humility and angels does not *ipso facto* illuminate our problem. Such commendable deference to one another cannot have been the object of attack in Colossians!

[70]Cf. Dibelius, *Botschaft und Geschichte*, 2. 64, where he understands the term to refer to a voluntary cult as opposed to national or state religion. Such a self-designation would hardly have distinguished Christian from Christian in that time.

[71]Cf. B. Reicke, "Zum sprachlichen Verständnis von Kol. 2:23", *ST*, 6 (1952) 46. Reicke assumes an objective genitive in τῶν ἀγγέλων (vs. 18), and renders the compound "pretended" or "quasi" worship.

[72]Reicke expresses approval of this English idiom.

[72a]Ralph P. Martin, *Colossians: The Church's Lord and the Christian's Liberty* (Grand Rapids, 1972) 92.

[72b]Eduard Lohse, *Colossians and Philemon: A Commentary on the Epistles to the Colossians and to Philemon*, trans. W. R. Poehlmann and R. J. Karris (Philadelphia, 1971) 119, n. 36.

[72c]Martin 92.

[73]Vs. 17 is based upon the Platonic metaphor of form and copy and is not at all to be interpreted as a statement of the comparative poverty of the errorists' practices. Cf. Philo, *Post.* 112, 114, 119, *Immut.* 177, *Flac.* 165, *Jos.* 140, *Spec.* 1. 26, 28 where Philo uses σκιά to communicate evanescence and unreality. However, when σῶμα is referred to in these passages it is in the elementary empirical sense and hence an aspect of the σκιά.

[74]The first of these (*Plant.* 17-27) is so fully analogous to Colossians that it merits being set out in detail. Philo says (*Plant.* 22), the strong yearning to perceive clearly the existent one gives the eyes of

the soul wings to attain not only to the last region of the upper air but to overpass the bounds even of all the κόσμος to speed to the uncreated. This is so because (*Plant.* 24) the divine spirit lightens and raises the mind to the utmost height, overcoming all powers (πάντα δυνατοῦ) and things below--this is especially true for the genuine philosopher. Such a one (*Plant.* 25) is not held down by bodily or earthly things, for he has sought to sever and estrange himself from these. Rather, he is borne upward (ἄνω φέρεται). Of course Moses (*Plant.* 26) is one who is called up (ἀνακαλεῖν). He produces (ἀνατυποῦν) the archetypes themselves (*Plant.* 27), which are exhibited to him clearly (τηλαυγέστερον), as in the sun. Bezaleel (*Plant.* 26) is also called up. He fashions (πλάττειν) shadows, which are exhibited to him as in a shadow (*Plant.* 27). Similarly, Philo (LA 3. 103) says that a prophet sees God "in a vision (ὅραμα) and in a shadow."

[75]*Jewish Gnosticism* 17 f. Perhaps we should note (against the Greek fathers) that σκιά itself does not have an anticipatory sense. Philo writes three times that a shadow follows its object (*Decal.* 82, *Virt.* 118, 181).

[76]It now becomes evident that the whole of 2:17 was a shibboleth of the errorists. With great skill the writer opposed the claim of that verse, arguing on the one hand that the errorists' practice was not a copy of Christ, and on the other hand that the Colossians shared in the very reality itself. Cf. Philo, *LA* 3. 95-103, *Plant.* 27, *Abr.* 119, 120, *Som.* 1. 188, 206, *Heres.* 72, *Agr.* 42, *Migr.* 12, *Conf.* 190, *Mut.* 243. Cf. also Heb 8:5, 10:1.

THE BACKGROUND OF EMBATEUEIN (Col 2:18) IN
LEGAL PAPYRI AND ORACLE INSCRIPTIONS*

Fred O. Francis

In previous papers and articles I have sought to identify the
disturbance that occasioned the epistle to the Colossians in terms of
ascetic, mystic trends of Hellenistic piety.[1]

A key term in understanding Colossian ascent mysticism is
ἐμβατεύειν one of several *hapax legomena* in the epistle. The following
is our translation of Col 2:18, in which the term occurs:

> Let no one disqualify you, being bent upon humility
> and the worship of angels, which he has seen upon
> entering (ἐμβατεύειν), being vainly puffed up by his
> mind of flesh.

We hold that the heavenly realm is the unexpressed object of
entering in Colossians 2:18. It is worth noting that certain of the
fathers explicitly employed ἐμβατεύειν with heaven as its object. For
example, Nemesius of Emesa (*De. Nat. Hom.*, Matt. pp. 63-65) states that
man enters (ἐμβατεύει) heaven by contemplation. But in this essay we are
concerned only to amplify our earlier treatment of two particular back-
grounds of the term. We turn immediately to that use of ἐμβατεύειν that
proves to be both most common in extant ancient literature and most available to the populace of the Graeco-Roman world, namely, entry into possession of property. We made only passing reference to this material in our
first article. Since then we have had opportunity for more thorough study
of the documents, and have come to appreciate the cultural/theological
significance of conceptions in the papyri for an understanding of Colossians.

*This essay is excerpted from a study in preparation on the occasion
and purpose of Colossians. An earlier form of the essay was read at
the 1969 meeting of the Society of Biblical Literature.

Entry into Possession

In legal papyri ἐμβατεύειν is used of entry into possession of property over a period of six centuries from the third century B.C. forward. The verb is employed in three areas of law: Property, Execution and Proceedings, and Inheritance.[2]

Petitions dealing with the protection of ownership or possession of property use ἐμβατεύειν with reference to seizure by force[3] and the possession of unattended property.[4]

The verb appears in three types of Hellenistic liens. In two of these ἐμβατεύειν is used of the creditor's expropriation of property put up as security in the event of default on payment. In the third case it is the creditor's entry into possession of the property used in lieu of interest until the discharge of the debt.[5] Furthermore, ἐμβατεύειν is used in contracts of sale in self-help clauses giving the purchaser the right to enter into possession of his previously paid-for purchase.[6]

In proceedings in circumstances of default[7] and in court cases dealing with the seizure of mortgaged property[8] ἐμβατεύειν refers to the creditor's confiscation of the property.

Wills used the verb for the heir's assumption of the inheritance.[9] The verb is also found in petitions concerning succession to an estate on intestacy.[10]

Regarding the syntax of ἐμβατεύειν in the papyri, it should be noted that several times ἐμβατεύειν is used absolutely, without an object, as in Colossians.[11]

There are several examples of the use of ἐμβατεύειν for entry into the possession of property in Hellenic texts. One of these, Euripides, *The Heracleidae*, 863-78, stands out because it is quite comparable to the LXX use of ἐμβατεύειν in Josh 19:49, 51. In Joshua the giving of the land constitutes the fulfillment of God's promises. As in *The Heracleidae*, to possess the land is to "have a portion in the Lord" and therefore to have the right to worship him (Josh 22:24-26).

The possession of the land in Joshua has an additional feature that merits attention. No land was given the tribe of Levi: their portion was the Lord God of Israel;[12] the priesthood of the Lord was theirs.[13] The fulfillment of promise was to have a portion in the Lord. For some this was an allotment of the land; for others it was a share in the service of the Lord.

The unexpressed object of ἐμβατεύειν in Colossians is *not* a plot of ground, but it *is* a portion in the Lord. Our view that Colossians' use of ἐμβατεύειν reflects such nuances of entry into possession is corroborated by the presence of several other "property related" theological terms in the epistle. The curious term, χειρόγραφον, in Col 2:14 is a noun frequently found in legal papyri. In the space of a few verses one encounters two New Testament *hapax legomena*, ἐμβατεύειν and χειρόγραφον, and they have only one common context outside the New Testament, namely property conventions. Moreover, the only extant papyrological instance of a third New Testament *hapax legomenon*, καταβραβεύειν appears in litigation concerning this very matter of entry into property. This becomes a pervasive theme with the addition of such terms as κλῆρος, κληρονομία, ἀνταπόδοσις, and θησαυροί.

What then is the connection between Col 2:18, *The Heracleidae*, and Josh 19:49, 51? It appears that all three employ common Hellenistic and Hellenic property conventions as a vehicle for theological reflection. More narrowly it may be asked whether Joshua inspires a measure of the terminology and thematic tendency of Colossians. Perhaps one should consider the possibility that Colossians draws upon a common body of traditional interpretation of Joshua.

Joshua's use of ἐμβατεύειν in the allotting of tribal inheritances certainly bridges to Colossians through the *Testament of Levi*. *T Levi* 2:10, 12, 4:2, 5:1-2 specifically relate Levi's portion and service to the Lord to heavenly entrance. *T Levi* 8:1, 18 emphasize that Levi's investiture is also a heavenly event. The occasion for Levi's entrance into possession of his inheritance is his entrance into heaven.

Having engaged in the preparatory discipline of humility, the Colossians sought to enter heaven in order to possess themselves of salvation, a portion in the Lord.

"Entering" at the Clarian Oracle

The Clarian oracle was one of the most important of the Graeco-Roman world. It was located in the same region as Colossae, and the inscriptions indicate that delegates from Laodicea (see Col 2:1, 4:13 ff.) had consulted the oracle more than once.

It is now possible to bring together eight Clarian inscriptions pertinent to the use of ἐμβατεύειν in Colossians.[14] Four employ the verb ἐμβατεύειν to enter: three from the site, one from Pergamum. Reference to mystery initiation appears in all four. Four other inscriptions from Claros refer to initiation. Arranged in chronological order and reduced to the key clauses, the inscriptions are these:

> Two delegates, having been initiated and having entered, consulted the oracle.
>
> Two others came who, having been initiated, entered.
>
> A delegate completed the mystery.
>
> A delegate completed the mystery.
>
> A delegate completed the mystery.
>
> Certain delegates [who were ini]tiated and ent[ered, consulted ...] ... the oracle
>
> Another delegate, having received the mystery, entered.
>
> Those present with a delegate were initiated, he being initiated with them.

It is clear that a mystery was celebrated at Claros in addition to the practice of the oracle. The question is, what was the nature of the "entering."

The Clarian apollo sanctuary was famous in its own time as an oracle--not as a mystery. And the inscriptions--those above and the larger body--record consultations with the oracle. The mystery was a secondary matter. Indeed, as Eitrem has suggested, the development of the mystery may have been a response to a growing sense of the importance of consulting the oracle. These facts are explicit in the first and sixth of the inscriptions above. Initiation and entrance are circumstantial details that lead to consultation of the oracle. One may take the distinctive mystery at Claros with full seriousness, but the fact remains that "entering" is to be understood as an act that facilitates consultation.[15]

This observation illuminates the other form of inscription in which "entering" occurs at Claros. In the second and seventh inscriptions above ἐμβατεύειν appears as a finite verb modified by a circumstantial

expression for initiation, with no explicit mention of consultation in
the statement. However, by recalling that these are inscriptions commem-
orating consultation of the oracle, one can see that this is simply a
short form of expression for the same three-fold procedure.

      This view is confirmed by the regular alternation in contemporary
oracle literature between fuller forms and those where a verbal expression
for entering itself stands for consultation.[16] Thus, when the Clarian
inscriptions say that "a delegate, having received the mystery, entered,"
they mean that he proceeded to consult the oracle.

      Various verbs are used in oracle texts for the entering by which
one presents himself for consultation. Most commonly they are compound
forms meaning "to go down." This, of course, is because oracles were often
practiced in subterranean grottos. Such was the case at Claros before
the period of the inscriptions. But when a large complex of buildings was
erected, and the oracle was "entered into" at ground level, it was appropriate to select a verb like ἐμβατεύειν for entering without descent.
Other oracle literature also evidences such verbs in connection with consultation.[17]

      The four inscriptions above that do not employ the verb "enter-
ing" also do not mention consultation. But one would have to say that much
as consultation is the necessary presupposition of the inscriptions, so
entrance to the place where consultation takes place is presupposed too.
Moreover, mystery initiation is mentioned precisely because it is the
feature that cannot automatically be assumed. This is certainly the implication of the eighth inscription above, which emphasizes that it was
because of the great piety of the delegate that those accompanying him
were initiated.

      If not everyone who came to consult the oracle was initiated,[18]
what was the special significance of initiation and what other rites were
practiced in connection with consultation?

      Analysis of the liturgical life of the Claros sanctuary is next
to impossible, because the inscriptions primarily serve as lists of officers and delegates. However, the diverse offices themselves evidence a
complex liturgical practice. Moreover, two aspects of the description
of the delegates are rather useful.

In the first place, the one activity of the delegates that is
recorded with any frequency at all is hymning the god with choirs brought
for the purpose. One inscription specifies that 'a choir of youths and
virgins, whose names were offered to the god along with the delegate from
Laodicea, together with the one sent to consult hymned the god at the
Clarian Apollo *according to the oracle*.[19] The parallel activity of the
inquirer and those accompanying him compares with the eighth inscription
above. This, plus the emphasis that their liturgical offering was *according to the oracle*, provides an alternative statement to the mention of
initiation. Another Laodicean inscription simply states that along with
the choral leaders and the inquirer, 'the youths and virgins were present
according to the oracle.'[20]

In the second place, the phrase, "according to the oracle," in
addition to the general sense of fulfilling the ritual procedure by the
oracle, must mean that the inquirers met the Clarian requirements for
purification and preparation. Regulation of the conditions of entry and
participation is not an uncommon theme in inscriptions relating to oracles
and mysteries.[21] Thus, one may infer from the Clarian inscriptions themselves a general liturgical practice that is occasionally supplemented by
mystery initiation. That is, there were three stages of activity in the
practice of the oracle: preparation, entrance, and consultation. Initiation was a distinct form of preparation.

But what of the special significance of mystery initiation?
With the second century renovation of the sanctuary, or before, initiation
could have been required for entrance to the innermost or particularly
important chamber at the sanctuary. In this circumstance the inscription
would serve to record a delegate's satisfaction of the conditions of such
entrance.

Eitrem explains ἐμβατεύειν as "le passage rituel du myste à
l'oracle," "le contact direct avec l'adyton."[22]

The point is that ἐμβατεύειν has the simple meaning that one is
led to expect from a study of verbs of "entering" in oracle literature: one
may have been enabled to *enter* an exceptional chamber at the oracle shrine
by exceptional preparation, namely initiation.

Our view that "entering" at Claros had no peculiar technical

meaning to distinguish it from other verbs of "entering" in contemporary
oracle literature appears to be confirmed by the uses of the verb in the
second century A. D. rhetorician Aristides. Aristides is a singularly
important witness to Clarian usage since he himself had consulted the
oracle at the time of the inscriptions (Arist. 312, 317) and spent his
life in the district. No less than four times (see the number of extant
inscriptions!) he uses ἐμβατεύειν and never in any technical sense he
might have learned at Claros. Aristides uses the verb for the entry of a
mob into a temple (!) and the entry of muses and graces into a city. In
addition, he shapes a figure drawn from the property conventions discussed
earlier when he says that Philip *entered into possession of Greek things*
as if receiving Greece overdue (Arist. 486). Finally, he extends the metaphorical possibilities of the verb stating that Athena indwells and
possesses the head of men, guarding the portents she gives (Arist. 10).
This last is a clear reference to oracle milieu, and yet "entering" is
used in the sense most commonly available in the Graeco-Roman world.

Aristides, who himself consulted the oracle at the time of the
inscriptions and used the verb in question with relative frequency, knows
only of the simple meanings "entering" and "entering into possession."

If this were not convincing enough, one could refer to the fourth
century sophist Himerius who also knows of the Clarian Apollo (*Or.* X 13)
and uses ἐμβατεύειν in the sense of entering into possession of the soul
(*Or.* IV 5).[23]

The application of the Claros inscriptions to the interpretation
of Colossians requires caution. The second century date of the inscriptions makes direct dependence or specific allusion far from certain.[24]
More importantly the other popular uses of "entering" appear to be behind
the use of the term at both Claros and Colossae, the two sharing--perhaps
independently--in a larger context of usage.

It would appear that the firmest connection that can be conjectured between the Apollo sanctuary and the Colossian church is the possibility that the employment of ἐμβατεύειν at Claros spurred popular use of
the verb in the areas to which delegates returned. The errorists may have
understood humility followed by visions seen upon entering "the heavenly
temple" to be analogous to preparation/initiation followed by reception of

oracles upon entering the Clarian oracle chamber. But even this may be saying too much, for the term was the common property of any man on the street. Entrance into heaven itself is saving, and it is the occasion for investigating, dwelling in, and possessing salvation.

Because the last of these, entrance into possession of salvation, is the ultimate goal, it is not surprising to find this very theme pervading the letter to the Colossians. Reciprocally, the letter's preoccupation with the theme provides a sufficient rationale for the choice of ἐμβατεύειν as the verb for entrance rather than another.

* * *

NOTES

[1]Morton Smith made a similar suggestion in his "Observations on Hekhalot Rabbati," *Biblical and Other Studies*, ed. A. Altmann (Cambridge, Mass. 1963) 156 f.

[2]Cf. R. Taubenschlag, *The Law of Greco-Roman Egypt in the Light of the Papyri (332 B.C.-640 A.D.)* (2nd ed., Warsaw, 1955), for a comprehensive survey of the subject. Cf. also F. Pringsheim, *The Greek Law of Sale* (Weimar, 1950) 286 f.

[3]P Par 14:19.

[4]P Lond 401:19. Cf. P SB 4512B.

[5]P Lond 1164d:11.

[6]P BGU 1130:14.

[7]P Oxy 1118:7; P Flor 86:23; P BGU 832:22; P Hib 197:7.

[8]P Oxy 653:18 ff.; P PSI 1411:29.

[9]P Eleph 2:14; P CPR 95:10, 13.

[10]P SB 4638:8; P BGU 1761:9.

[11]As a finite verb: P Oxy 653:18 ff.; as an infinitive: P Eleph 2:14, P BGU 1130:14; as a participle P SB 4370:32.

[12]Cf. LXX Josh 13:14, MT Josh 13:33.

[13]Cf. Josh 18:7.

[14]For a comprehensive treatment of the material on Claros, cf. C. Picard, *Éphèse et Claros* (Paris, 1922). The Clarian mystery receives special attention in pp. 303-11 in this work. The inscriptions were published in T. Macridy, "Altertümer von Notion," *JÖAI* 8 (1905) 155-73, and Macridy, "Antiquities de Notion," *JÖAI* 15 (1912) 36-37. Further information on the excavation is found in T. Macridy-Bey and C. Picard, "Fouilles du Hieron D'Apollon Clarios a Colophon," *BCH* 39 (1915) 33-52. Picard, "Un Oracle d'Apollon Clarios a Pergame," *BCH* 46 (1922) 190-7, publishes two additional inscriptions (one of which also appears in his *Éphèse et Claros*).

[15]Cf. M. Dibelius, *An Die Kolosser Epheser an Philemon* (1st ed., Tübingen, 1912). W. Ramsay, "Sketches in the Religious Antiquities of Asia Minor," *ABSA* 18 (1911-12) 45-8, conjectures a two stage ritual in which ἐμβατεύειν was the climax following "the *muesis* proper." He relates his conjecture to his reconstruction of the hall of the sanctuary of Men in Antioch. He suggests that two stone slabs standing near the center of the hall formed the "entrance" through which the initiate passed. It is hardly persuasive to attempt to clarify one conjecture by another. Picard, *Éphèse et Claros* 307, rightly denies that Ramsay can explain Claros by the Antioch sanctuary--though Picard himself follows Ramsay in saying that ἐμβατεύειν represents the second degree of initiation at Claros (*BCH* 46. 193, n. 7).

There is no evidence that ἐμβατεύειν at Claros is the climax of initiation in the sense of being the concluding constituent segment of it. That ἐμβατεύειν follows initiation seems to be clear, but that says very little. The fact that the same verb for initiation appears both with and without ἐμβατεύειν suggests that the latter is not constitutive of the former. The proposition that ἐμβατεύειν is a second, higher initiation is sheer guess work, having no foundation in the inscriptions.

Cf. Eitrem, *Orakel und Mysterien am Ausgang der Antike* (Zürich, 1947) 72: "Unzweifelhaft müssen wir nämlich das 'Hineinschreiten' von den Einweihung trennen."

[16]Cf. Plutarch *Mor* 397A, 407D, 408D, 437D, 438B, Pausanius, *Descript*. 9. 39, 5 ff.

[17]Cf. Picard, *Éphèse et Claros* 660-71, 45-50, concerning the place of second century developments in the history of the sanctuary. It will be remembered that the inscriptions in question are of a second century date. Cf. Dibelius, *Kol*. (2nd ed.) 26.

One must wonder whether "going down" to the Merkabah in Jewish mysticism derives, as a verbal idea, from the predominance of "descent" in Hellenistic oracles.

As examples of other verbs for entrance, cf. Strabo, *Geog*. 17. 1, 43: παρελθεῖν; Pausanias, *Descript*. 10. 24, 5: παρεῖναι.

[18]With S. Eitrem, "EMBATEYΩ, Note sur Col 2:18," *ST* 2 (1948) 91, it is to be noted that "la myese n'est pas obligatoire à tous les consultants de l'oracle. Les consultants ordinaire n'ont pas été initiés, à ce qu'il semble."

[19]Cf. Macridy, *JÖAI* 8. 167: III, 1.

[20]Ibid., III, 2.

[21]Cf. G. Dittenberger, ed. *Sylloge Inscriptionem Graecarum* (2nd ed., Leipzig, 1900), 2. 939, 1-11; 563, 103; 790, 30-42; 653, 36-7. Eitrem, *Orakel* 72, finds the connection between initiation and consultation understandable in the view of the increasing importance of oracles in the second century A.D.

[22]*ST* 2. 91.

[23]Cf. Aristides 10, and 4th cent. A. D. church fathers who speak
of God entering (ἐμβατεύειν) the heart. Cf. Picard, *Éphèse* 711-21,
xxviii, 124 ff., on the Clarian Apollo in the fourth century.

[24]S. Lyonnet, "L'Epitre aux Colossiens (Col 2:18) et les
mysteres d'Apollon Clarien," *Biblica* 43 (1962) 433, states that *embateuein*
could neither be written nor read in the area of Colossae without bringing
to mind Claros. On the contrary, it would bring to mind other associations;
see Aristides!

Although this volume contains essays spanning nearly a century,
its purpose has not been retrospective, not a history of research. The
editors wanted to point to the on going task of formulating historical-
critical theories, particularly with regard to the problem of "the opponents"
in polemical documents. Colossians is an instructive case, and one worth
carrying forward in its own right. We chose articles that reflect important theoretical and methodological alternatives in this area.

J. B. LIGHTFOOT's essay marks out the present conceptual bound-
aries of efforts to identify the opponents at Colossae. Lightfoot recognizes two elements in the Colossian heresy, the one Judaic and the other
gnostic. Two important qualifications give breadth and openness to Lightfoot's model. First, he indicates that he uses the term Gnosticism "to
express the simplest and most elementary conceptions of this tendency of
thought" and not as "a distinct designation of any sect or sects at this
early date." Thus, the term embraces theosophic speculation, shadowy
mysticism, and spiritual intermediaries, as well as intellectual exclusiveness, speculative cosmology and theology (ending in dualism and a doctrine
of emanations), and asceticism (or license). Second, when Lightfoot proceeds to delimit the Judaic element as Essene Judaism, he notes that he
does not "assume a precise identity of origin" between the Essene movement
and the Colossian opponents--even though he thinks one can make a case for
the presence of Essenism in contemporary Phrygia and Asia Minor--"but only
an essential affinity of type." The marks of this Essenism are speculation,
asceticism, and exclusiveness. The correspondence between these characteristics and Lightfoot's formulation of Gnosticism enables him to label the
Colossian heresy Essene Judaism of a gnostic character.

Lightfoot's construction has the virtue of calling attention to
certain important features of the data in Colossians--the indications of
sectarian Judaism, the presence of other features of Hellenistic religiosity,
and the probability that these two cultural trends constitute one entity
at Colossae. A property of Lightfoot's model which is at once a strength
and a weakness is its diffuseness or openness. Lightfoot enables one to
see phenomena in Colossians that might go unobserved if one were compelled

to identify the opponents with a particular sect of antiquity. Yet, if one's conceptualization is like no particular history, but only like some generality of Hellenistic phenomena, one must ask whether it is sufficiently analytic. Surely Gnosticism and Essenism are not umbrella-terms for exotica in Hellenistic religiosity. Lightfoot's model needs to be modified by elements of another.

MARTIN DIBELIUS proposes a very specific construction of the problem of the opponents at Colossae. He argues that members of the Colossian church entered into association with outsiders in a cultic life devoted to the powers. These Christians joined with their non-Christian teachers without abandoning their Christianity. Dibelius finds in *embateuein* a technical term of the strange cult. On the basis of his analysis of the inscriptions from the Clarian Apollo he believes *embateuein* signifies mystery initiation. The Colossian Christians were initiated into a cosmic mystery devoted to the elements. While Dibelius' essay emphasizes the constitution of the Colossian heresy as a mystery, he also characterizes it as a *gnostic* mystery. Since he takes the practice of the strange cult to have been independent of the church, he believes this to be an instance of pre-Christian Gnosticism. He then postulates the beginning of Christian Gnosticism through such double initiation into church and gnostic mysteries.

Dibelius' view of the opponents at Colossae is a good example of the impact of new data on model building. The first edition of his commentary on Colossians appeared shortly after the initial publication of inscriptions from the Clarian Apollo. Following issuance of additional inscriptions, the essay included in this volume was written. Dibelius found in the Clarian inscriptions the factor that had been missing from previously known instances of *embateuein*: a plausible cultic setting for some of the peculiar symbols and practices of Colossians.

Models are abstractions from the data itself, and in that sense leave out certain features of the data. Dibelius' preoccupation with *embateuein* in the Clarian inscriptions is the most important factor in his conceptualization of the Colossian heresy. This led him to give no weight to the fact that the clarian Apollo was an oracle sanctuary and no oracle is indicated in Colossians. Similarly, Dibelius fixes so strongly on the independent, pagan character of the strange cult that he flatly dismisses

Jewish influence at Colossae.[1]

> For all modern interpreters of Colossians, Dibelius'
> assessment of the heresy has been as important a
> consideration in the development of models as the
> nineteenth century synthesis represented in Light-
> foot has been. Eduard Lohse employs Dibelius'
> model with great fidelity. While he recognizes the
> Colossian allusions to apparent Jewish tradition, he
> argues that the regulations are not a sign of the
> Israelite covenant, and, therefore, that the heresy
> is neither the Essenism isolated by Lightfoot nor
> heretical Judaism. Rather, it is a gnostic or pre-
> gnostic mystery cult. Some Colossian Christians
> thought initiation and submission to the powers would
> perhaps open the way to Christ.

> Ernst Lohmeyer's conception of the opponents has
> the appearance of a polar radicalization of Light-
> foot's model. Lohmeyer sets in bold relief the
> Gnostic and Judaic aspects of the problem identified
> by Lightfoot. They are Hellenistic nature philosophy
> of Gnostic self-redemption and heretical Jewish
> ethical/ritual practice. The speculative philosophy
> is the key; the Jewishness of the opponents is of
> less significance for Lohmeyer than for Lightfoot.
> Lohmeyer rejects the idea of a mystery cult which is
> at the center of Dibelius' model.

GÜNTHER BORNKAMM's treatment of the Colossian heresy may be said
to represent a re-casting of Lightfoot and a correction of Dibelius.
Although Bornkamm, as Lightfoot, concludes his essay by sketching out an
assertedly analogous sect from a period later than Colossians, on the
whole Bornkamm's conception appears to be less diffuse, more defined.
Bornkamm understands the heresy as Gnosticism of a Jewish origin. In that
respect he is closer to Lightfoot than to Dibelius. Bornkamm retains
Dibelius' notion of the practice of a mystery, but moves it into the church.
The heresy is a Christian error in which Christ is given an integrated
place among the powers. There is no opposition nor dual allegiance for the
Colossians. The decisive characteristic of the heresy is the opponents'
teaching regarding the powers. Bornkamm is again closer to Lightfoot than
to Dibelius by giving first consideration to speculative theology rather
than mystery practice. The speculation and the mystery are connected, of
course, for the "philosophy" has the character of revelatory teaching which

is the "tradition" of the mystery. The rule of the divine elements over
the world is understood by Bornkamm as the speculative dualism of Gnosticism.

Because models are not identical with the data, they inevitably
incorporate features not in the data. For example, Bornkamm seems to have
recognized that Dibelius' conception was problematic in locating the source
and actual practice of the heresy outside the church even though Colossians
does not. Bornkamm brings it back in. But to do that and retain something
like Dibelius' reading of the error, Bornkamm has to postulate that the
opponents gave Christ an integrated place among the powers. However,
Colossians does not provide that information either.

> Hans Conzelmann and Hans-Martin Schenke are nearest to
> Bornkamm's conception of the heresy. An all-
> pervasive Gnosticism is at the heart of the matter.
> Yet, whereas Dibelius seems to have anticipated
> Bultmann's assumption of the existence of pre-
> Christian gnostic congregations, Conzelmann sees
> Gnosticism as a broad spiritual movement, not
> properly a religion. It was a change of attitude
> toward the world which affected all religions in
> the Mediterranean Basin in the Hellenistic age. As
> with Bornkamm, the source of the error is pre-
> Christian Jewish Gnosticism. Schenke and Conzelmann
> believe the gnostic opponents in the church under-
> stood themselves as Christians. Conversely, the
> writer of Colossians employed radicalized Gnosticism
> to put down the heresy.
>
> One of the real difficulties in developing an adequate
> model for the Colossian controversy is the unstable
> character of the models of Gnosticism often used to
> interpret Colossians. There is a vast difference
> between members of a church being initiated into
> another, pagan assembly, and a church reflecting the
> broad outlook of a culture.[2] A number of scholars
> seek to conceptualize the Colossian problem without
> reference to Gnosticism.

STANISLAS LYONNET argues that the apparent pagan gnostic vocabulary of Colossians is not what it seems. Some terms often taken to be
crucial for the gnostic background of the letter are simply vocabulary
familiar to Paul drawn from popular usage. Other terms have a Jewish background, as may be seen in comparable language in Galatians and 2 Corinthians. Lyonnet believes it is imprudent to build a whole theory of a pagan

mystery at Colossae on the basis of one term, namely *embateuein*. Instead he finds in the Qumran material an illustration of Jewish interest in calendar, dietary regulations, visions, and angels. He is attracted to the opinion that the worship or religion of angels is the pattern of regulations of the moral life intended to honor the angels who assisted in the giving of the Mosaic law.

Lyonnet's theory illustrates one of the ways in which one's construction of a body of data may be shaped by prior models. The choice of a "Jewish" model over a "pagan" one seems to presuppose another rather widely held view of early Christian history: that Jewishness is to be identified with both temporal priority and doctrinal purity. The seeming self-evidence of this theory relieves Lyonnet of the responsibility of giving reasons why the "Jewish" *possibility* is more *probable* than the "pagan".[3] Beyond this, Lyonnet in effect selects one half of Lightfoot's construct but does not consider the possibility that Jewish and non-Jewish factors may be found in combination as Lightfoot sees it.

> Ernst Percy's work is reductionistic on this and other grounds. He holds that the opponents were observant Jewish Christians with a strong interest in late Greek speculative philosophy and ascetic piety. According to Percy, most of the key terms and phrases are critical, ironic comments of the writer or textual corruptions. The approach of Werner Foerster largely compares with Percy's though he takes Dibelius more seriously and casts the Jewishness of the opponents more in the sectarian terms of Lightfoot, but the Essene-type group is outside the church. Foerster reads the text of Colossians in a more straightforward, descriptive-- less ironic--manner than Percy.

> Harald Hegermann claims to be in agreement with Dibelius and Bornkamm, but his 'modification of only particular points' entails an exclusion of Gnosticism from his model in favor of Hellenistic Judaism of Philonic stamp. He does wish to re- tain Dibelius' mystery religion. Yet, one must ask if this is possible in view of the question- ableness of actual cultic practice in the Philonic mystery.

> Johannes Lähnemann combines the main features of the models of Lightfoot--Phrygian Judaism--and Dibelius--mystery cultus--though he excludes

> Gnosticism. According to Lähnemann, the Jewish
> community in the region of the Lycus River provided
> the Hellenistic, sectarian setting for the combina-
> tion of cultural factors analogous to Phrygian nature
> religion with its ecstatic rigorism, Iranian myth-
> ology regarding the elements, Greek wisdom, and
> mystery religion. He holds that the non-Christian
> opponents incorporated Christ into their pleroma.

FRED FRANCIS formulates a model of the error at Colossae that
highlights a distinct form of Hellenistic piety, namely ascetic mysticism
directed toward visionary ascent and entrance into heaven. According to
Francis, the angelic powers were not the objects of worship. The phrase
"worship of angels," Col 2:18, is understood to be a subjective genitive:
the angels worship--worship God. What the opponents insist upon as a
standard of piety is the vision of and even participation in the angelic
liturgy. On this view, the pre-eminence of Christ over the powers is not
at issue; that is the common ground from which the argument proceeds. The
opponents saw Christ as a pattern rather than primarily the one who acted
on their behalf. As he put off the body, so they too had to handle it
with severity; as he took his place above all power, so they too sought to
enter the heavenly realms. Through a re-examination of the Claros inscriptions and a study of legal papyri, Francis concludes that *embateuein* is not
an indication of the practice of a mystery, but a broad word for "entering"
which in the Colossian context takes heaven as its implied object. Asceticism prepared one for entrance into heaven.

In the humanities as in the natural sciences, knowledge is cumula-
tive. New models incorporate the successful features of previous ones. As
other students of the Colossian problem, Francis conceptualizes the error
at Colossae within the bounds of the Jewish-Hellenistic piety marked out
by Lightfoot, though he makes no use of the Essene-gnostic labels. The
asceticism, cosmological theology, and exclusiveness Lightfoot isolated
are taken up into Francis' model. At the same time, new models frequently
differ significantly from previous ones and require substantial modification
or ever abandonment of assumptions that have long seemed unquestionably
self-evident. According to Francis, the pre-occupation with mystery initiation stemming from Dibelius' construct rests on a mistake and should be excluded from future model building. Similarly, the all but universal

assumption that the Colossian opponents worshipped angels amounts to the
repetition of a rather ancient error based on meager, irrelevant evidence.
Yet, again, Francis' model does *not* thereby exclude other observations
that have been made concerning correspondences between the text of Colossians and phenomena of Hellenistic religion--whether these be called gnostic
or not.

The real challenge for the construction of models of the Colossian controversy is to be critical of diffuse collections of data that pur-
port to be actual syncretistic entities of antiquity. The appearance of
syncretism may be just an expression of the interpreter's unanalytic grasp
of the data. The massive impact of Dibelius' hypothesis concerning the
practice of a mystery at Colossae stems from the fact that such a hypothesis
provides an integrating cultic center for the heresy. The question is:
if a mystery cult can no longer be posited, can the ascent mysticism and
angelic liturgy proposed by Francis be seen to provide the cultic/ethical
nucleus for future model building?

We conclude by bringing together a few of the methodological
issues that emerge from this research.

1) The basic problem is our need to know. We want to understand
a document better than we do. Many factors restrict our understanding,
for example language itself and other cultural shifts, but a primary obstacle is that we are outsiders to the original communication. The writer
could presuppose that the Colossians knew certain things. Other matters
could be brought to the readers' minds by the merest allusion. Some things
that are explicit are so peculiar to the particular relation of the writer
and the Colossians that we find ourselves seeming outsiders to the flat
statement. (This sometimes leads scholars to say that a document is confused or corrupt. But this conclusion should be steadfastly resisted in
spite of its possible truth. The problem is that a corollary of attribut-
ing nonsense to a document is a reduced responsibility to understand.
Better to err on the side of insisting that a document makes sense, and
we need to know it better.)

2) We never know anything in isolation. Context and coherence
and correspondence are basic to historical understanding. The differences
in the interpretations of Colossians are partly due to each interpreter's
location of the letter in a somewhat different historical context.

3) The establishment of historical context for a document is a constructive task involving the development of models by which we organize the data. As we saw above, models vary in specificity and openness. They highlight certain features of Colossians and of Hellenistic religion generally, often leaving out other elements while incorporating still others not actually in the data.

4) Unresolved historical questions regarding cultural phenomena that are offered as context for a document such as Colossians naturally make the shaping of historical theories somewhat problematic. To a degree, the evolution of interpretation of Colossians across the years is a result of the changing understanding of Gnosticism and Judaism.

5) Ideally, the literary form and context of a document ought to be of paramount importance in constructing an historical model. The line of argument in Colossians--its phases and their inter-connectedness--must be weighed carefully. The difficulty lies in he opaque allusion, the enigmatic statement, even the unexpressed presupposition. A distinct problem in Colossians and some other documents is to know the function of traditional material (hymns, other formulae).

6) Unfortunately, difficulties in developing a compelling correspondence between substantial argumentative units of Colossians and a specific movement in Hellenistic culture have led some scholars to construct models on the basis of an atomistic treatment of individual terms in the letter. Often even confessing confusion about the meaning of sentences and paragraphs, they take individual words to be significant verbal symbols.

7) The occurrence of individual words and phrases--occasionally sentences and paragraphs--is often accounted for in the various models of Colossians by assigning the expressions differing polemical functions. The phrase "according to the elements" (Col 2:8) may be the *quotation* of a slogan of the opponents, a *description* of their thought and practice, or a *condemnatory*, perhaps *ironic*, attribution to them of something they deliberately avoid. Is Christ said to be head of all rule and authority because the *opponents believed the opposite* (so that the positive assertions of the writer seemingly mirror the opponents)? Or is this simply the *writer's view* in any case?

8) If the data of a text are treated atomisticly, no control over meaning is possible. Once the key features of a model are posited, the model itself becomes the chief interpretive device, assigning meaning to bits of information and then circularly "discovering" that they fit the model. Critical control over this self-reinforcing pragmatism is had only by repeated reference to the text as a whole and major structural elements in it. That structure is the basis for evaluating models. A better model reflects more of the structure of the text itself. Admittedly, this structure is often not self-evident--again, there is the problem of unexpressed presuppositions. But one's argument must be judged on the basis of what is evident in the text. Subtler matters are in the nature of model building itself.

9) The problem of control involved in taking words and phrases in isolation is compounded when several words in a passage are assigned differing polemical functions. The identification of a term as ironical is difficult for the historian at best, and should be done with greatest caution, for such identification asserts that the expression does not mean what it says. Yet, what the text says is the primary basis for meaning.

10) Careful attention must be given to establishing the common ground between writer and opponents in controversialist documents such as Colossians. One cannot carry on an argument if everything is at issue. Perhaps the traditional material functions at least in part as common ground.

* * *

NOTES

[1] In the third edition of Dibelius' commentary (M. Dibelius and H. Greeven, *An Die Kolosser, Epheser, an Philemon* [Tübingen, 1953]) the concession is made that Bornkamm's essay on the heresy (see below) makes a good case for a Jewish factor in the problem. But this is not really integrated into the model by Dibelius himself.

[2] Cf. C. Colpe, *Die Religionsgeschichtliche Schule: Darstellung und Kritik ihres Bildes vom gnostischen Erlösermythus* (Göttingen, 1961),

and U. Bianchi, ed., *The Origins of Gnosticism* (Leiden, 1967).

[3]Cf. S. Lyonnet, "St. Paul et le gnosticisme: la lettre aux Colossiens," *Origins of Gnosticism*, 538-551, where he argues more fully for caution in characterizing the opponents at Colossae as Gnostics.

SELECTED BIBLIOGRAPHY

I. Studies in this Volume

Bornkamm, Günther. "Die Häresie des Kolosserbriefes," *TLZ* 73 (1948) 11-20.

Dibelius, Martin. Die Isisweihe bei Apulejus und verwandte Initiations-Riten. SAH. Heidelberg, 1917.

Francis, Fred O. "Humility and Angelic Worship in Col 2:18," *ST* 16 (1962) 109-34.

Lightfoot, J. B. *St. Paul's Epistles to the Colossians and to Philemon.* London and New York, 1879.

Lyonnet, Stanislas. "L'étude du milieu littéraire et l'exégèse du Nouveau Testament: #4 Les adversaires de Paul à Colosses," *Biblica* 37 (1956) 27-38.

II. Studies Discussed in Epilogue

Conzelmann, H. *Die kleineren Briefe des Apostels Paulus* Neues Testament Deutsch 8. Göttingen, 1965.

Foerster, W. "Die Irrelehrer des Kolosserbriefes" in *Studia Biblica et Semitica*. Festschrift Th.C. Vriezen, Wageningen, 1966. 71-80.

Hegermann, Harald. *Die Vorstellung vom Schöpfungsmittler im hellenistischen Judentum und Urchristentum.* TU 82. Berlin, 1961.

Lähnemann, Johannes. *Der Kolosserbrief, Komposition, Situation und Argumentation.* SNT. Gütersloh, 1971.

Lohmeyer, E. *Die Briefe an die Philipper, an die Kolosser und an*

Philemon. Meyer Kommentar 9 (additional notes by W. Schmauch) Göttingen, 1964.

Lohse, Eduard. *Colossians and Philemon: A Commentary on the Epistles to the Colossians and to Philemon*. Translated by W. R. Poehlemann and Robert J. Karris. Philadelphia, 1971; German revised edition 1968.

Percy, E. *Die Probleme der Kolosser- und Epheserbriefe*. Lund, 1946.

Schenke, Hans-Martin. "Der Widerstreit gnostischer und kirchlicher Christologie im Spiegel des Kolosserbriefes," *ZTK* 61 (1964) 391-403.

III. Additional Resources

Bandstra, A. J. *The Law and the Elements of the World: An Exegetical Study in Aspects of Paul's Teaching*. Kampen and Grand Rapids (n.d. about 1964).

Beare, F. W. *The Epistle to the Colossians*. Interpreter's Bible 11. New York/Nashville, 1955.

Benoit, P. *Les épitres de saint Paul aux Philippiens, aux Colossiens, etc*. La sainte Bible, Paris, 1949.

Benoit, P. "Qumran and the New Testament," *Paul and Qumran*, ed. J. Murphy-O'Connor. London, 1968.

Best, E. *One Body in Christ*, London, 1955.

Bieder, W. *Die kolossische Irrlehre und die Kirche von heute*, Theologische Studien, 33. Zürich, 1952.

Dibelius, M., Greeven, H. *An die kolosser, Epheser, an Philemon*. Handbuch zum Neuen Testament, 12. Tübingen, 1953.

Eitrem, S. "EMBATEYΩ: Note sur Col 2:18," *ST* 2 (1948) 90-94.

Francis, F. O. "Visionary Discipline and Scriptural Tradition at Colossae," *Lexington Theological Quarterly* 2 (1967) 71-81.

Gabathuler, H. J. *Jesus Christus. Haupt der Kirche--Haupt der Welt.* Der Christushymnus Kolosser 1, 15-20 in der theologischen Forschung der letzten 130 Jahre. Zürich, 1965.

Gewiess, J. "Die apologetische Methode des Apostels Paulus im Kampf gegen die Irrlehre in Kolossä," *Bibel und Leben* 3 (1962) 258-70.

Grässer, E. "Kol 3:1-4 als Beispiel einer Interpretation secundum homines recipientes," *ZTK* 64 (1967) 139-168.

Holtzmann, H. J. *Kritik der Epheser- und Kolosserbriefe.* Leipzig, 1872.

Hugedé, Norbert. *Commentaire de l'Épître aux Colossiens.* Geneva, 1968.

Käsemann, E. "A Primitive Christian Baptismal Liturgy," *Essays on New Testament Themes.* London, 1964.

Kehl, N. *Der Christushymnus im Kolosserbrief.* Stuttgart, 1967.

Lohse, E. "Christologie und Ethik im Kolosserbrief," *Apophoreta.* Festschrift E. Haenchen. Berlin, 1964, pp. 156-168.

_____ "Pauline Theology in the Letter to the Colossians," *NTS* 15 (1969) 211-220.

Lyonnet, S. "Saint Paul et le gnosticisme: la lettre aux Colossiens," *The Origins of Gnosticism,* Leiden, 1967, pp. 538-551.

_____ "Col 2:18 et les mystères d'Apollon Clarien," *Biblica* 43 (1962) 417-35.

222

MacRae, G. W. "The Coptic Gnostic Apocalypse of Adam," *Heythrop Journal* 6 (1965) 27-35.

Masson, Ch. *L'épitre de saint Paul aux Colossiens.* Commentaire du Nouveau Testament 10. Neuchatel/Paris, 1950.

Moule, C. F. D. *The Epistles of Paul the Apostle to the Colossians and to Philemon.* The Cambridge Greek Testament Commentary. Cambridge, 1957.

Mussner, Franz. *Der Brief an die Kolosser.* Geistliche Schriftlesung 12, 1. Düsseldorf, 1965.

Reicke, B. "Zum sprachlichen Verständnis von Kol 2:23," *ST* 6 (1952) 39-52.

Scott, E. F. *The Epistles of Paul to the Colossians, etc.* Moffatt New Testament Commentary. London, 1930.

Thompson, G. H. P. *The Letters of Paul to the Ephesians, to the Colossians and to Philemon.* Cambridge Bible Commentary. Cambridge, 1967.

Schweizer, E. *The Church as the Body of Christ.* Richmond, Va., 1964.

_____ "Die 'Elemente der Welt' Gal 4:3-9; Kol 2:8-20," *Verborum Veritas.* Festschrift Gustav Stählin. Wuppertal, 1970, pp. 245-259.

Williams, A. Lukyn "The cult of Angels at Colossae," *JTS* o.s. 10 (1909) 413-38.

Yamauchi, E. "Qumran and Colosse," *Biblioteca Sacra* 121 (1964) 141-152.

Printed in the United Kingdom
by Lightning Source UK Ltd.
120477UK00001B/58